Android Developer Tools
Essentials

Mike Wolfson

O'REILLY®

Beijing · Cambridge · Farnham · Köln · Sebastopol · Tokyo

Android Developer Tools Essentials

by Mike Wolfson

Printed in the United States of America.

Published by O'Reilly Media, Inc., 1005 Gravenstein Highway North, Sebastopol, CA 95472.

O'Reilly books may be purchased for educational, business, or sales promotional use. Online editions are also available for most titles (*http://my.safaribooksonline.com*). For more information, contact our corporate/institutional sales department: 800-998-9938 or *corporate@oreilly.com*.

Editors: Andy Oram and Rachel Roumeliotis	**Indexer:** Ellen Troutman
Production Editor: Rachel Steely	**Cover Designer:** Randy Comer
Copyeditor: Gillian McGarvey	**Interior Designer:** David Futato
Proofreader: Charles Roumeliotis	**Illustrator:** Rebecca Demarest

August 2013:   First Edition

Revision History for the First Edition:

2013-08-13:   First release

See *http://oreilly.com/catalog/errata.csp?isbn=9781449328214* for release details.

ISBN: 978-1-449-32821-4

[LSI]

Table of Contents

Preface

If you are reading this book, it's likely that you already know a little about Android development and how challenging it can be. Learning to effectively use the standard Android Developer Tools (ADT) can make the development process easier and improve the quality of your code, thereby producing a more refined and robust end product.

Requirements for Android Developer Tools

Android is very different from other mobile platforms currently available. It is not managed by a single organization, but by a group of companies named the "Open Handset Alliance," which is committed to providing a mobile OS that is free, complete, and open source. While this approach ensures decentralized control of the platform, it does create some complexities. These include:

Multiple screen sizes
> Android devices come in a multitude of different screen sizes. Success of your app can hinge upon how your app looks across devices.

Fragmentation
> It is up to the carrier and manufacturer to update their devices when a new version of the OS and runtime are released, which doesn't always happen in a timely manner. It is therefore necessary to support older versions of the OS and runtime.

Different hardware capabilities
> Android phones come in all shapes, sizes, and capabilities. It is necessary to ensure that you degrade unsupported features gracefully when the hardware is limited. Another important consideration is the particular hardware components on which you can or cannot rely (for instance, some devices don't have cameras, GPS sensors, or keyboards).

Resource limitations

Developing applications targeted to the mobile environment is different from developing for the desktop. CPU speed and memory are limited compared to desktops or servers. Mobile device users don't put up with apps that tie up their devices (blocking the UI), consume too many resources, or crash their devices.

Development Process for Android Developer Tools

Google manages ADT development, as well as the standard Android platform. However, the two products are managed very differently, particularly in regards to the open-source nature of the products. The ADT project is developed by a different group from the one that manages the main platform. The tools are released separately from the standard SDK and follow their own release cycle, which is frequently (but not always) tied to the platform release.

The standard OS is developed behind closed doors—contributions are not accepted to the current code base. The source code is released to the public at some point after the group releases it to manufacturers and other insiders.

The first line on the ADT website (*http://tools.android.com/*) makes it clear that this project is different. It reads: "The Developer Tools for Android are being developed entirely in the open and [the project] is accepting contributions." ADT is developed as a series of open source projects with publicly accessible Git repositories (*https://android.googlesource.com/*) and a public bug tracker (*http://b.android.com*). The management group solicits contributions from the community and considers them for implementation in current releases. You can find information on how to contribute on their website (*http://tools.android.com*).

Development on a Variety of OS Platforms

Just as Android is designed to run on many different devices, it is also possible to use many different computer configurations when developing Android applications. This book provides examples based on the Windows 7 64-bit OS and Mac OS X, using the Eclipse Integrated Development Environment (IDE). One chapter introduces the new Gradle-based Android Studio. But you should be able to follow along with any OS and IDE, as the tools have been ported to work on a large variety of platforms. It is also worth noting that it is possible to develop for the Android platform without using an IDE at all, as most of the tools can be run directly from the command line.

Conventions Used in This Book

The following typographical conventions are used in this book:

Italic

Indicates new terms, URLs, email addresses, filenames, and file extensions.

`Constant width`

Used for program listings, as well as within paragraphs to refer to program elements such as variable or function names, data types, and XML keywords.

`Constant width bold`

Shows commands or other text that should be typed literally by the user.

`Constant width italic`

Shows text that should be replaced with user-supplied values or by values determined by context.

This icon signifies a tip, suggestion, or general note.

This icon indicates a warning or caution.

Using Code Examples

This book is here to help you get your job done. In general, if this book includes code examples, you may use the code in your programs and documentation. You do not need to contact us for permission unless you're reproducing a significant portion of the code. For example, writing a program that uses several chunks of code from this book does not require permission. Selling or distributing a CD-ROM of examples from O'Reilly books does require permission. Answering a question by citing this book and quoting example code does not require permission. Incorporating a significant amount of example code from this book into your product's documentation does require permission.

We appreciate, but do not require, attribution. An attribution usually includes the title, author, publisher, and ISBN. For example: "*Android Developer Tools Essentials* by Mike Wolfson (O'Reilly). Copyright 2013 Mike Wolfson, 978-1-449-32821-4."

Supplemental material (code examples, exercises, etc.) is available for download at *https://github.com/mwolfson/ToolsDemo*.

If you feel your use of code examples falls outside fair use or the permission given above, feel free to contact us at *permissions@oreilly.com*.

Safari® Books Online

Safari Books Online (*www.safaribooksonline.com*) is an on-demand digital library that delivers expert content in both book and video form from the world's leading authors in technology and business.

Technology professionals, software developers, web designers, and business and creative professionals use Safari Books Online as their primary resource for research, problem solving, learning, and certification training.

Safari Books Online offers a range of product mixes and pricing programs for organizations, government agencies, and individuals. Subscribers have access to thousands of books, training videos, and prepublication manuscripts in one fully searchable database from publishers like O'Reilly Media, Prentice Hall Professional, Addison-Wesley Professional, Microsoft Press, Sams, Que, Peachpit Press, Focal Press, Cisco Press, John Wiley & Sons, Syngress, Morgan Kaufmann, IBM Redbooks, Packt, Adobe Press, FT Press, Apress, Manning, New Riders, McGraw-Hill, Jones & Bartlett, Course Technology, and dozens more. For more information about Safari Books Online, please visit us online.

How to Contact Us

Please address comments and questions concerning this book to the publisher:

O'Reilly Media, Inc.
1005 Gravenstein Highway North
Sebastopol, CA 95472
800-998-9938 (in the United States or Canada)
707-829-0515 (international or local)
707-829-0104 (fax)

We have a web page for this book, where we list errata, examples, and any additional information. You can access this page at *http://oreil.ly/Android_Essentials*.

To comment or ask technical questions about this book, send email to *bookquestions@oreilly.com*.

For more information about our books, courses, conferences, and news, see our website at *http://www.oreilly.com*.

Find us on Facebook: *http://facebook.com/oreilly*

Follow us on Twitter: *http://twitter.com/oreillymedia*

Watch us on YouTube: *http://www.youtube.com/oreillymedia*

Acknowledgments

Special thanks to my wife Dana. Without your support and encouragement, this book (and many other things in my life) wouldn't be possible. I love you and appreciate everything you do for me.

Thanks to the tech reviewers who stuck with me and provided great feedback throughout the long writing process: Jason Douglas, Maija Mednieks, Charlie Meyersohn, and especially Peter Van Der Linden, whose thorough review and excellent comments improved the quality of the book and made my job much easier. I couldn't have done it without you.

Thanks to Donn Felker for your last-minute help on Android Studio. Your content really improves the quality of this book. Looking forward to shipping more products together!

Shout-out to Heatsync Labs in Mesa, AZ and CO+HOOTS in Phoenix, AZ for providing spaces that foster creativity.

## CHAPTER 1

Getting Started

It's fairly easy to set up the Android developer environment. The steps are basically the same for all supported platforms (with small variations on each OS). I'll describe them in detail so you can be sure you have everything configured correctly.

 Installation instructions might change over time. These basic steps are consistent with the latest release. However, they might change, so you should always check the online documentation (*http://bit.ly/XUepi1*) to make sure you are installing and using the most up-to-date version.

The basic steps are:

1. Make sure your computer meets minimum requirements.
2. Install the Java Development Kit (JDK).
3. Install the Android SDK.
4. Install the Eclipse Integrated Development Environment (IDE).
5. Install the Android Developer Tools (ADT) plug-in for Eclipse.

Minimum Requirements

To develop for Android, you'll need a reasonably responsive computer. You will likely be running a few memory-intensive processes (including emulators) and IO-intensive things (such as building your code or packaging a release artifact). The published base requirements for Android make it possible to develop on a variety of very low-powered devices (such as netbooks), but for practical purposes I suggest using a development environment with more widely available resources. Guidelines for practical minimum requirements are listed in Table 1-1.

Table 1-1. Practical minimum hardware requirements

	Windows	Linux	Mac OS X
OS Version	Windows XP (32-bit)	Ubuntu, RedHat, and others	OS X (10.4.9 +)
Hard Disk Space	25GB	25GB	25GB
System Memory	3GB	2GB	4GB
Processor	Dual Core +	Dual Core +	x86 Only
USB	USB 2.0+	USB 2.0+	USB 2.0+

Installing Java

The Android development platform is built on the standard Java framework. Android applications are built on top of the Java platform, so you will need to install it in order to do anything with Android. Make sure you get the Java Developer Kit (JDK) as opposed to the Java Runtime Environment (JRE) (which may already be installed on your system). The JDK has the compiler, debugger, and other tools you will use to develop software; the JRE is a runtime for executing those tools. Download the latest version, choosing the default settings (it is not necessary to have any of the optional packages that are available).

> Currently, Android is designed to target Java version 1.6. If you download a version newer than this (which is likely), you will need to set the Java Compiler level to be compliant with 1.6. In Eclipse, a Java Compiler option in the properties of your Android project allows you to set this.

You can download the JDK installation packages for each supported OS from the Java download site (*http://bit.ly/TEA7iC*).

> Optionally, if you are on Linux, you can use a package manager (such as *apt* or *yum*) to download and install Java. For instance, on Ubuntu or Debian, use the following command:
>
> ```
> sudo apt-get install sun-java6-jdk
> ```

In general, Mac OS X developers aren't required to install Java manually. On the Mac OS, Java comes preinstalled, with a custom packaged version directly from Apple. Updating to newer versions of Java is only possible when Apple releases an update through their own channels. To confirm that the correct version of Java is installed, the following command can be run from any terminal window to display this information:

java -version

More information about Java on Mac OS X is available here: Mac OS Java site (*http:// bit.ly/15U7ZkF*).

Installing the Android Software Development Kit

The Android Software Development Kit (SDK) is the collection of libraries, tools, documentation, and samples that are required to run and develop Android apps and to use the tools. It is not a complete development environment, and contains only the base tools needed to download the rest of the necessary components. Downloading tools and components will be discussed in detail in the section about using the "SDK Manager" on page 11.

In order to get started, you will need to download the "ADT Bundle." This is a new packaging style (as of ADT version 21) that includes all the components required to develop for Android packaged as a single, integrated download. Previous to this release, it was necessary to download and install each of the required components separately, and then set them up to work together. This manual approach is more error-prone, but is still supported, particularly if you wish to use an IDE other than Eclipse. The manual procedure is described on the Android Developers web page titled Setting Up an Existing IDE (*http://bit.ly/13LJtmy*). I strongly recommend you use the ADT Bundle to install the tools. It streamlines the process, minimizes the chances of error, and creates a standard directory structure for the tools. The bundle includes each of these components:

- The Eclipse IDE, including the ADT plug-ins, and all the required extensions
- The SDK Tools
- The Platform Tools
- The latest Android Platform
- A CPU image compatible with the latest platform

Installing the ADT Bundle

The most recent release of the tools provides a convenient single package containing everything necessary to develop Android. It makes installation easy.

Downloading the ADT bundle

On the main page of the SDK site (*http://bit.ly/XUepi1*), you will notice a button to download the package, which currently looks like Figure 1-1. This link will automatically download the version for the OS you are using. Make sure you have good Internet connectivity (it is a large download—at the time of this writing, over 400MB).

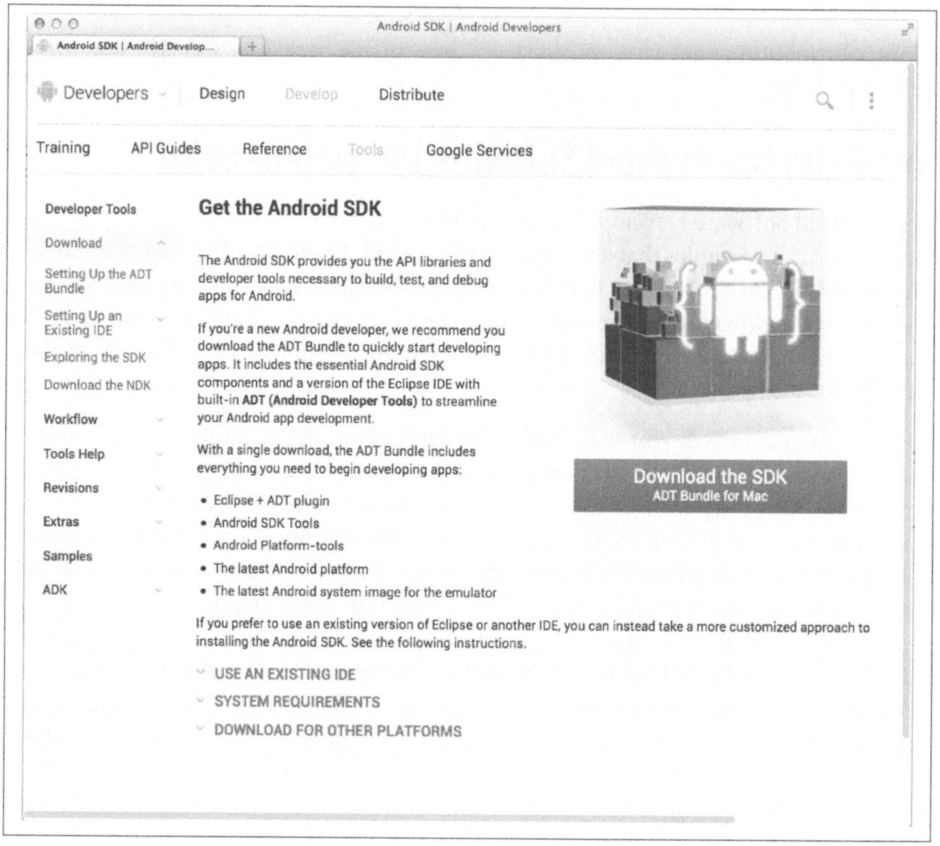

Figure 1-1. Downloading the ADT Bundle

Extracting the tools to Android Home

The next step in the installation is to extract the artifacts to an appropriate location on your filesystem. You will need to select the location to install the tools, which can be wherever you wish. I suggest placing this directory at a high level in the filesystem, in order to make it easier to reference, locate, and back up. Here are some suggestions:

If you are on a single-user machine or want to put everything in a common location, you could use the following locations:

- Windows: *C:\android*
- Linux or Mac OS X: */usr/dev/android*

It is common and perfectly acceptable to put Android in your home directory. For instance:

- Windows: *C:\Users\youruserid\android*
- Mac OS X: */Users/youruserid/android*
- Linux: */home/youruserid/android*

Unzip the downloaded artifact to the Android folder

Use the appropriate utility (such as WinZip on Windows, tar on Linux, or just double-click the file on Mac OS X) to extract the Bundle into the folder you chose in the previous step. If you do this correctly, you should see the *android-sdk* folder in the *Android Home* folder you created in the previous section. On Windows, this is *C:\android\sdk*, and on Mac OS X or Linux, it's */usr/dev/android/sdk*.

Setting your PATH variable

Next, you will need to append the location of the Android executables to your PATH environment variable. This is not strictly required, but makes it much easier to use the Android tools from anywhere on your system (and will be assumed in the examples in this book). All the executables we want to use from the command line can be found in the *platform-tools* and the *tools* directories in your Android installation.

Setting your PATH is different on each OS. Instructions about how to do this can be found on the help pages of each operating system, or in this article, which contains a great overview (*http://bit.ly/14smsVa*) of how to set and use PATH and other environment variables.

You can verify that your path is set correctly by opening a new terminal window and typing **android** at the command prompt. This will launch the SDK Manager, which signifies you did everything correctly and that you have successfully installed the Android SDK. You will use the SDK Manager to download additional components, but won't need to use it now, since the ADT Bundle already has the current platform included.

Validating the installation

To validate that everything was installed correctly, launch the Eclipse executable by clicking on or running *${android.sdk}\eclipse\eclipse*. Eclipse will start, and prompt you to enter the location of the *workspace*. This is the location where your project-specific assets (source code, images, build scripts, and so on) will be stored. You can select whatever location you prefer, or just use the default value supplied. Eclipse will start, and you will see a customized version of the tool (named the Android Developer Tools – ADT). Congrats, your installation was successful.

Developing Without Eclipse

Although it is recommended that you use an IDE to help in the development process, the tools provided in the SDK can also be used on the command line or with other IDEs. You will be able to do almost anything you need (including compiling, building and packaging artifacts, launching emulators, and using the tools) strictly using the command line or other tools.

Command-Line Usage

To start using the tools from the command prompt, simply start a terminal window, and type the name of the tool you want to start at the command prompt. If you set your PATH variable properly (according to the instructions in "Setting your PATH variable" on page 5), you will be able to execute the various command from anywhere on your filesystem. Some examples of command-line usage can be found in "Android Debug Bridge (ADB)" on page 17. The main way you will access the tools is through Eclipse, but you can also access them from the command line. This is useful for scripting or automation. It is not recommended to use them exclusively, as the tools integrated into Eclipse are excellent, make a lot of tasks simpler, and will likely make your coding more efficient.

 Windows users can use Explorer to navigate to their *C:\android\sdk\tools* folder, highlight the full address, and simply replace it with *cmd*. Press Enter, and the command prompt starts at the location.

Using a Different IDE

It is not strictly necessary to use Eclipse for development. Many people have had success using Netbeans or IntelliJ. At the time of this writing, the officially supported IDE is Eclipse, which is the tool we will focus on for this book. In general, I suggest using the officially supported tools. This will ensure that you are able to get the latest updates and are using the most stable tool. Another important reason to stick with the suggested tools is that you will be using the same tools as a majority of the development community, so bugs you come across will likely be easier to fix because they'll be encountered by a larger community of users.

The open-source nature of the Tools projects means that they are designed to be platform- and tool-agnostic. This means the development team takes care to ensure the tools run well everywhere. If you do have a preference for other development tools, you most likely will be able to use them for your Android projects. There are robust communities supporting various platforms, and in many cases, the alternate tools do things better than Eclipse.

At Google I/O 2013, the Android tools team announced support for a new IDE named "Android Studio" (Chapter 6 describes how to use it). This looks like an exciting alternative for the future. However, it is currently a very early release, so it is not ready for production usage.

The NetBeans IDE also supports Android development. Information about using this can be found on the Android Plug-in for NetBeans (*http://bit.ly/14cHF1f*) page on the Kenai website.

Configuring a Device for Development

The simplest way to test your applications is often by using an Android device. You can use almost any Android device for development, as long as you make a few changes in order to enable communication with the development tools.

1. Configuring a Physical Device for Development.

   The instructions for setting up your device to be used as a development device are covered in "Configuring a Physical Device for Development" on page 26.

2. Change phone settings.

   Launch the Settings app on your phone, then select Applications → Development → USB-Debugging. Check the box next to "USB debugging" to enable this functionality. The result should look like Figure 1-2.

3. Download the ADB driver.

   In order to connect an Android-powered device for testing on Windows machines, it is necessary to install the appropriate USB driver. This is not necessary on Mac OS X or Linux.

   You can find drivers at the website of the manufacturer of your phone. You may be able to find a driver through the Android Document website (*http://bit.ly/18gFmi4*), which contains a list of links to software for many original equipment manufacturers (OEMs).

4. Validate debugging on the phone.

   Connect your device to your computer. If everything went well, you will see a notification (▣) from your operating system, indicating that the device is installed and ready to use.

   You will also notice two new entries in the notification drawer of your device (shown in Figure 1-3). These will show that you are successfully connected. You can select them to launch the Settings application.

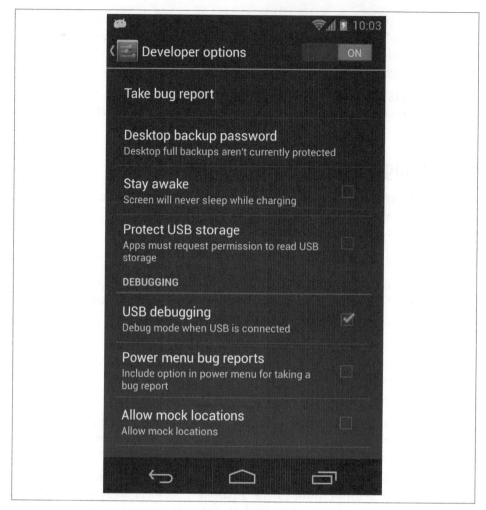

Figure 1-2. Debugging enabled for testing apps on a phone

Figure 1-3. Debugging notification

Congratulations! You have successfully installed everything you need to develop and test Android applications.

## CHAPTER 2

Essential Tools

This chapter describes the fundamental tools that you need in order to start developing Android applications. In it, I will show you how to use the SDK Manager to download various development resources, and discuss using the command-line tools (in particular the Android Debug Bridge – ADB).

SDK Manager

The SDK Manager is a GUI tool designed to make it easy to download and install the required components. It is likely the first tool you will encounter, and the one you will use most often. The SDK Manager allows you to update the Android SDK and install additional components.

SDK Components

The Android SDK has a modular structure, which means that the major components of the SDK are collected into separate packages. This makes it easy to install only the components you need for your particular unique use case. The packages you install are determined by the version of the OS you are targeting, if you use third-party services (like Google Maps or Analytics), and if you plan to support specific hardware (like a particular chipset or a dual screen). The modular structure has two important benefits. The first is that disk storage is not wasted on downloading unnecessary components. This is important because each platform requires at least 100MB of space, and this can grow rapidly when optional packages are included. The other advantage is that managing dependencies within a project is streamlined because it is possible to control exactly which software you are working with, and install only the components you require.

It is important to understand the various components that are available. They are organized into categories:

SDK Tools

> These include the various utility tools you will use to develop apps. These are essential tools required by all developers. You can think of them as the core system tools of the platform. These include android, ddms, apkbuilder, and emulator, among others. You can find these in the *android-sdk/tools* directory.

Platform Tools

> These are additional tools that are developed alongside the core platform, and are typically updated in concert with the release of a new version of the platform. These include adb, fastboot, dx, aidl, and others. You can find these in the *android-sdk/platform-tools* directory.

Android Platform

> An SDK platform is released for every version of Android. Each release includes a compliant library, system image, emulator skins, and platform-specific tools. Patches and point releases to the platform are also located here (*http://bit.ly/1ccVmY5*).

Google APIs

> The additional libraries required to use Google-specific services such as Google Cloud Messaging or Maps.

Drivers

> This contains driver files that allow an Android device to communicate with a computer. USB drivers here can be or downloaded from here.

Samples and documentation

> Here you'll find the sample code and documentation for each platform release. This includes example projects containing documented code that can and should be used when designing your own code. As with the SDK, it is generally a good idea to use the latest release because updates include the best examples with the least bugs.

Third-party add-ons

> This category includes tools and libraries for third-party add-ons, including the Android support package and the Analytics SDK. This also includes third-party add-ons such as a Samsung Galaxy Tab skin, Motorola SDK add-ons, and the Nook Color SDK add-ons. You can also find customized, fully compliant Android system images representing particular devices.

Starting the SDK Manager

The SDK Manager can be launched as an independent application, directly from the OS or from inside Eclipse. Follow these steps depending on how you will be launching the SDK Manager:

Windows

> Start → All Programs → Android SDK Tools → SDK Manager

Linux/Mac OS X

> Open a terminal, and run *android.*

Eclipse (all platforms)

> Look for the 🔲 icon in your Eclipse toolbar. Click on it to launch the SDK Manager.

> On all platforms, you can also launch directly from the menu: Window → Android SDK Manager.

The SDK Manager GUI launches, as shown in Figure 2-1.

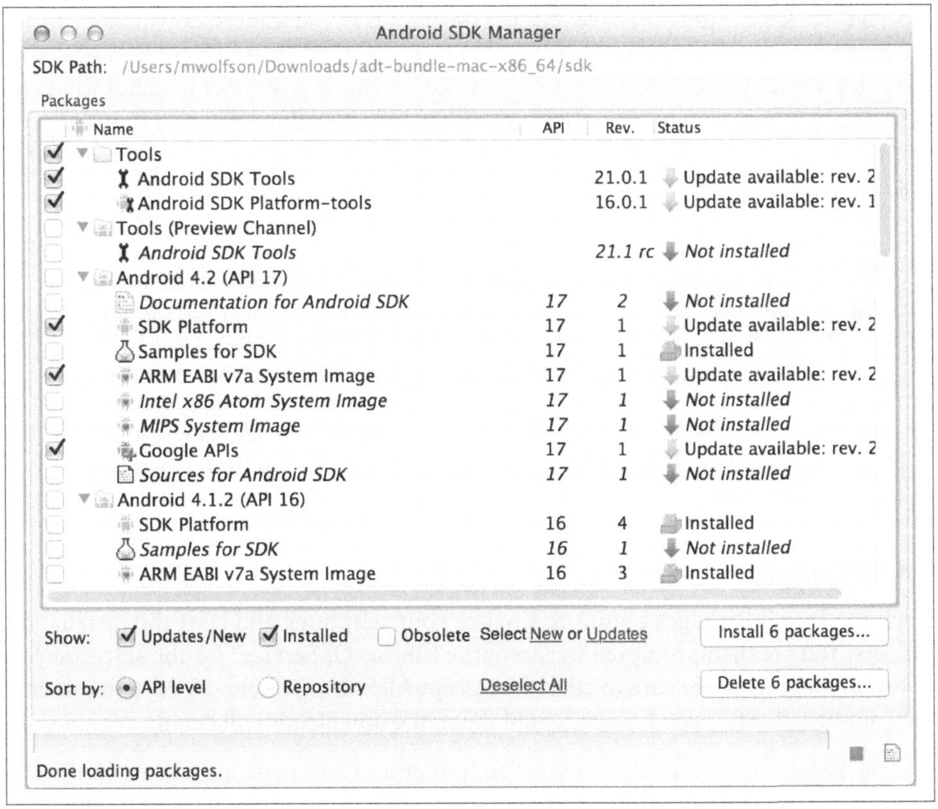

Figure 2-1. SDK Manager

Viewing Installed and Available Components

After launch, the SDK Manager will present a list of all the packages available for download from the SDK repository. The components are organized into those defined in

"SDK Components" on page 11. You can click on the white triangle (▷) next to any particular platform to expand the tree and see more detail about the compatible resources available. Figure 2-1 shows the *Android 4.2* and *4.1.2* sections expanded to expose more details about the compatible downloads available. In this view, you will see additional information about a particular package (this is the column on the right). This includes version information and install status. If there is a newer version of a component available, it will appear in the status column. In Figure 2-1, you will notice that there is an update available for the Tools.

Selecting packages

Next, select the packages you want to download. Place a checkmark next to each individual component that interests you, or select every package in a release by marking the top-level package. After you have selected the packages you want to download, you are ready to proceed. The button on the bottom right (marked "Install X packages...") now indicates the number of selected packages. Confirm that this number matches what you expect, as it is common to have packages marked for download that you didn't expect, and this is not always obvious (especially if something is marked in a platform that is not expanded).

 The various packages can take up a lot of space on your computer (for instance, each of the core platforms are around 100MB, without the docs or samples). It is important to decide which packages you want to support, and limit your downloads to those that are important to you. There are a lot of things to consider when making this decision, and a discussion of this is outside the scope of this book. This discussion (*http://bit.ly/13THhp6*) covers it well, and is recommended reading.

Installing packages

Click the Install Packages button to finalize your selections and start the installation process. You are then prompted to accept the "Terms Of Service" for the software you are downloading. Make sure to click the Accept All button, or else all the components may not install. After you have accepted them, the downloads will begin.

The packages are downloaded to your computer and automatically stored in the appropriate folder in the location where you installed Android (see "Extracting the tools to Android Home" on page 4). The components are downloaded into the following subdirectories:

Platforms	*platforms/android-API_level*
Add-ons	*add-ons*
Samples	*samples/android-API_level*
Documentation	*docs* (there is only one copy, because old docs are replaced)

In some cases (such as when installing device drivers), you need to run the software you downloaded to complete the installation. Other components, including the Platform components, are automatically installed during the download process and don't require additional installation steps.

Deleting and updating components

In order to delete a package, follow the same process as you did when you installed it. Select the packages to delete, and then click the Delete Packages button. If there are packages that need to be updated, select them and click the Install Packages button. Don't forget to confirm that the number of packages shown on the button is correct, so you don't accidentally remove something you need.

Managing dependencies

For the most part, Android developers don't need to worry about package dependencies too much. For the most part, the components are designed to run independently of each other. As long as you are extra careful and double-check which packages you are installing or removing, you shouldn't have many problems managing installed components. If you do make an error, you now know how easy it is to use this tool to manage your installed components.

ADT Preview Channel

The ADT team releases new code frequently. This can include bug fixes, or previews of new features. You may want to try a particular release if it has a particular bug fix you require or new tools that you would like to try. The ability to download and install a preview is integrated directly into the "SDK Manager" on page 11, which makes switching to it very simple. For the most part, you should use the officially released tools, because they are more stable, but having the ability to switch to the newest tools can be useful in some situations.

Enable the Preview Channel

The Preview Channel is not enabled by default. You can access this setting (as shown in Figure 2-2) from the following menu: Tools → Options → Check "Enable Preview Tools."

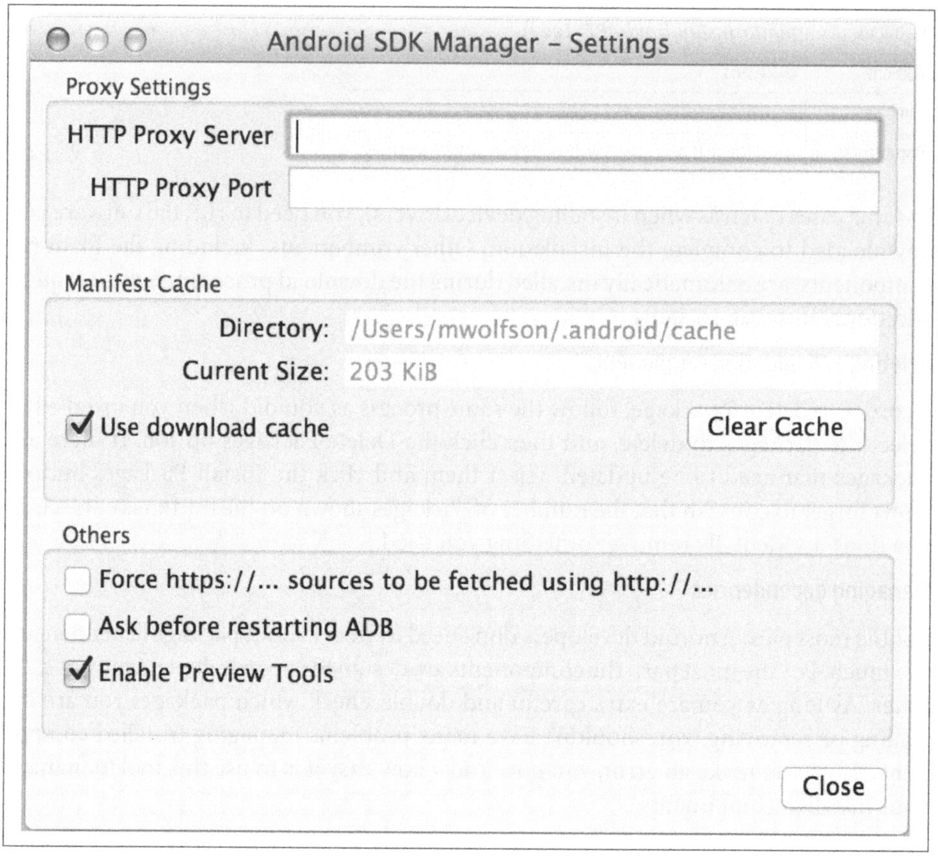

Figure 2-2. Enabling the Preview Channel

Installing Preview Tools

After enabling this option, you will see the Preview Channel option, shown in Figure 2-3, appear in the list under the "Tools (Preview Channel)" heading. To install it, select it, then click the Install Packages button to use that version of the tools.

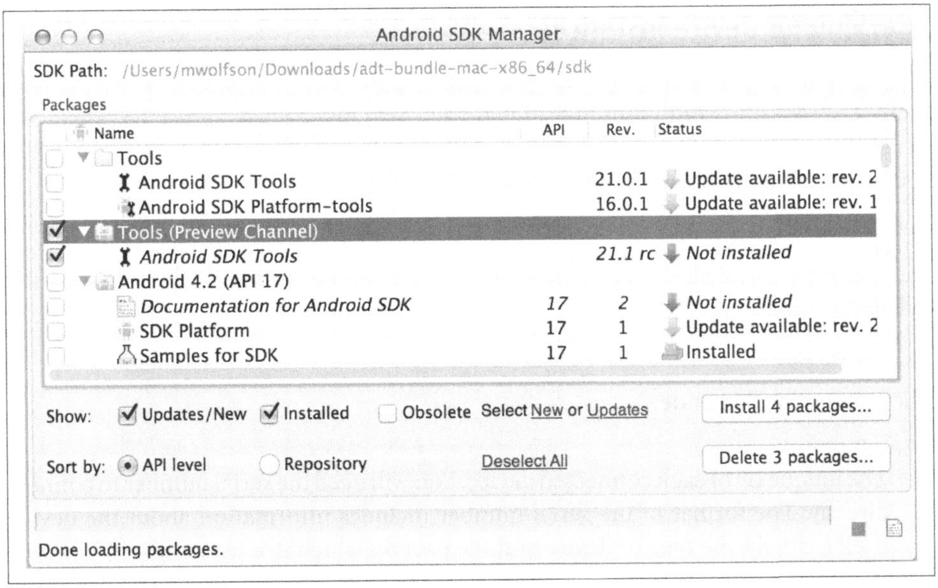

Figure 2-3. Verifying that the Preview Channel is enabled

Reverting to released tools

If you would like to revert to the released version, simply reinstall that version by selecting it and then clicking the Install Packages button again.

Android Debug Bridge (ADB)

ADB is the main tool that allows you to interact with your emulator or a connected device. The ADB process is actually a client/server program. The server component communicates with a variety of clients (such as the command line or DDMS). The daemon process on the device facilitates communication of activities such as:

- Push/pull of data or apps
- Issuing shell commands
- Restarting the device
- Reading system logs

Starting ADB

Start the ADB client using the command line. To start the process, simply execute the following command:

```
adb
```

Querying for Device Instances

The ADB server automatically connects to all of the devices or emulators that are currently connected to your computer. If you have only one device connected, it will automatically connect to that single instance. If you have more than once device connected, you will need to direct commands to a specific instance.

Find connected devices

You can get a list of all devices that ADB is able to communicate with by issuing the following command:

```
adb devices
```

The response will include:

Serial number
> The unique ID of each connected device. You will need the serial number to connect directly. The format of the serial number includes information about the device itself (namely, the type of device and the port on which it is listening).

State
> The connection state of the device. This will be *offline* if the device is connected but not responding. It will be *device* if is available and connected. Otherwise, the response will be *no devices*, which indicates there are no active devices that ADB can communicate with currently.

Directing a command to a specific device

Now that you know what devices are on your system, you can direct a command to a specific instance by issuing the following command:

```
adb -s  serialNumber
        command
```

The example below shows how you would target a command to a particular device, when more than one is connected. The first step is to issue the *devices* command to display a list of connected devices. The list shows two connected devices: the first is a physical device, and the second is an emulator (which is clear from the name). The next step is to use the -s option to target the preferred device. In this example, we are using ADB to find the ADB version number of the attached emulator.

```
$ adb devices
List of devices attached
emulator-5556    device
emulator-5554    device

$ adb -s emulator-5556 version
Android Debug Bridge version 1.0.31
$
```

If there is only one device connected, ADB automatically defaults to use that instance. I usually keep only one device connected at a time. This makes issuing ADB commands simpler because I don't need to specify a device argument anymore (ADB will default to the only running device). For example, you can eliminate the targeting step during the deploy cycle, which speeds up this common task.

Issuing Commands

Now that ADB knows which device to target, we can interact with it. It is possible to do a variety of useful things with this interface. Let's walk through a few examples:

Transferring files

It is very easy to transfer files between your computer and your device using the *push* and *pull* commands. *push* goes from your computer to the device, whereas *pull* does the opposite. You can include additional path parameters if you would like to specify a particular location for the files. If a path is not specified, the commands will use the current directory of your computer for the local location and the data folder on the device for the remote location. *push* and *pull* can also copy complete directories (recursively), which can be very useful.

The syntax of *push* is:

```
adb push    local-directory
            remote
```

An example of using this command is shown here. We are using ADB to push a file named *foo.txt* from the current directory to the SD card. The syntax for this is:

```
adb push foo.txt /sdcard/foo.txt
```

To move the file off the SD card and back onto your machine, in a new directory and with a new name, type:

```
adb pull /sdcard/foo.txt C:/tmp2/foo2.txt
```

This looks like this, when executed from the command line:

```
$ adb push foo.txt /sdcard/
0 KB/s (8 bytes in 0.019s)
$ adb pull /sdcard/foo.txt /tmp/foo2/txt
1 KB/s (8 bytes in 0.004s)
$
```

Managing applications on a device

A very common process is to install or remove applications from a device. This is easy to accomplish using ADB. Simply issue the *install* command and supply a valid APK file. This installs the app on your device.

The syntax of the command is:

```
adb install    foo.apk
```

The syntax is similar to remove an app, except that you need to supply the package name instead of the APK filename as an argument.

The syntax of the command is:

```
adb uninstall    com.example.masterd
$ adb install foo.apk
2134 KB/s (222527 bytes in 0.101s)
    pkg: /data/local/tmp/foo.apk
Success
$ adb uninstall com.tools.demo
Success
$
```

The Shell Command

The Android Framework is built upon a modified Linux kernel. The creators of Android added their own middleware, libraries, and APIs to the Linux kernel to develop the framework. This means that it includes a command-line interface that will look familiar to Linux users. The *shell* interface will have many of the same tools developers are used to, but not all of them. Additionally, the tools themselves may be different, and likely won't support every operation you expect. For instance, the *ls -l* command works, but *ls -x* does not.

The binaries for the included tools are stored on the device in the */system/bin* folder. I suggest you look in that folder to familiarize yourself with the commands that are available. Some frequently used commands that are not available include *more, less, cp,* and *file.* Some common tools that are included are *ls, ps,* and *rm.* It is definitely worth reviewing the contents of the */system/bin/* directory. It contains not just the standard command-line tools, but also a variety of additional tools designed specifically for Android development (like *monkey, logcat, dumpstate,* etc.). You may get frustrated by the limitations of the Android shell, especially if you are used to the more feature-rich options available in full Linux distributions. You should spend some time learning how to use these tools effectively; they may be limited, but they still are still very useful.

You can use ADB to access the command shell of a device directly. You can issue commands as one-line executables, or interact with the shell interactively by issuing a series of commands.

Interactive mode

Interactive mode allows you to execute more than one command successively on the device. To start interactive shell mode, type:

```
adb shell
```

You will see a # symbol, which indicates that you are in shell mode. When you are ready to exit the remote shell, you can use Ctrl+D or type **exit** to end the shell session.

The example belows shows accessing the shell, using common Linux commands to navigate the directory structure, reading the contents of a file, and finally, exiting the shell back to the command prompt.

```
$ adb shell
root@android:/ # pwd
/
root@android:/ # cd /system/etc
root@android:/system/etc # pwd
/system/etc
root@android:/system/etc # cat ./hosts
127.0.0.1          localhost
root@android:/system/etc # exit
$
```

One-off mode

It is also possible to execute commands noninteractively. To do this, type the command you want to execute after the shell keyword.

```
adb shell     command
```

The next example shows how you would read the */system/etc/hosts* file by issuing a single command that executes, but does not maintain, an open connection to the remote shell.

```
$ adb shell cat /system/etc/hosts
127.0.0.1          localhost
$
```

Retrieving system data

There are many cases in which you need detailed information about the various systems on your device. Some useful commands can dump huge amounts of information about the system, including service status, system statistics, and error logs. You may want to collect these statistics if you are trying to analyze trends or specific details about your application.

adb shell dumpsys
> Outputs data about specific system services to the screen. For example, *adb shell dumpsys alarm* will output details about all the alarms currently registered on the system.

adb shell dumpstate
> Detailed system data representing a device at a particular state in time (includes dumpsys information as well).

adb shell dmesg
> Outputs the contents of the kernel's ring buffer to the screen. This output is quite verbose, and contains a lot of key information from the system kernel, including

information about the CPU, memory, OS version, system mount points, and lots more. It can be useful, especially when trying to debug hardware issues, or when writing software that interacts directly with the system hardware.

adb shell logcat -b radio
> This command provides access to the cellular radio log. This information is useful when interacting with the networking stack. Some of the information available in this log includes time of events, a listing of commands used by the system to communicate, SMS information, IP information, and cellular network data.

Using the Activity Manager

Shell access allows much more granular access to the device. You can use this to start applications or even single activities in a controlled way. This can be very useful if you need to test different entry points to an application that may be hard to simulate by stepping through the UI. Use the *Activity Manager* to launch a specific screen with a specific set of *Intent* parameters.

An example of starting an activity named *com.foo.FooActivity* directly would be:

```
adb shell am start -n com.foo/.FooActivity
```

In Figure 2-4, I start my app at a particular activity (MemDemoActivity), which is not the activity defined in the manifest as the main launcher activity.

```
adb shell am start com.tools.demo/.MemDemoActivity
```

ADB Does a Lot More

The ADB tool has a variety of additional functionality that is beyond the scope of this book. It is worth becoming familiar with these additional features, as they provide a lot of useful and important functionality.

Some functionality worth highlighting includes:

- Modify network configuration options like port forwarding (example: *adb forward tcp:7101 tcp:8101*)
- Access your device as the root user (example: *adb shell su*)
- Restart the device in alternate modes, such as recovery mode (example: *adb reboot recovery*)
- View system logs, such as the radio or event buffers (example: *adb logcat -b events*)
- Show kernel debug info (example: *adb shell dmesg*)
- Examine system utilization (example: *adb shell tail | top*)

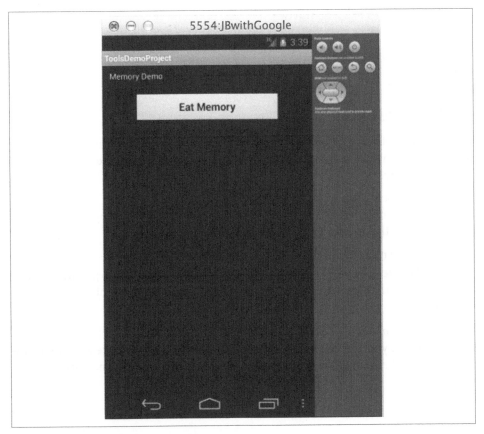

Figure 2-4. Activity Manager example

There is a lot of other functionality we aren't able to cover. For a complete list of all available commands and their parameters, type *adb -help* without any additional arguments to get a listing of all options.

Resetting the ADB Server

There will be times when ADB loses connectivity, or encounters other issues that require resetting the process. To do so, stop the existing ADB process, and then restart it by issuing the following two commands in order:

1. adb kill-server

2. adb start-server

```
$ adb kill-server
$ adb start-server
```

```
* daemon not running. starting it now on port 5037 *
* daemon started successfully *
$ adb devices
List of devices attached
emulator-5554    device

$
```

Additional Resources

There are many features of the ADB tool that I am not able to cover in this chapter. If you would like to learn more about the advanced capabilities of this tool, there are a few excellent resources.

Command Reference (http://bit.ly/1extzNM)
> The command reference on the official Android page has a listing of all the commands and their options.

XDA Devs ADB Guide (http://bit.ly/13LJZko)
> The XDA Devs website has a very complete explanation of how to get started using the advanced features of ADB, and is targeted towards people wanting to root their devices.

Embedded Android Book (http://bit.ly/embedded-android)
> This book by Karim Yaghmour contains in-depth explanations relating to the internals of the ADB tool and using it to control embedded environments.

## CHAPTER 3

Configuring Devices and Emulators

When developing mobile applications, it is necessary to test your code on many different devices. Because there is such a large variety available for Android (at the time of this writing, there are over 3,000 devices supported in the Google Play Store), this can be particularly challenging. It is necessary to test your app to ensure it runs well on the majority of devices; you also need to test out a few different screen sizes. You may also need to account for different hardware capabilities, including OS levels, existence of sensors, amount of memory, or CPU. Fortunately, ADT provides tools that make handling these challenges easier. I'll describe how to test on real devices, and also how to use emulators when the devices you need aren't available.

Using a Physical Device for Development

For many activities, it's important not to rely completely on an emulator, but to check your app on an actual device. For instance, this is particularly useful when you are testing advanced graphics rendering, utilizing location services, or making use of advanced sensors. It is not strictly necessary to own an Android device to develop for Android (see "Using Hardware Acceleration" on page 33 for details), but it is a common and simple way to start testing with minimal effort. This section will go through the steps required to use an Android device as a development aid.

If you don't already have a device, it is easy to acquire a cheap used handset; check Craigslist or eBay for older devices. Other alternatives are outlined later in this chapter (including HAXM and Genymotion).

Capabilities and Limitations

As I mentioned, there are reasons to use a physical device instead of an emulator. Here is an overview of the most important capabilities and limitations:

Capabilities

- Making real phone calls and sending real SMS text messages.
- Using multitouch on a screen.
- Having access to actual location data, in multiple locations and when in motion.
- Using advanced sensors, such as a compass, gyroscope, or barometer.

Limitations

- Certain core services of a phone might be locked down by the device manufacturer or service provider. It might be difficult to change networking parameters or access resources as the *root* user.
- Testing on a device, particularly if it is one you rely on, could mess up your phone.
- Simulating distant locations is a no-go (for example, if you want to test a location in Egypt and your device is in Belize).

Configuring a Physical Device for Development

Almost any Android phone can be used for development. In order to configure a device, enable the option in the Settings app on the device. To do this, open the Settings app, then select Applications → Development. Place a checkmark next to USB debugging (if you are running a device with OS 4.0+, the setting is located in a slightly different place within the Settings app, namely "Developer options"). The result should look like Figure 3-1.

Using an Emulator for Development

We all agree that it is necessary to test Android apps on a variety of different devices and hardware. As it is practically impossible to own every physical device, you will need to use an emulator to check configurations of hardware you don't have. Some of the important reasons to use emulators include:

- Testing on different hardware configurations
- Validating on different versions of the Android OS
- Simulating load or other stress tests
- Viewing your UI on various screen sizes and resolutions

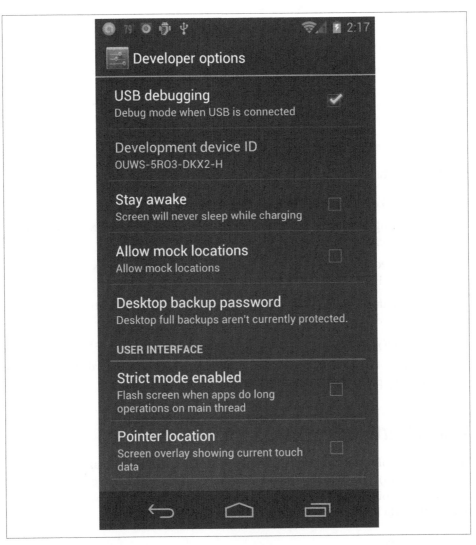

Figure 3-1. Enable USB debugging on a physical device

Supported Features

The emulator included in the standard toolkit is feature-rich, however there are some constraints.

Supported features

- Simulating telephony, including latency and connectivity
- Simulating text messaging

- Simulating both a single location or a path

- Simulating a variety of hardware configurations (see "Emulator Options" on page 32 for options)

- Modifying networking (including port redirection, DNS settings, and proxy settings)

- Simulating various processor types, including ARM and Intel (see "Using Hardware Acceleration" on page 33)

- Using multimedia (video only, not audio)

Unsupported features

- Cannot make real phone calls or send real text messages

- No accessing of Google services such as Gmail, Google Play Store, and other Google-specific applications

- No advanced graphics support without using native x86 processor support; see "Using Hardware Acceleration" on page 33 for a workaround

- No simulating of touch events (in particular multitouch, or gestures); see Chapter 4 for a workaround that allows you to use a device to simulate sensors

- No accessory integration (USB, headphones, or other peripherals)

- No support for performance-sensitive applications—the standard emulator does not reliably perform as a real device would in all situations

Android Virtual Devices

To test a variety of devices, you will want to create different emulator images (to represent different devices). These configurations are stored in files with the *avd* extension, which stands for Android Virtual Device (AVD). It allows you to specify hardware and software options that will be used by the emulator to model an actual device.

Creating AVDs

There are two primary ways to create AVDs. The easiest way is to use the graphical AVD manager. It is also possible to configure AVDs from the command line by passing configuration parameters to the *android* tool. For the most part, you will likely want to use the graphical tool, as it is simple to use. You would use the command-line option when working with scripts or other noninteractive operations (for instance, if you are creating emulator images on a build server, or using a batch operation to test your code on multiple device configurations).

AVD Manager

Next, let's look at the AVD Manager, a GUI tool designed to make configuring AVDs simple. Start it by clicking on the 🖿 icon or running the android tool from the command line. The first time you launch it, you will see something similar to Figure 3-2. The screen will display a list of existing emulator configurations. You will be able to create, edit, repair, start, or see details of the various AVDs you have configured.

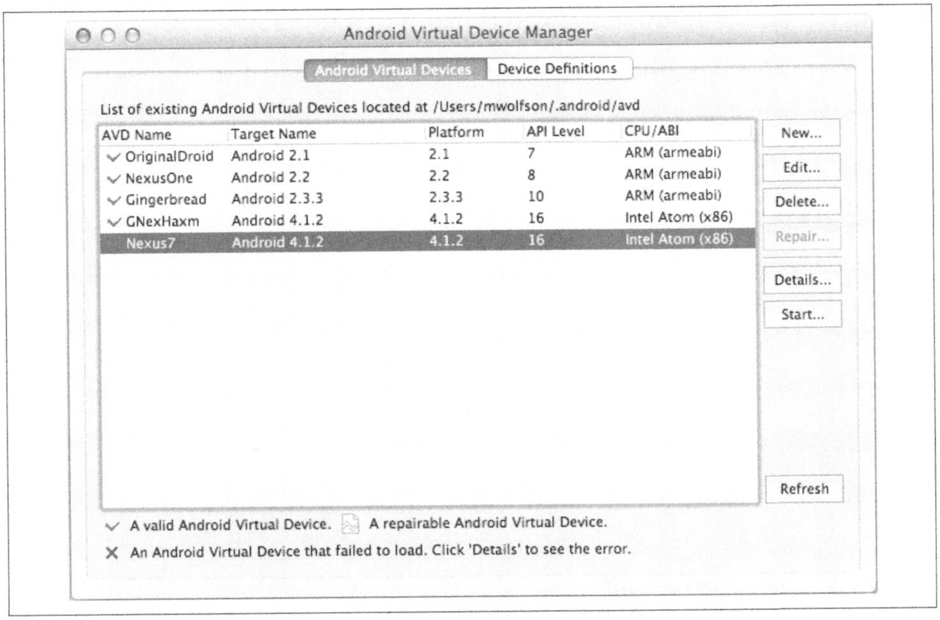

Figure 3-2. AVD Manager

To create a new emulator configuration, click the New button to launch the "Create new Android Virtual Device (AVD)" wizard (see Figure 3-3). You will then use this simple form to set the various configuration options necessary.

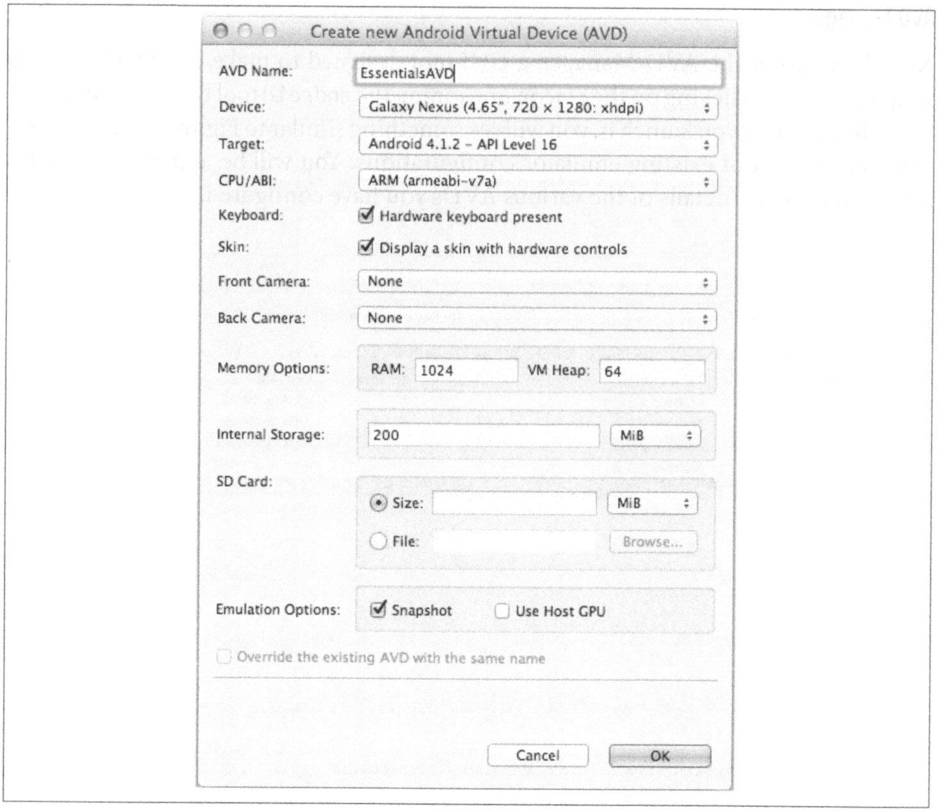

Figure 3-3. Create AVD wizard

To configure an AVD, you need to supply a variety of configuration parameters. They will be used to define the specific hardware parameters you wish to emulate. The options include:

Name

Identifies your current configuration image. This can be anything you like, but you should choose a name that lets you identify the specific options offered by the AVD. I usually name these according to the device I am trying to emulate, e.g., Galaxy-Nexus, SamsungS4, or HTCOne.

Device

Allows you to select a preconfigured image based on a variety of common devices.

Target

Specifies the version of the platform the device will run. The tool will allow you to specify only those platforms that you have downloaded to your environment. In other words, if you have not used the SDK Manager (Chapter 1) to install the API you wish to use, you will not be able to create an emulator running that version.

CPU/ABI

Specifies a particular hardware configuration to use (currently either ARM or Intel Atom). See "Using Hardware Acceleration" on page 33 for information on how to enable it.

SD Card

Simulates an SD card. You can specify the size and location on your local disk (the default is the ~/.android folder).

Snapshot

Enabling this feature gives you the ability to save and restore an emulator's state to a "snapshot" file. This can be useful for saving the state of an emulator, allowing you to quickly boot to a specific state, avoiding lengthy boot times. For more information, see "Using the Emulator" on page 39.

Skin

Allows you to specify a particular screen size and resolution. It provides a set of standard screen configurations for a particular platform, or you can specify custom values.

Creating AVDs from the command line

It can be useful to generate AVD images from the command line when you are scripting or using an environment where employing the GUI isn't practical. To create AVDs using this method, you need to pass command-line parameters to the android tool.

To create an AVD, run the android create avd command and include parameters that specify the particular configurations. Required parameters are a name for the AVD and the system image that should run on the emulator when it is invoked. If you want, you can also specify other options, such as SD card size, OS platform, skin, or a specific location in which to store user data files. The syntax of the command is:

```
android create avd -n name -t targetID/ [option value] ...
```

As an example, if we wanted to create an AVD named **ToolsAvd**, targeting the **Android 2.3 Platform**, with a **WVGA800** display, the command would look like this:

```
android create avd -n ToolsAvd -t 5 --skin WVGA800
```

Location of the AVD files

When you create an AVD image (regardless of whether you do it using the GUI tool or command line), a variety of files are stored on your system in a default directory named *.android*. This directory contains the AVD configuration files, the user data image, the SD card image (if configured), and any other relevant files. The root of this directory will also contain a file named *AVD_name.ini*. This file contains the location of the directory containing the AVD files.

The default location of this directory is:

- *~/.android/avd* on Linux or a Mac
- *C:\Documents and Settings\user\.android* on Windows XP
- *C:\Users\user\.android* on Windows 7 or Vista

If you would like to specify a different default location for this directory, you can create an environment variable named *ANDROID_HOME* and set it to the new default location. It is also possible to specify a different location for a specific AVD by including -p *path* as an option when you create the AVD. If you do set a custom location for the *.android* folder, make sure you put it on a local directory and not a network drive.

Emulator Options

There are many options available when creating an AVD. I will describe a few of the most common ones you will likely want to set for each emulator you create. If you want to learn about all the available options, this AVD Command Reference (*http://bit.ly/1bwMSJX*) is an excellent source.

Device RAM size

Sets the amount of physical RAM available on a device (in MB or megabytes). The default value is 96, which is quite low. I suggest increasing this value substantially to improve emulator performance. I generally set it to 512, but you can set it higher if your hardware can support it.

Keyboard support

Defines whether the device will support the physical keyboard on your computer. I always set this to "yes," because it makes interacting with the device easier. You will be able to use your computer keyboard to interact directly with the Android OS, which makes typing much easier than trying to use the onscreen keyboard with your mouse.

Camera support

Defines whether your emulator will support camera functionality. If your app requires a camera, make sure to set this value, as the default is "no." You can specify if your emulator will support front, back, or both cameras.

GPS support

Will allow your device to support location functionality. The default for this is "yes," so you will need to change it only if you specifically want to disable this functionality.

Cache partition size

This value is used by the Google Play Store to determine whether a device can download an app from the market. This value differs greatly between devices (for instance on an HTC Wildfire, it is 30 MB, and on the Nexus S, the size is 500 MB). It is worth testing with a variety of settings to make sure your app will work on many different devices. I suggest setting this to 1024 MB, especially if you see *Installation error: INSTALL_FAILED_INSUFFICIENT_STORAGE* messages when trying to install an app.

Advanced Emulator Configuration

Working with the emulator can be frustrating. Some of the most common tasks (like starting or deploying an app) can take a long time. There are a few simple things you can do to make it faster, including using VM hardware acceleration, eliminating unnecessary functionality, and dedicating a CPU core to the emulator.

Using Hardware Acceleration

People running development machines on Intel processors can use the Hardware Accelerated Execution Manager (Intel HAXM) to speed up the Android emulator on the host computer. Using it can improve performance significantly, but there are also limitations to consider.

Benefits

Key benefits of HAXM include:

- Improved emulator performance, in particular, quicker startup and shorter deploy times.
- Better performance of graphics-intensive applications, particularly those that make use of OpenGL.
- Better use of native hardware: if your development computer is robust, using HAXM will allow you to use it to its full potential.

Limitations

There are also some limitations to consider:

- HAXM doesn't support Google APIs, which means you can't test apps (such as Maps or Cloud Messaging) using this code.
- The performance characteristics of the emulator are not the same as you would find in the real world, because most current Android devices use different (ARM-based) processors.
- HAXM offers support only for certain API levels: currently only APIs 10, 15, 16, and 17.
- It has very specific hardware requirements: your processor must support VT-x, EM64T, and the Execute Disable Bit.

Downloading the components

In order to use HAXM, you need to install some software on your host computer. The easiest way to do this is using the SDK Manager (see "SDK Manager" on page 11). Download and install the following components:

- Android SDK Platform that supports HAXM (the only supported API levels are 10 and anything over 15)
- Intel Atom x86 System Image (consistent with the platform version)
- Intel Hardware Accelerated Execution Manager Driver (from the Extras section)

As an example, if you want to create a HAXM enable emulator compliant with API 16, you need to ensure your selections look like those in Figure 3-4.

Installing the HAXM software

It is not enough to just download the tool; you also need to install it. On Windows and Mac OS X, you can do this by running the executable available in the *${android.sdk}/ extras/intel/Hardware_Accelerated_Execution_Manager* directory. You need to launch the installer process and accept the license agreement to complete the installation.

In order to use this functionality on Linux, you also need to install the KVM software package. Instructions for this vary based on the particular version of the OS being used. The official documentation, HAXM Linux Install Guide (*http://intel.ly/19S6mbE*), describes the additional steps required for running on Linux.

Configuring an AVD

Once you have downloaded and installed the correct components, follow the usual procedure to creating an AVD. You will see additional options for using the Intel-based system for your emulator. When you create an AVD and specify a compatible Target (in this case API 16), you will be able to specify a particular CPU/ABI image to use. Select the "Intel Atom (x86)" option to enable HAXM. The dialog should look like Figure 3-5.

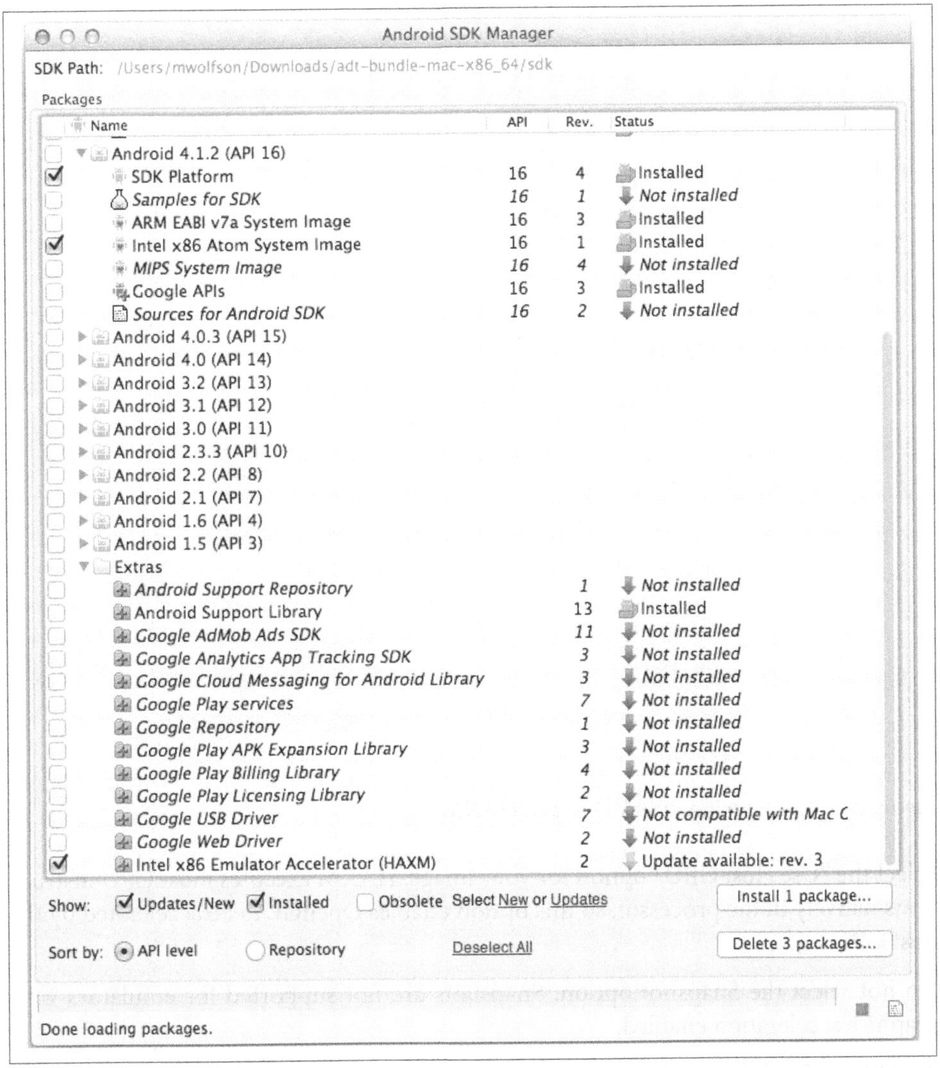

Name	API	Rev.	Status
▼ Android 4.1.2 (API 16)			
☑ SDK Platform	16	4	Installed
Samples for SDK	*16*	*1*	↓ *Not installed*
ARM EABI v7a System Image	16	3	Installed
☑ Intel x86 Atom System Image	16	1	Installed
MIPS System Image	*16*	*4*	↓ *Not installed*
Google APIs	16	3	Installed
Sources for Android SDK	*16*	*2*	↓ *Not installed*
▶ Android 4.0.3 (API 15)			
▶ Android 4.0 (API 14)			
▶ Android 3.2 (API 13)			
▶ Android 3.1 (API 12)			
▶ Android 3.0 (API 11)			
▶ Android 2.3.3 (API 10)			
▶ Android 2.2 (API 8)			
▶ Android 2.1 (API 7)			
▶ Android 1.6 (API 4)			
▶ Android 1.5 (API 3)			
▼ Extras			
Android Support Repository		*1*	↓ *Not installed*
Android Support Library		13	Installed
Google AdMob Ads SDK		*11*	↓ *Not installed*
Google Analytics App Tracking SDK		*3*	↓ *Not installed*
Google Cloud Messaging for Android Library		*3*	↓ *Not installed*
Google Play services		*7*	↓ *Not installed*
Google Repository		*1*	↓ *Not installed*
Google Play APK Expansion Library		*3*	↓ *Not installed*
Google Play Billing Library		*4*	↓ *Not installed*
Google Play Licensing Library		*2*	↓ *Not installed*
Google USB Driver		*7*	↓ *Not compatible with Mac C*
Google Web Driver		*2*	↓ *Not installed*
☑ Intel x86 Emulator Accelerator (HAXM)		2	↓ Update available: rev. 3

Show: ☑ Updates/New ☑ Installed ☐ Obsolete   Select New or Updates   [Install 1 package...]

Sort by: ⦿ API level ◯ Repository   Deselect All   [Delete 3 packages...]

Done loading packages.

Figure 3-4. Example of selecting necessary components to run HAXM

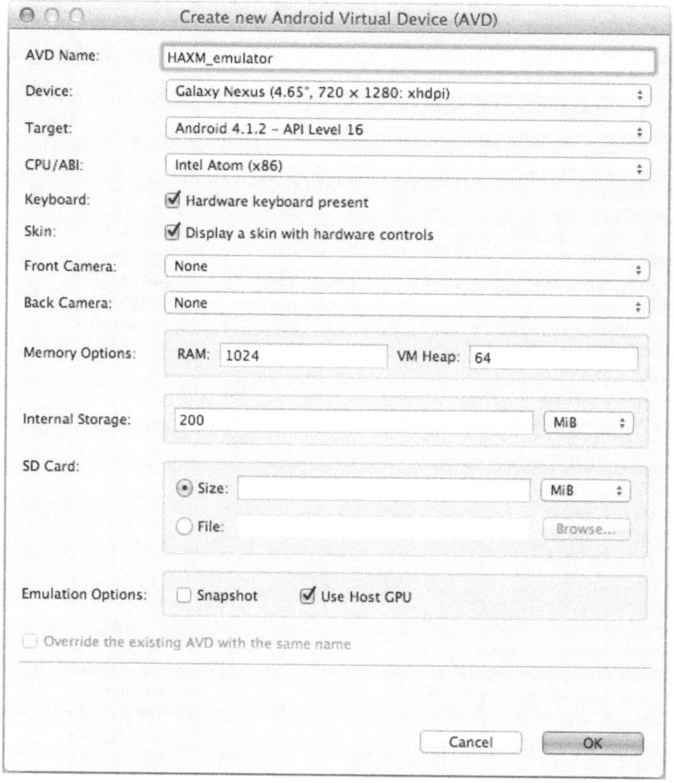

Figure 3-5. Configuring an AVD to use HAXM

Select the "Use Host GPU" option for your image. HAXM executes most CPU instructions natively in the processor, so this option enables OpenGL to be accelerated by the host GPU.

Do not select the Snapshot option. Snapshots are not supported for emulators with graphics acceleration enabled.

Validating that HAXM is running

After you have installed all the correct components and started your correctly configured AVD, you can easily validate that everything is running correctly. If it is, a notification indicating success is displayed in the console during startup (Figure 3-6).

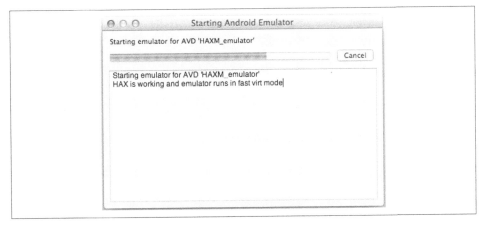

Figure 3-6. Validating that HAXM is running

Disabling the Boot Animation

When the emulator starts up, it displays a boot animation. Generally this isn't something you need to see, and it's preferable not to waste precious seconds while it displays. You can disable the boot animation by adding the `-no-boot-anim` option to your AVD start command. For example:

```
emulator -avd myAvd.ini -no-boot-anim
```

On Windows: Dedicating a Core to the Emulator

If you are running on a Windows machine and have a multicore processor, it is possible to dedicate one of the CPU cores to a running emulator process. This prevents it from contending for a CPU with other resource-intensive processes (such as Eclipse). To do this, start the Windows Task Manager, select the Processes tab, right-click on the running emulator process, and click on "Set Affinity option ()." Then you will be able to check or uncheck the CPU processor core(s) on which you want to run the application (see Figure 3-7). Finally, click OK to finish the setup.

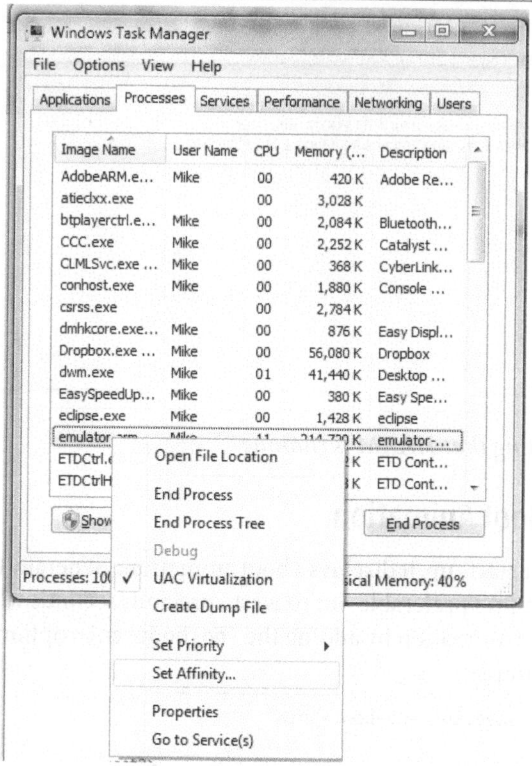

Figure 3-7. Dedicating a core to the emulator

## CHAPTER 4

Using Devices and Emulators

Using the Emulator

In the previous chapter, we learned how to create emulators. Now we'll discuss their use. An emulator is a very powerful tool that makes testing easier and allows the developer to simulate a variety of things that would be difficult to accomplish under real-world conditions. For instance, if you are writing a mapping application, you might need to test locations all over the world, and it would be impractical (although quite a bit of fun) to actually travel to each of these locations. The emulator provides the capability to simulate networking configurations, hardware/software configurations, and sensor events. It eliminates the need to have physical devices to represent each configuration that you need to test. For instance, you will use emulators to mock various screen sizes and memory configurations. This chapter describes how to use the emulator to effectively test various parameters.

For the most part, emulators and physical devices interact with the ADT tools in the exact same way. In other words, the operations we discuss in this chapter perform the same way on an emulator as they will on a physical device. In most cases, a physical device is more limited, because options (such as changing network configurations) are locked down by the service provider.

You will likely use many different combinations of physical devices and emulators to test thoroughly. You can run as many different emulators and devices as you like. If you plan on running a lot of emulator instances, you will need a powerful computer to support it (depending on configuration, each emulator can require 1 GB+ of dedicated memory). It is common for a developer to have many different emulator and physical devices running at the same time, then use each of them throughout the test cycle. It is worth noting that the emulator doesn't support certain actions, such as simulating accelerometer activity, or simulating some sensor activity (such as the magnetometer).

You should review the "Capabilities and Limitations" on page 25 discussion to determine whether the emulator suits your needs.

Starting the Emulator

In the previous chapter, we discussed using the AVD Manager to create AVDs ("Creating AVDs" on page 28). This tool is also used to start the emulator instances as well. It provides options to control runtime parameters of the emulators you created.

To start it from within Eclipse, click the 🖥 icon from the main toolbar.

Or start it from the command line with the following command:

```
android avd
```

When you launch the AVD Manager, you will see a screen similar to Figure 4-1. This screen displays a list of all the AVDs you have configured on your system, and some options for managing them. To start an emulator, select a particular AVD and click the Start button.

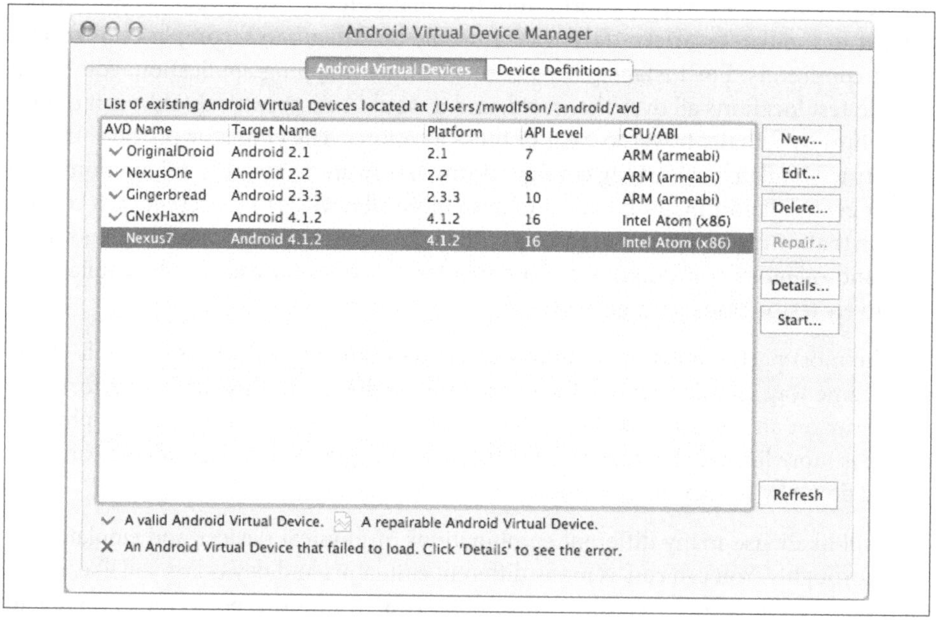

Figure 4-1. AVD Manager tool

You are then presented with a secondary screen (Figure 4-2) that has a variety of options specific to running an emulator instance.

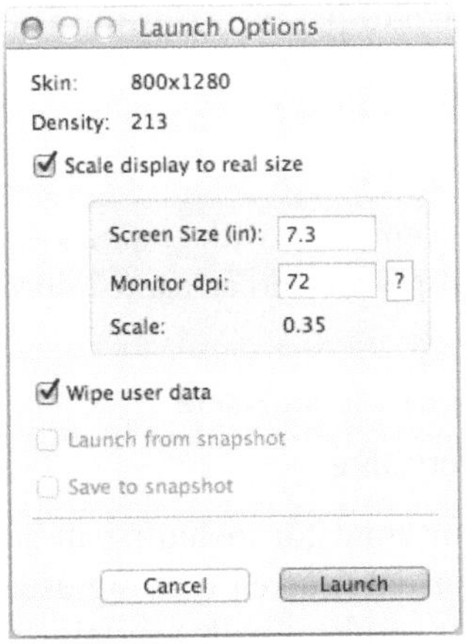

Figure 4-2. AVD launch options

AVD launch options

It is important to understand the launch options, and what they do. Using them allows you to change the size, performance, and data of your emulator.

Scale factor
    This allows you to adjust the size of the emulator on your computer screen. To specify a particular screen size, place a checkmark in the Scale Factor box. Next, click the ? next to the dpi option to set the particular resolution of your computer. Enter the resolution and size of your display. Then type a number in the Screen Size box. Your emulator will be started with the screen size you entered.

Snapshot
    This lets you save an emulator's state to a snapshot file and restore it later. This can be useful if you would like to preconfigure an emulator to start in a particular state every time, or would like to avoid the lengthy boot process when starting from scratch. This is a great way to speed up the time to boot an emulator, and will save a lot of time. Emulator boot times can be reduced from many minutes to just seconds.

Starting an emulator from the command line

It's not absolutely necessary to use the AVD Manager to start an emulator. You can also start it from the command line. This is useful when using scripts, or if you would like to run an emulator without the overhead of Eclipse. There are a variety of configuration options you can use when starting an emulator this way. There are options relating to networking, graphics acceleration, sensor abilities, and more. To see a complete list of options, type:

```
emulator -help
```

The command to start an emulator has the following syntax:

```
emulator -avd    avd_name
                 [option
                 [value] ]...
```

For example, you could start an emulator with graphics acceleration turned on and boot animation disabled (two good options you can use to improve performance). This would look like:

```
emulator -avd Nexus7 -gpu on -no-boot-anim
```

Using snapshots to improve performance

The snapshot is a view of your emulator including all data, the current UI being displayed, or any other sensor or data currently being used. This snapshot can be very useful if you wish to start your emulator with a certain configuration or state multiple times. In order to use snapshots with a particular AVD, it needs to be configured appropriately. Reread "Creating AVDs" on page 28 to review how to do this.

You will notice three options in the snapshot section of the launch configuration tool.

Wipe user data
    Refreshes your emulator image to remove all data and resets it to a clean configuration (just as if it were started for the very first time).

Launch from snapshot
    Allows you to restore your emulator to the state it was in when the last snapshot was taken. If there is no snapshot in memory, this option is not enabled.

Save to snapshot
    Triggers the system to save a snapshot of the current state of the emulator when you close it.

 I use snapshots as a way to save a clean emulator that I can recover quickly. I save a snapshot the first time I start the emulator, right after it has completed the boot sequence. From that point forward, I make sure I don't check the "Save Snapshot" box. If I need a clean emulator image, I can just restart this emulator and thanks to snapshots, I will have a fully booted clean emulator ready to go.

Saving and retrieving a snapshot

Snapshots are such a great way of speeding up your emulator usage, it is worth going through an example to show exactly how they work. Let's step through setting up an emulator using snapshots so you can actually see it for yourself.

The first step when using this functionality is to enable it for the AVD you are using. If you haven't done this already, review "Creating AVDs" on page 28 to do it.

When you start your emulator, the options for snapshots will be enabled. The first time you start your emulator, you should select the "Wipe user data" and "Save to snapshot" options (as shown in Figure 4-3). This starts the emulator with a brand new image, and allows you to save your state when you close it down. Once you have these checkmarks selected, you can press the Launch button to start the emulator. Depending on the speed of your hardware, this can take a long time (anywhere from 90 seconds to many minutes). After the wait, you have an emulator booted to its clean state (Figure 4-4).

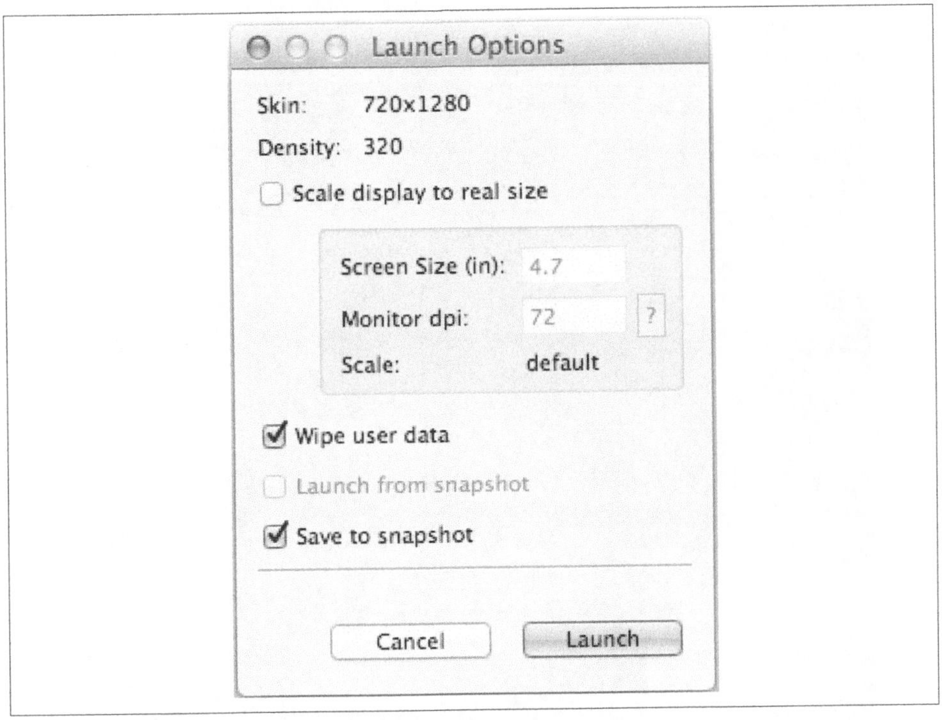

Figure 4-3. Enabling the options to save the initial snapshot

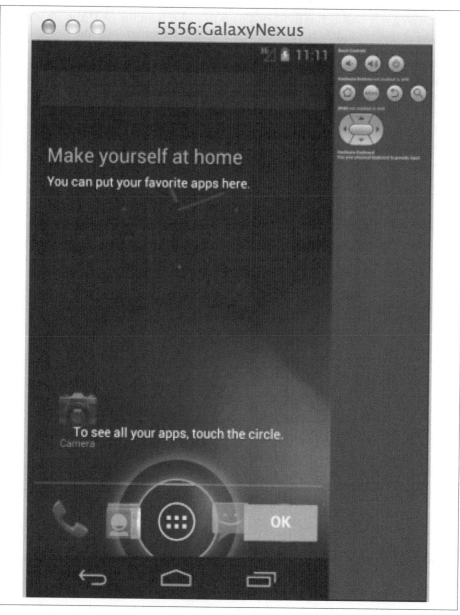

Figure 4-4. AVD snapshot initial instance

Now configure your device to a state you would like. In this example, the state we'll save is the emulator started with the main Activity of an app displayed (see Figure 4-5). Now close the process; in this case, that means clicking the red circle on the top left to kill the window. This will take a little bit of time (maybe up to a minute) because a "snapshot" of the current state of the emulator is being saved, which will allow you to recover to this state easily.

Figure 4-5. AVD snapshot saved state

The next time you start your emulator, you can select the middle selection: "Launch from snapshot" (see Figure 4-6). When you select this option, and press the Launch button, instead of the emulator starting from scratch (which takes many minutes), it starts up to the state we saved when we shut down the emulator in the previous step. Because the emulator doesn't need to go through the entire boot process, startup time is drastically improved (the emulator will start to a snapshot state in around 10 seconds). You will see your emulator booted right to the same place (as shown in Figure 4-7).

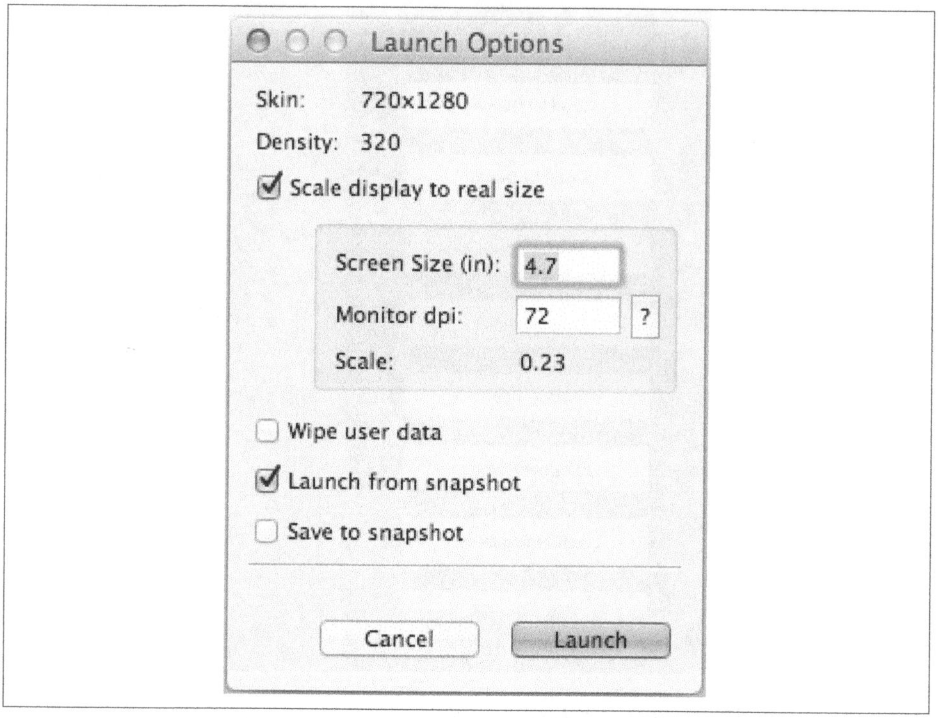

Figure 4-6. Enabling the options to launch from snapshot

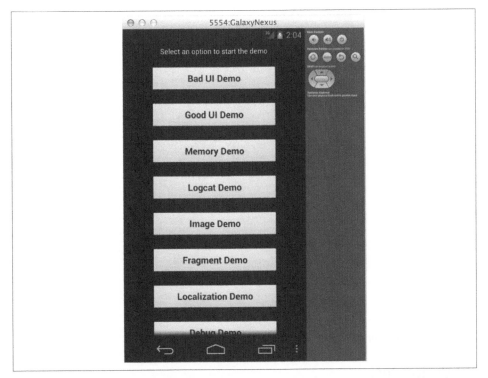

Figure 4-7. AVD after loading snapshot state

The Emulator Application

The emulator you start will look similar to the one in Figure 4-8. The emulator consists of a screen and optionally a keyboard or navigation buttons, if they were enabled when you created your AVD ("Creating AVDs" on page 28). The emulator runs like a native application in your operating system, and can be closed or minimized just like any other window (by clicking an X or red button at the top of the window).

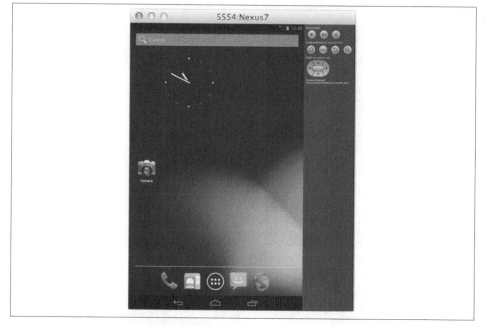

Figure 4-8. Emulator anatomy

The Devices Tool

So how do you keep track of the emulators or devices you have hooked to your computer? You can use the Devices tool (shown in Figure 4-9), which allows you to see and control the various devices or emulators connected to your computer. This will be the central location where you control your devices. You will start a variety of important operations from this window (including memory inspection, location and network simulation, and UI inspection). I cover these operations in the DDMS section ("Dalvik Debug Monitor Server (DDMS)" on page 152).

I'll also highlight frequently used, essential functionality you that you will access directly from this tab.

The primary way to access the Devices tool is from a tab at the bottom of your screen (see Figure 4-9). The devices tab should be there by default. If it is not there, you can add it from the menu: Window → Show View → Other → Android → Select Devices from list.

Name		
▼ 📱 Nexus7 [emulator-5554]	Online	Nexus7 [...
com.android.exchange	1254	8600
com.android.inputmethod.latin	1135	8601
com.android.deskclock	1305	8602
com.android.email	1425	8603
android.process.acore	1191	8604
com.android.launcher	1369	8605
com.android.quicksearchbox	1532	8606
com.android.phone	1168	8607
com.android.systemui	1117	8608
android.process.media	1352	8609
system_process	1007	8610
com.android.contacts	1382	8611
com.android.mms	1485	8612
com.android.calendar	1274	8613
com.android.settings	1180	8614
com.android.providers.calendar	1318	8615
▶ 📱 emulator-5556	Online	GNexHax...
📱 003e0f1ccb51a895	Online	4.2.2

Figure 4-9. Viewing running devices using the Devices tool

 There is also a version of the tool that can be run from the command line without Eclipse. This is particularly useful for team members that might not have the full development suite installed, but could still benefit from using these tools. The tool is named Android Debug Monitor, and can be started with the following command:

```
{$android.sdk}\tools $ monitor
```

The upper left corner contains the *Devices* view. This will show you all the devices (both physical devices and emulators) that are currently connected and available. You can use the arrow on the left to collapse or expand a particular device tree in order to see details about the current running processes. In Figure 4-9, you'll see different devices connected. The first two are emulators (the icon and their name both signify this), and the last one in the list (with the funny name that is a mix of letters and numbers) is a physical device.

There are a variety of useful operations that can be launched from this tab, including:

Debugging
The first button on the top (☀) allows you to enter debugging mode. In this mode, you can attach the debugger to an application that is already running. This means that you can start an application, run it until it gets to the place you would like to test, and then start debugging from that point. This can be an efficient way to directly debug exactly the code you want and avoid other code paths.

Heap

> The second set of buttons allows you to start inspection of the memory (heap) of a running application. See Chapter 10 for more information.

Device screen capture

> The next button (📷) launches a utility that allows you to take a screenshot of what is currently displayed on your device. Pressing this will launch the dialog in Figure 4-10. The dialog shows an image of whatever is currently displayed on the screen of your device, along with buttons across the top that will enable you to save, rotate, or refresh the image.

Reset ADB

> The upside-down triangle (▿) is a particularly important button. Pressing this allows you to access the controls to reset the ADB process. This resets connectivity between the computer and the devices. You can use it if you encounter connectivity issues between your computer and device.

Keyboard Shortcuts

If you enabled keyboard support when you created your AVD (see "Emulator Options" on page 32), a variety of keys will be mapped between your computer keyboard and the emulator. I have listed some of the more useful mappings in Table 4-1. A description of each option can be found in the emulator documentation (*http://bit.ly/14cIuY2*) on the Android developer website.

Table 4-1. Popular shortcuts

Key	Effect
Home	Android Home
F2	Menu
Esc	Back
Ctrl-F11 (Cmd-F11 on Mac)	Rotate landscape/portrait
Keypad 4/6/5/8/2	D-Pad: left/right/center/up/down
Ctrl-F8	Toggle Cell Network On/Off

File Explorer

ADT provides a GUI tool that makes exploring and interacting with the files on the device very easy. It allows you to navigate the file system to discover which files are on the device, move files onto and off the device, and modify the file system by adding and rearranging folder locations. To use this tool, open the DDMS perspective, select a device, and select the File Explorer (📁) tab. This allows you to do a variety of things, including:

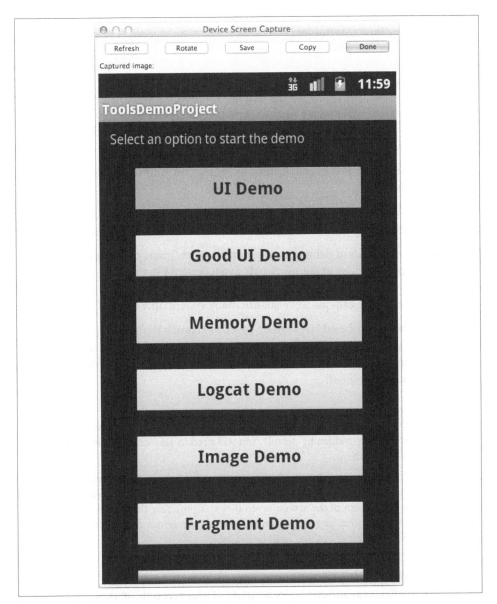

Figure 4-10. Capturing a screenshot using the Devices tool

- Push files to a device (🖼)
- Pull files from the device (🖼)

- Delete a file from the device ($-$)
- Create a new directory/folder ($+$)

Developer Tools Application

One more important tool that we need to explore is the "Developer Tools" application. It is installed by default on all system images included with the SDK, and is preinstalled on your emulator.

This application allows you to enable various settings on your device that will make it easier to test and debug.

The application incudes some of the basic items you might expect (such as "Stay Awake When Connected" or "Allow Mock Location").

In addition to the standard debugging options, there are many other tools designed to help debug applications by enabling visuals when certain events occur (such as touch events, or the UI thread being locked). These tools are very useful when you are testing on a real device, as you can quickly visualize many system operations.

You can find the icon (labeled "Developer Tools") to launch the application in the main app drawer. It allows you to do a large variety of activities relating to testing, instrumenting, and inspecting the state of various systems on your device. A brief list of some of the core functions follows:

 If you are running a device with Android 4.2 and up, the developer options are hidden by default. You will need to know the "secret" way to enable them.

To enable them, open the Settings app, scroll to the bottom, then click "About phone" (or "About tablet") and then tap on the Build number at the bottom of the screen seven times. After doing this, you will see a message that says "Congratulations, you are now a developer," and the "Developer options" will be available.

Accounts Tester
    Allows you to access and configure a variety of user accounts on the emulator. Very useful if you need to test logins or similar authorization functionality.

Bad Behavior
    Allows you to simulate a variety of issues, like creating ANR (Activity Not Responding) events, or crashing key systems (like the main app thread or the system server).

Configuration

Displays the current configuration values for the keyboard and display parameters. You can also see things like system locale, keyboard type, and display metrics (such as density). This can be extremely useful when trying to determine how your app looks on different resolution devices.

Connectivity

Allows you to modify the networking parameters or modify the WiFi connectivity of the device. This is useful when you need to test connectivity issues or how your app will perform without connectivity.

Development Settings

Does a variety of things such as enable debugging, show system statistics (such as running processes, CPU, and memory usage) or display UI hints (like showing the coordinates of touch points or flashing the screen during updates).

Instrumentation

Runs unit tests directly on the device.

Media Scanner

Scans the media folder of your SD card and identifies any media available for use.

Package Browser

This tool should look familiar, as it is the same tool you use to manage apps from the Android Settings app installed on your device. It serves the same purpose (managing applications) here as well.

Pointer Location

Displays visible lines and coordinates that allow the developer to closely determine specific touch points.

Running Processes

Presents a list of processes currently running.

Sync Tester

Tests third-party sync adapters.

Terminal Emulation

Opens a terminal, allowing command-line access to the Linux shell.

This application relies on many system-level permissions that aren't available to third parties. If you would like to run this on an actual physical device, it is necessary to build a custom system image and sign the Dev Tools APK with the same key as the system image. After signing the app correctly, you will be able to install it and run it on a device. This means that you can only run it on a rooted device, or on a device for which you built the system image. The system image signing key is generally only available to the hardware manufacturer.

## CHAPTER 5

Developing with Eclipse

ADT provides a robust and powerful development environment in which to build Android applications. Designed as a plug-in to the Eclipse IDE, it leverages many Eclipse features including code completion, syntax highlighting, and JUnit integration. There is also a rich ecosystem of plug-ins and additional features available to download and install from third-party developers. In addition to the standard IDE, there are a variety of Android-specific tools that have been integrated. These include wizards for resource creation, the logcat Viewer, the Hierarchy Viewer, and the Visual GUI Builder, among others.

The close integration makes developing easier, so I recommend ADT as the fastest way to get started with Android development. Throughout this section (and this book), I highlight many of the ways you can leverage the IDE to improve your experience writing Android code.

Anatomy of the Eclipse Workspace

You will be spending a lot of your development time within Eclipse, so you'll need to familiarize yourself with how it is organized. Figure 5-1 shows the standard Eclipse layout. Let's look at a few key areas:

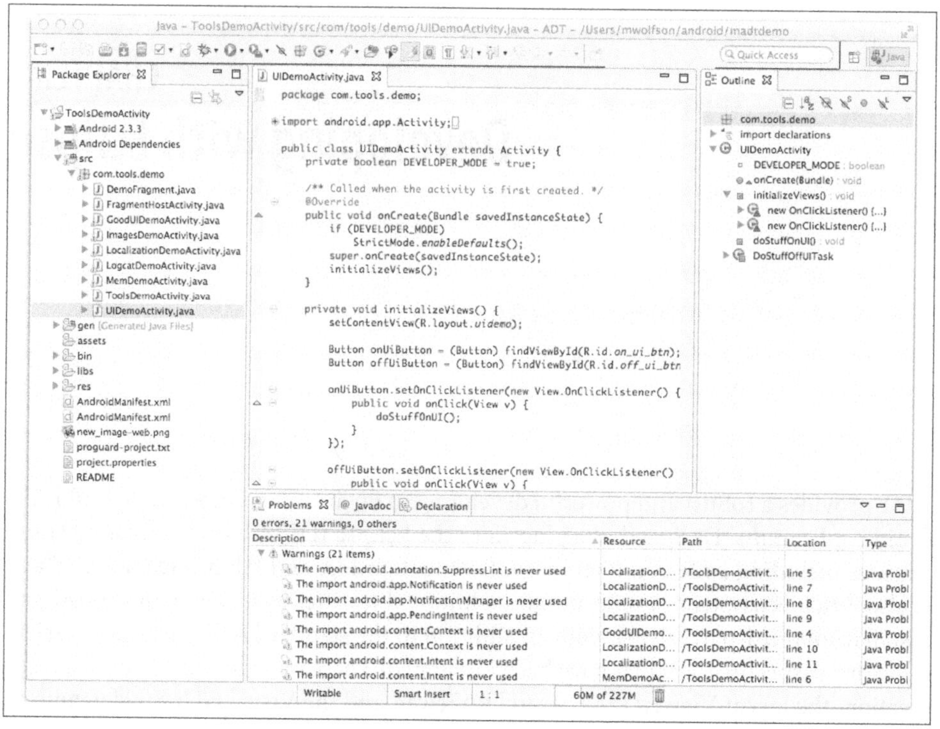

Figure 5-1. Standard Eclipse layout

Package Explorer

The window on the far left allows you to view all the code components included in your project. You can click on the small triangles (▼) to expand or minimize a particular tree, which will expand or minimize that section of the code appropriately.

Code Editor

Seen in the middle of the screen, this is the area where you make changes to your code. The source code is color-coded to highlight different elements of syntax. For instance, variable definitions are displayed in blue, and method modifiers are displayed in purple.

Outline

The view on the far right displays the main sections of the code in a structured way. You can click on the triangles to expand and minimize certain sections, just as in the Package Explorer view. Refer to "Quick Outline for XML" on page 68 for an alternate way to view this.

Problems

This tab appears at the bottom of the screen and displays any warnings or errors in your project. If there is an error in your code, it will be listed here (in red). You can click on any of the messages that appear here. This will open the code with the error and place the cursor at the location where the problem exists.

Uncovering Additional Tools and Views

The default layout for Eclipse likely won't have all the components you need to use. Several additional tools are available, as well as a few different ways to customize what is displayed (Figure 5-2).

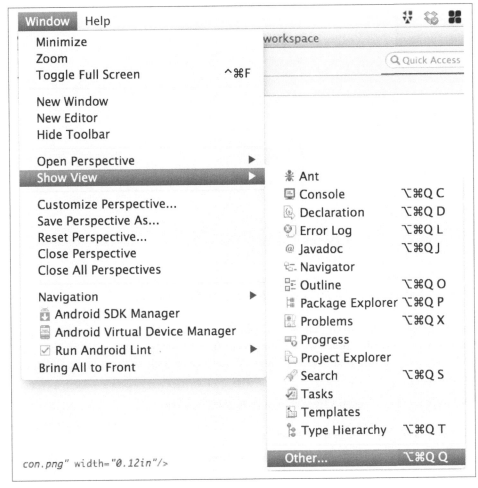

Figure 5-2. Adding views to Eclipse layout

You can display the additional Android tools by selecting Window → Show View → Other → Android.

This displays a long list of tools under the Android section, as shown in Figure 5-3. To add one of these to your Eclipse layout, select it from the list. Once it is placed in your screen, you can drag and drop the tab to move it wherever you would like.

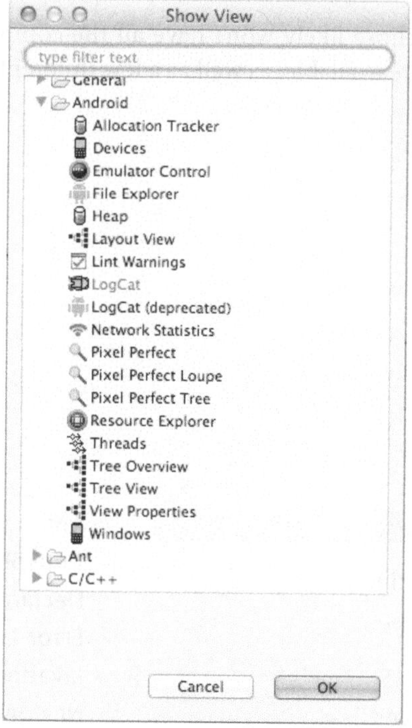

Figure 5-3. Viewing the options available in the Android menu

The *perspectives* concept in Eclipse is a collection of tabs and tools organized in a pre-defined way. Android comes with a few preconfigured perspectives: DDMS, the Hierarchy Viewer, and the Pixel Perfect View. We will cover each of these in detail later in the book.

The steps to open a perspective (shown in Figure 5-4) are:

1. Select Window → Open Perspective.
2. Select the perspective you would like to display.

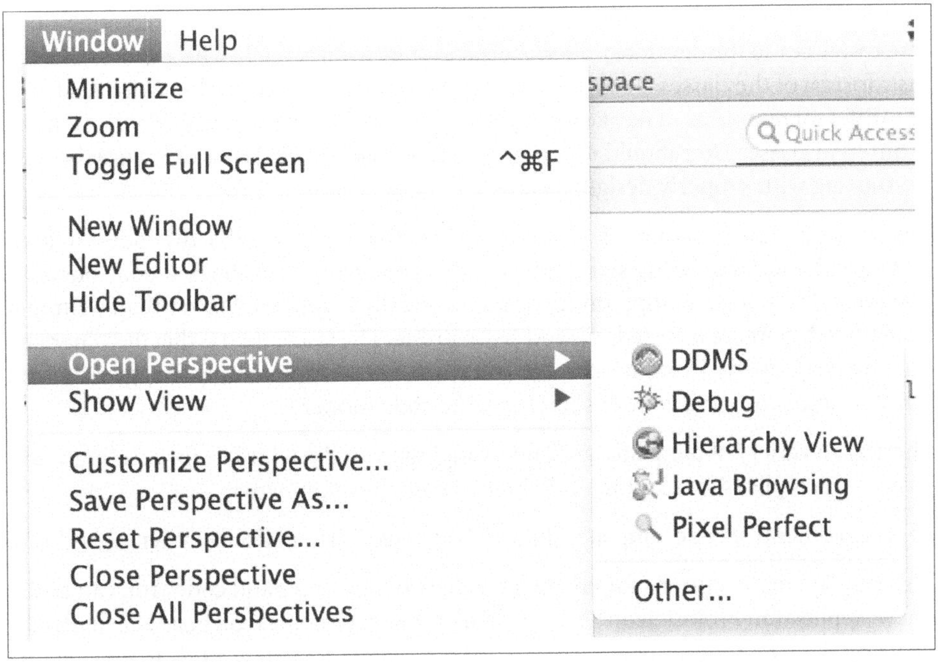

Figure 5-4. Eclipse perspectives

Quick Button

There is a small button at the top of the menu bar (⏺▾) that is easy to overlook. This button is a shortcut to run your project. It has the same functionality that is executed by invoking the Run as... menu (which you can access by right-clicking on your project). This button is the simplest way to run your app, as it is just a single button click (as opposed to navigating a menu). It is important to note that this works only if you are editing a Java file. If you are editing an XML file, nothing happens when you click the button (not even an error dialog).

Code Templates

It can be difficult to understand the proper way to create Android classes. You need to know the proper naming standards, which methods are required, how to tie various resources together, and other patterns for creating proper classes.

ADT now provides the "Code Templates and Wizards" tools to assist in creating these base resources so the developer doesn't need to start from scratch. This ensures that the basic format of the classes is correct and that they match the standard style for Android. The different templates make it easy to get started quickly and are available for a variety of different classes. You should use these to create your initial classes to ensure that you are starting with properly designed code.

Generating code this way has a few important benefits. The first is that the code is written to Android and Java coding standards, so you are starting with the best code possible. The second is that generating this code automatically is generally faster than writing it from scratch, which can be tedious and error-prone. The last benefit is that the generated code works properly from the start, so you won't need to spend time fixing errors and can start implementing your business-specific code sooner.

There are a variety of templates available, ranging from the template for creating a new project to templates for creating individual resource components.

To access a menu of code templates (Figure 5-5), select File → New → Other → Android.

This displays many options for creating a variety of resources and code. You can create a new Application Project, Icon Set (see "Working with Graphics" on page 182 for details on using this), or code snippets. This tool allows you to launch wizards that will guide you through creating these various components. After the wizard walks you through the process, the system generates all the required code, resources, and dependencies and puts them directly in your project.

As an example, I will show how you would use a code template to generate a master/detail flow. This is a common UI pattern where there is a list of items on one side of the screen and a detail view of that item is displayed in a panel on the other side when it is selected.

1. First, select the desired option from the templates option screen.

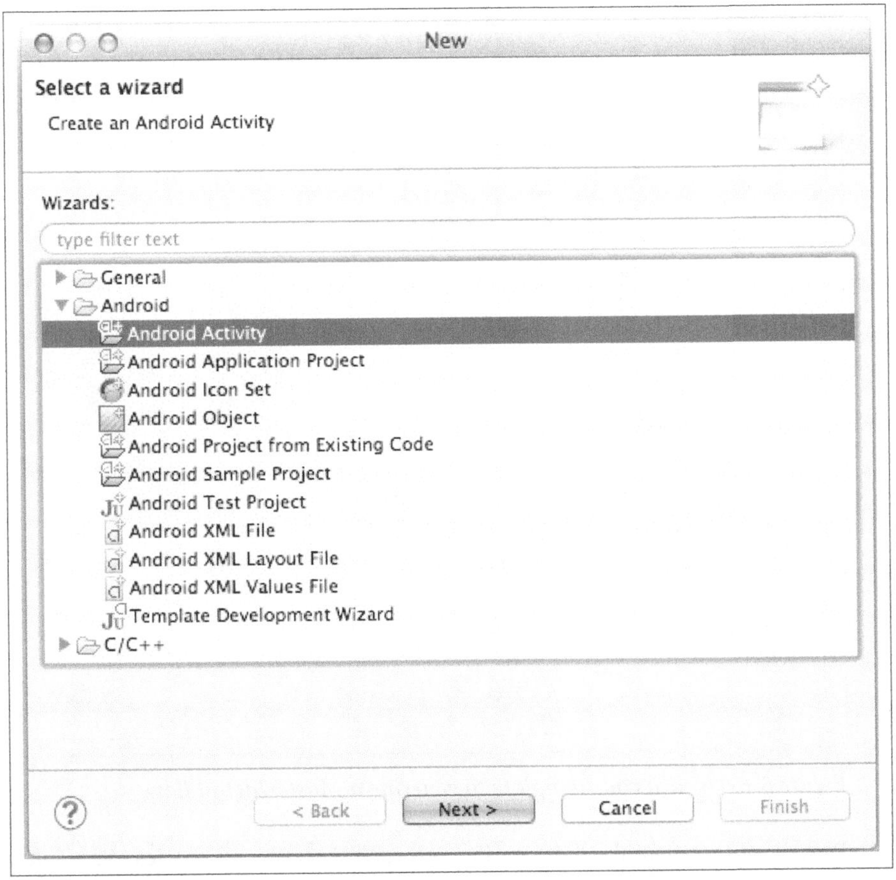

Figure 5-5. Viewing Code Templates menu

2. Enter the details about your code in the wizard (Figure 5-6).

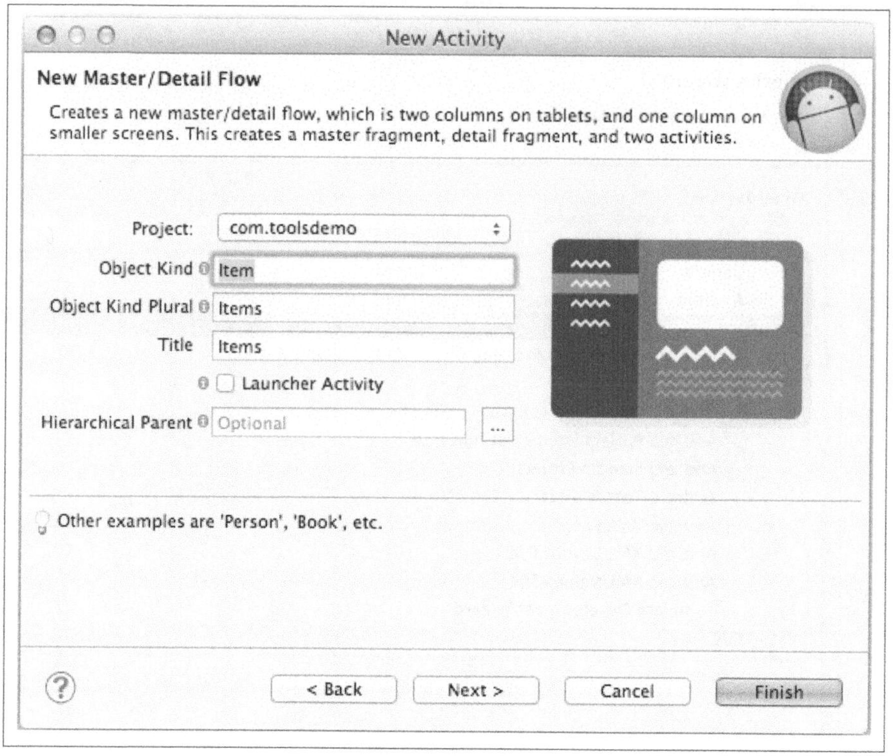

Figure 5-6. Using a code template to generate a Master/detail flow

3. Review and confirm the data you have entered. Accept your entries to complete the wizard (as shown in Figure 5-7).

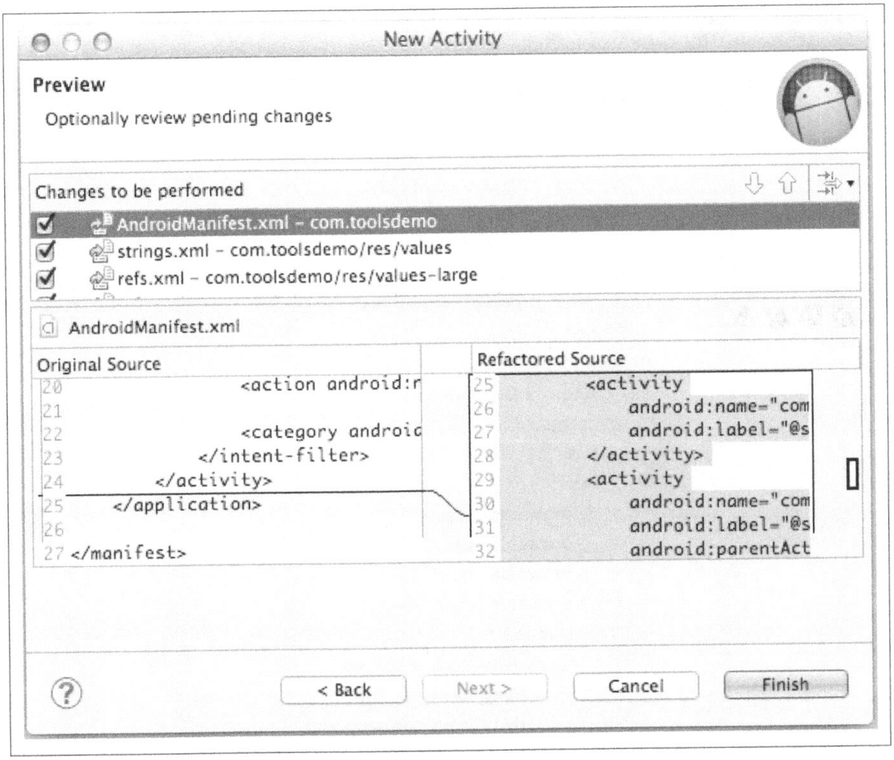

Figure 5-7. Confirming the generated code

4. The system then automatically generates the appropriate code. For the master/detail flow, quite a bit of code is created. All of the activities, fragments, layouts, and resources that are shown in Figure 5-8 were created using this template.

Figure 5-8. Viewing the code generated from the Master/detail

You should explore each of the code templates that are available. There are many different possibilities including various activity types, Android-specific XML files, and unit testing assistance. Having the ability to create framework code that is written correctly and works is something I can't recommend enough. It will eliminate time spent debugging and ensure that your code is written to standards.

You are not limited to using only the existing templates. There is a syntax that allows you to create your own templates. There is a good article by Roman Nurik titled ADT Template Format Documentation (*http://bit.ly/15WgRc1*) that outlines how to do this.

Properties Editors

ADT includes editors designed to create XML files without requiring direct editing of the file. You can use these editors to enter values into a form, which is easier than trying to enter the properly formatted XML tags manually.

A good example of this is the Manifest Editor. Every Android application has a manifest file (which must be named *AndroidManifest.xml*). This file contains information about the application that the Android system must have before it can execute the code. The manifest file contains information about application permissions, the components of the application (activities, services, etc.), API level, instrumentation classes used by profilers, and a variety of other important data. This file is critically important to Android development, and is modified frequently.

The Manifest Editor tool makes editing this file easy, and less error-prone. This tool is launched when you edit *AndroidManifest.xml* (which is located in your project root directory). The tools will look like Figure 5-9.

The manifest wizard groups common elements together. Each can be accessed by clicking its tab on the bottom of this window. The tabs are organized as follows:

Manifest
Allows you to change general information about your app (like OS level, screen support, package name, version number, etc.)

Application
Describes application-level components, as well as general application attributes. You will list the components you use (activities, services, etc.) here, and can specify a variety of parameters specific to the app execution: for instance, whether it is debuggable, or information relating to optional backup configurations.

Permissions
Lists the Android permissions your app requires. For instance, `android.permis sion.INTERNET` grants the app the ability to send or receive data over the Internet in your application.

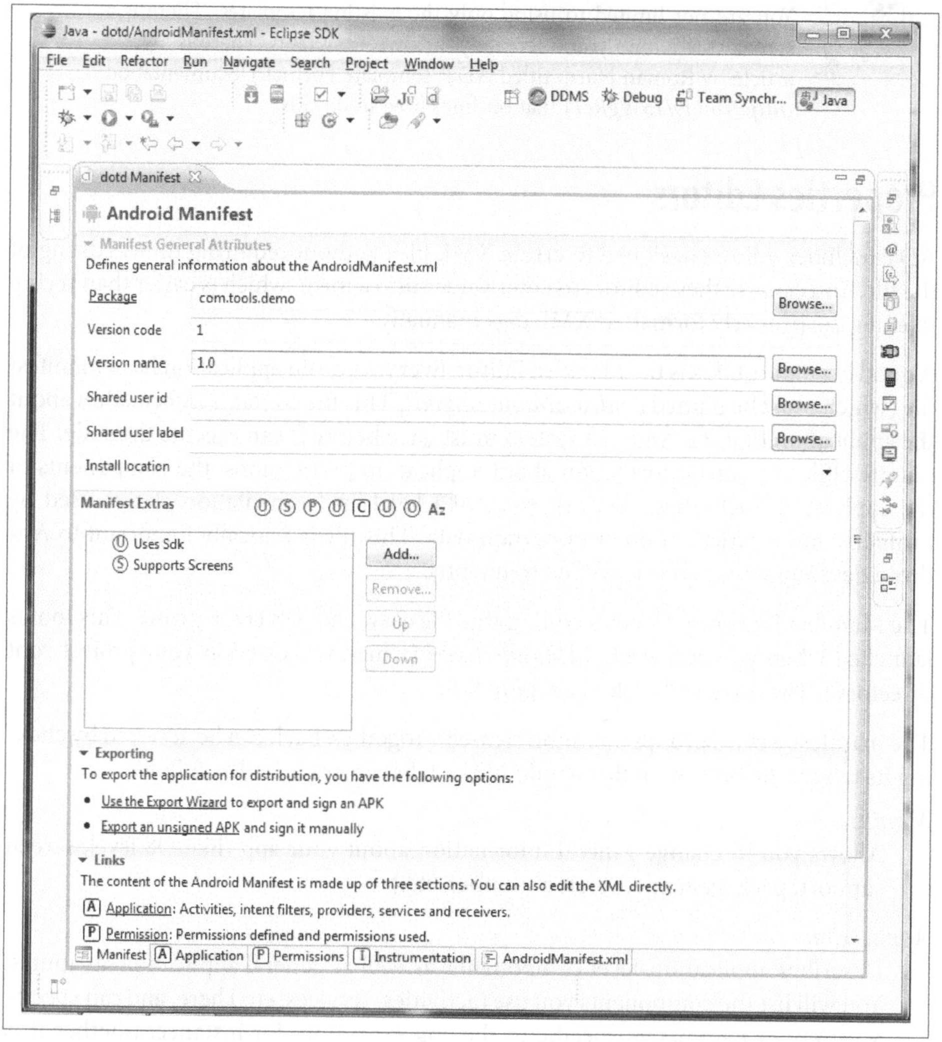

Figure 5-9. Android Manifest Editor

Instrumentation

> Allows a developer to designate a class that will be instantiated before any other component in the application. This class can be used to monitor an app's interaction with the system, or set up test functionality.

AndroidManifest.xml

> Allows you to edit the XML directly, if you prefer that.

XML Formatter

You probably know that the layout files in Android are designed using a hierarchy of XML tags to describe the various views in your interface. These files can get complicated quickly, and often become disorganized and difficult to read. ADT provides a very useful key sequence that allows you to quickly format XML files. In addition to aligning the whitespace, the tools go a step further, and reorder the attributes within each tag.

On Windows or Linux, you will use the keys Ctrl+Shift+F and on Mac OS X, you will use Command+Shift+F.

By default, this will reorder the attributes to a default standard that the Android team has determined is best for a wide variety of developers. This default order should work for most people, but it is possible to specify your own order if you prefer. You can specify your own preferences in the following location: Window → Preferences → XML → XML Files → Editor.

You can learn more about this in "XML formatting" on page 178.

The Android Key

This keyboard combination is worth mentioning because it provides quick access to a few operations that are frequently used. Using this shortcut makes performing these tasks quicker, and speeds up the development workflow. You can access these shortcuts with the following keystrokes: on Windows and Linux, use Alt+Shift+A, and on Mac OS X, use Option+Shift+A.

When you use this key combo, a small dialog opens at the bottom right of your IDE (as seen in Figure 5-10) that contains three shortcuts allowing you to do the following things:

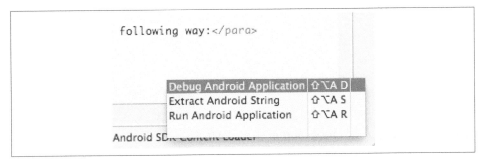

Figure 5-10. Using the Android key to access shortcuts

Run Android Application
Launches your app to a running emulator (or starts one if necessary).

Debug Android Application
Launches your app in debug mode.

Extract Android String
Launches a dialog allowing you to extract a string out of any file and place it in the *strings.xml* file.

Quick Outline for XML

Use this key sequence to launch a UI (as shown in Figure 5-11) that shows the structure of the current XML document or Java class you are editing inline with your editor. You can then quickly navigate to any location in the file. This is a giant time saver, and is my primary way of navigating within my files. On Windows and Linux, use [Ctrl]+[O], and on Mac OS X, use [Command]+[O].

Figures 5-11 and 5-12 show how the outline looks in XML and Java classes.

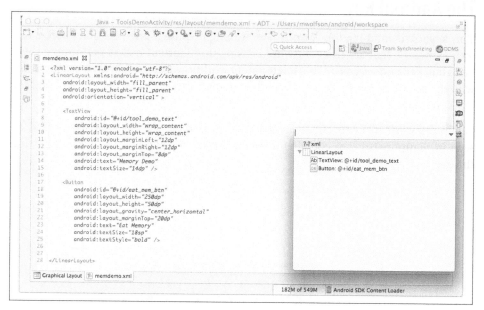

Figure 5-11. Viewing the Quick Outline in an XML file

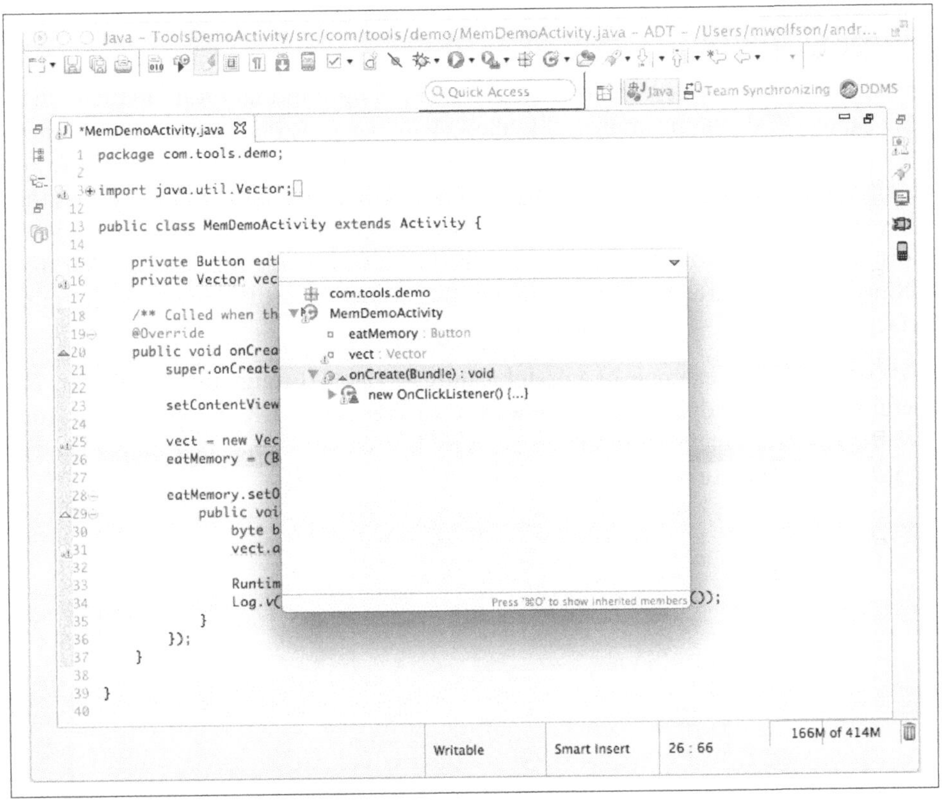

Figure 5-12. Viewing the Quick Outline in a Java class

Other Essential Eclipse Shortcuts

It is worth mentioning a few other key shortcuts that make development easier, but aren't Android-specific.

Ctrl/Command+Shift+R

Open any file quickly without browsing using the package manager or navigator.

Ctrl/Command+Q

Go to the last location you edited (particularly useful for going right back to the last place you were working).

Ctrl/Command+F6

Quickly navigate to any open editor.

There are a lot more than I have space to mention here. You can access the full list of shortcuts from the following menu: Help → Help Contents → Java Development User Guide → Reference → Menus and Actions.

Refactor Menu

There is one more top-level menu with some useful options that I want to mention in this chapter. As the name implies, this allows you to do a variety of useful refactors to your project. These are great shortcuts to help rearrange or clean up your code. For example, one provides a way to extract strings and there are convenience utilities that allow you to modify your layout when you are editing a layout file. You should use these shortcuts to modify your layouts. This can be much less error-prone and quicker than editing the XML directly. You can access this feature from the menu by selecting Refactor → Android → Extract Style.

"Extract Style" is an example of a useful feature available through this menu. This is a useful pattern in Android, which allows you to keep your style independent of your layouts. This convenient shortcut makes it simple to extract elements from your layout into *styles.xml* (Figure 5-13).

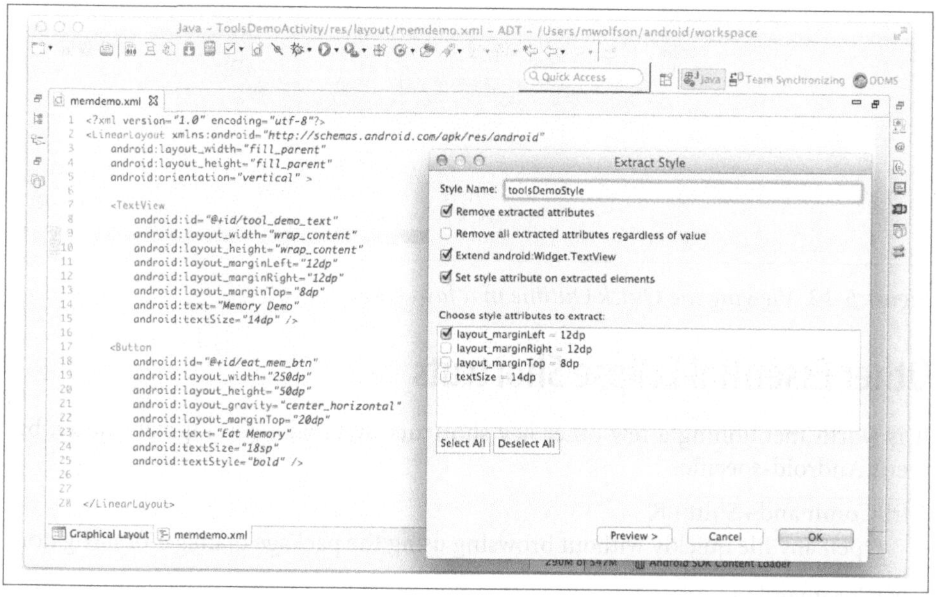

Figure 5-13. Using the tools to extract style information

ADT version 21.1 included some additional functionality that makes it easier to rename item IDs. Previously this was challenging, as the developer was responsible for manually changing the names in each file where it occurs. This makes it easier to rename a resource XML file, drawable name, field name, or ID. If you are using the layout editor, renaming any of these resources will automatically launch a refactoring routine that updates all resource references.

## CHAPTER 6

Developing with Android Studio

Donn Felker

Android Studio (shown in Figure 6-1) is the IDE for Android that was announced in May 2013 at the Google I/O developers event, and is intended as an alternative to Eclipse. At the time of this writing, Android Studio is currently in Early Access Preview, with the most recent version being 0.0.5. At this time, Android Studio is not ready for full end-to-end Android application development, but should be ready in the coming months. I highly advise you review this chapter, as this is where Android development is migrating to in the future. Android Studio is based on the Java IDE called IntelliJ. If you've worked with other products by JetBrains (developer of IntelliJ), such as RedMine, PyCharm, PhpStorm, WebStorm, or AppCode, you will find yourself at home. All IntelliJ products share the same shell IDE, which you'll see as soon as you open up Android Studio. In this chapter, I intend to familiarize you with Android Studio and show how you can use it for Android development.

Although Android Studio is a brand new IDE, it is important to note that most of your IDE skills from Eclipse apply to Android Studio as well. Most of the tooling in Android Studio is very similar to Eclipse, such as shortcuts, designers, and code editors. You'll still export signed APKs, view logcat, and edit code virtually the same way in Android Studio as if you were in Eclipse. Think of Android Studio like this: if Eclipse were a trusty old power drill used in construction, Android Studio is the new cordless high-powered version of that same drill. Android Studio has some of the same options, and some new ones that you'll need to familiarize yourself with. In the end, you'll still feel comfortable enough to use the tool to get the desired result—an Android app.

Installing Android Studio

Google has made installing Android Studio as simple as possible. Just visit the Android Studio page (*http://bit.ly/1cQuSJE*) and download the installer for your platform. Supported platforms include Windows, Mac OS X, and Linux. Follow the installation

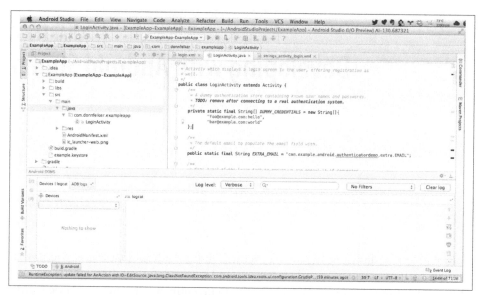

Figure 6-1. Android Studio with the Editor, Project, and Android panels

instructions for your platform to install the application. Installation instructions are not provided in this chapter because installation instructions change often. If you encounter issues, please visit the Android Studio installation page (*http://bit.ly/1cQuSJE*).

Bundled SDK

Android Studio comes bundled with its own version of the Android SDK, which is preconfigured to be used with Android Studio upon installation. On Mac OS X, it is located in the package contents for the application, as I determined by choosing Android Studio → Show Package Contents (see Figure 6-2) and checking the resulting screen (as shown in Figure 6-3). This means that if you already have an SDK installed, Android Studio will not use the previously installed SDK by default. If you would like to use the existing SDK on your machine, follow these steps from Stack Overflow (*http://bit.ly/135ZsgO*).

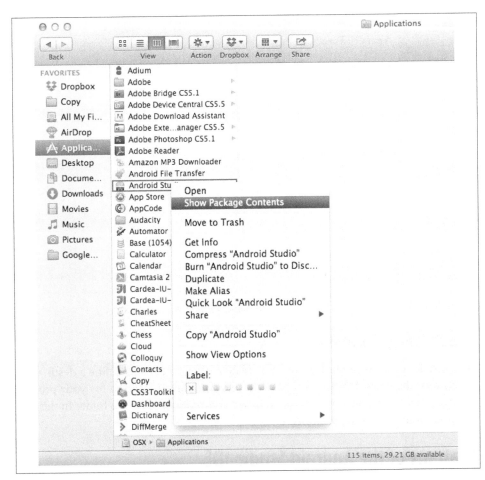

Figure 6-2. Showing the package contents of the Android Studio application

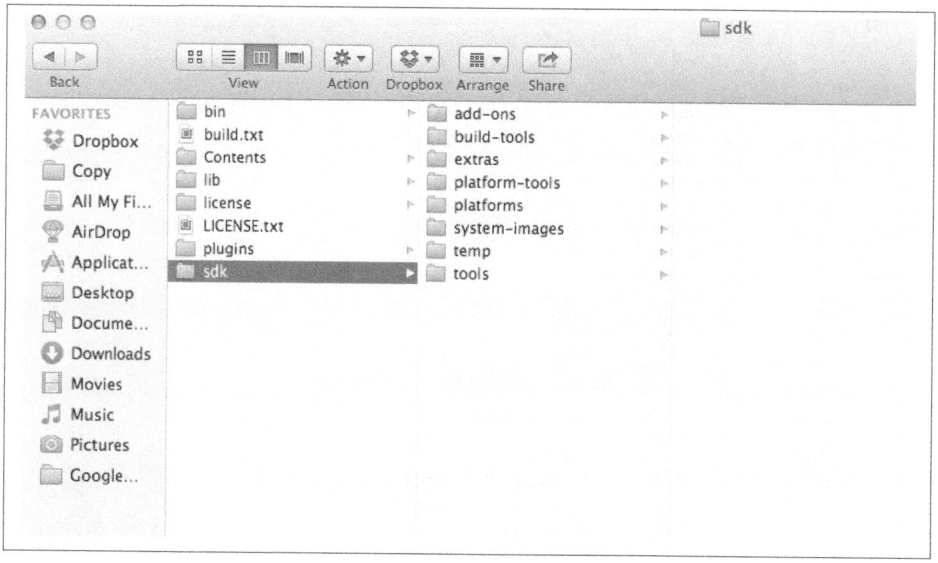

Figure 6-3. The SDK folder in the Android Studio package contents

Default Project Location

After installing Android Studio, you can create a new project and define a destination location for the project files. If you don't explicitly define a location for your project, Android Studio will place your files into the *~/AndroidStudioProjects* folder in the current user's folder on your machine.

Anatomy of the Android Studio IDE

The Android Studio IDE is comprised of a vast array of panels, tools, and functions to help you become as productive as possible at developing Android applications. I'll cover the most common panels, windows, and toolbars with which you'll be interacting.

Panels

The main panels that you will interact with during your day-to-day development of Android apps appear in Table 6-1.

Table 6-1. Important panels in Android Studio

Panel	Description
Project Panel	Allows you to navigate through the file hierarchy of your project and select, open, edit, and perform various other actions on your files.
File Editor	The main editing window in Android Studio. This is where you write your code.

Panel	Description
Android Panel	Presents the devices (emulators and physical devices) connected to your system, and allows you to view the logcat output, filter the output, and view ADB logs.
Messages Panel	Here you'll find any important messages that the IDE presents, such as compilation errors.
TODO Panel	Shows all the TODO comments sprinkled throughout your project's code.
Find Results Panel	Here you can examine the results of any find command that you execute. Examples include the Find Results command (Edit → Find → Find) and the Find Usages command (Edit → Find → Find Usages).
Maven Panel	If your project is Maven-based, interact with this panel to perform Maven activities.
Gradle Panel	If you're utilizing the new Gradle build system, you can find the tools necessary to interact with Gradle here.
Event Log Panel	At times, the Android Studio IDE may encounter an unexpected error or have important events that need to be visible to you, the developer. This panel will show you these events.

The final area, which is of utmost importance, is the status bar at the bottom of Android Studio, shown in Figure 6-4. This is where the majority of status updates will occur when background processes run. Some of these background processes include updating indices on the files, Maven or Gradle background processing, and event errors. The rightmost box shows the IDE's memory usage.

Figure 6-4. The Android Studio status bar

Toolbars

Android Studio ships with a highly customizable toolbar that is easily accessible from the top of the display. The default toolbar that ships with Android Studio is shown in Figure 6-5.

Figure 6-5. The default toolbar in Android Studio

Table 6-2 describes each set of tools from left to right.

Table 6-2. Tools in the default toolbar

Tool	Description
File Actions	Actions such as Open, Save, and Synchronize.
Undo/Redo	Undo and redo the previous action.
Cut/Copy/Paste	Quickly cut, copy, and paste from the toolbar.

Tool	Description
Find/Replace	Find and replace values in the project files.
Navigation	Navigate forward and backward in the most recent files that you've accessed or edited recently.
Build/Run/Debug/ Attach	These buttons are some of the most common buttons that you will use in Android Studio, as they allow you to build, run, debug, and attach to a running Android process for debugging.
Settings	These access the IDE Preferences and Project Structure.
Android Actions	The Android Action Group allows you to sync your project with the Gradle files, open the AVD or SDK Manager, and open the Android Monitor application.
Help	Where you can go for help in using Android Studio.

Useful Actions in Android Studio

In addition to the various panels and toolbars, Android Studio has a wide feature set that is accessible via the top menu and various contextual menus. Table 6-3 shows a few of the common actions that you'll want to familiarize yourself with.

Table 6-3. Common actions

Action	Description
New Module/ Library/Java Library	You can easily add a new Android Module, Android Library, or Java Library to your application by simply choosing the File → New Module or File → Import Module file option and following the wizard through the process.
Preferences	At times, you may want to customize Android Studio. You can do this by accessing the Preferences through the Android Studio → Preferences menu. Some options you can edit are the theme of the IDE, font sizes, keymap, toolbars, and many other options.
Project Structure	An Android project is comprised of modules and libraries, and at times you may need to edit the settings for these modules and libraries. To do so, you'll need to enter the project structure by visiting the File → Project Structure menu.
Showing Additional Windows	Although the default windows that ship with Android Studio are usually sufficient for day-to-day Android development, there may come a time when you need to get into the gritty details of the IDE. To explore the various other windows that are available to you (such as file structure, commander, VCS changes, etc.), visit the View → Tool Windows menu.
Right-Click to Explore	Anytime you're unaware of the actions you can perform in the IDE, simply right-click the area in which you would like to see the various options. Android Studio will present you with the array of options (if available) that are possible in the given context of the IDE panel in which you're working.

Navigation

Navigation shortcuts are used for navigating around your code base at the speed of light. Master the shortcuts in Table 6-4 and you'll increase your productivity immensely.

Table 6-4. Keystroke shortcuts in Android Studio

Action	Shortcut on Mac OS X	Shortcut on Windows\Linux
Go to Class	Command + 0	Ctrl + 0
Go to File	Command + Shift + 0	Ctrl + Shift + 0
Go to Definition	Command + B	Ctrl + B
Back / Forward	Command + [or]	Ctrl + [or]
Code Editor Tab Nav	Command + Alt + Left or Right	Ctrl + Alt + Left or Right
File Switcher	Ctrl + Tab	Ctrl + Tab
Find Usages	Alt + F7	Alt + F7
Find	Command + F	Ctrl + F
Replace	Command + R	Ctrl + R
Find in Path	Command + Shift + F	Ctrl + Shift + F
Replace in Path	Command + Shift + R	Ctrl + Shift + R

The New Structure of an Android Project

When you first open up Android Studio and create your first new project in the IDE, you'll notice that Android Studio introduces a new paradigm in regards to folder and file placement that is not congruent with what you may be used to in Eclipse. Almost all of your files are located in the *src* directory. The new file structure is in place in order to support the new Gradle build system.

A Tour Around the New Structure

As noted, the new file structure puts the majority of your files in the *src* folder, as shown in Figure 6-6. The files in this folder are the source files for your project. These are the files you'll be editing the majority of the time. This file structure provides more flexibility and will eventually provide the ability to provide multiple build variants (different types of builds with the same project). Everything in your project will still behave the same for the most part.

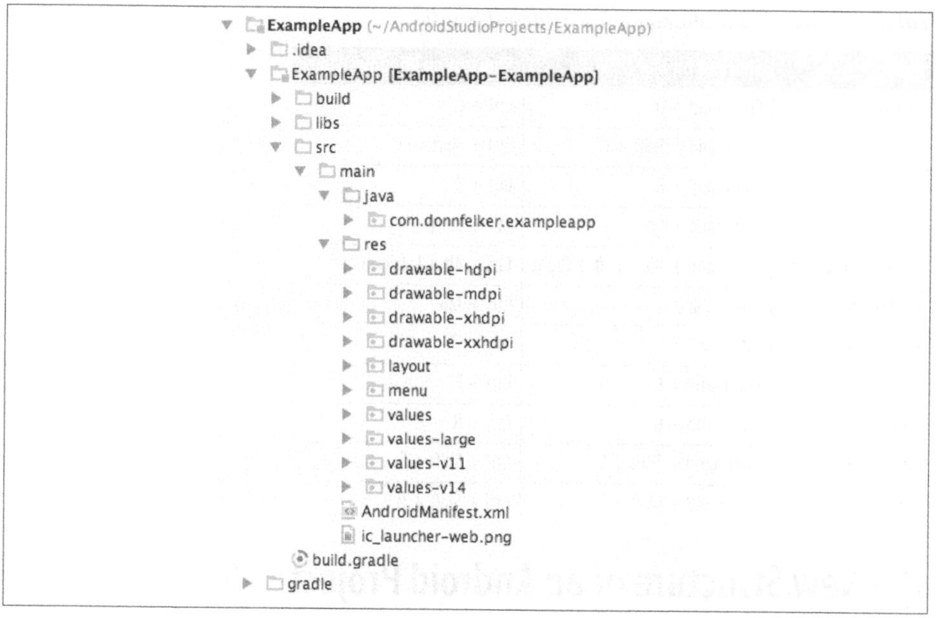

```
▼ 🗂 ExampleApp (~/AndroidStudioProjects/ExampleApp)
   ▶ 📁 .idea
   ▼ 🗂 ExampleApp [ExampleApp-ExampleApp]
      ▶ 📁 build
      ▶ 📁 libs
      ▼ 📁 src
         ▼ 📁 main
            ▼ 📁 java
               ▶ 📁 com.donnfelker.exampleapp
            ▼ 📁 res
               ▶ 📁 drawable-hdpi
               ▶ 📁 drawable-mdpi
               ▶ 📁 drawable-xhdpi
               ▶ 📁 drawable-xxhdpi
               ▶ 📁 layout
               ▶ 📁 menu
               ▶ 📁 values
               ▶ 📁 values-large
               ▶ 📁 values-v11
               ▶ 📁 values-v14
                 📄 AndroidManifest.xml
                 📄 ic_launcher-web.png
         📄 build.gradle
   ▶ 📁 gradle
```

Figure 6-6. An example of the Android folder structure in Android Studio

> Build variants are not implemented at the time of this writing.

Running and Debugging an Android Project

When you're ready to deploy your app to a device or an emulator to test and/or debug it (see "Debugging" on page 98), you can easily do so with Android Studio. The three various methods for this are Run, Debug, and "Attach Debugger to Android Process." All three of these commands are available via the Run menu or the main toolbar in Android Studio, as shown in Figures 6-7[1] and 6-8.

---

1. The "Attach Debugger to Android Process" item is at the very bottom of this long menu and has been removed from this screenshot for brevity.

Run
Tools
VCS
Window
Help
Run 'ExampleApp-ExampleApp'
^R
Debug 'ExampleApp-ExampleApp'
^D
Run...
^⌥R
Debug...
^⌥D
Edit Configurations...
Stop
⌘F2

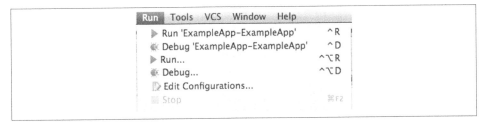

Figure 6-7. The Run menu

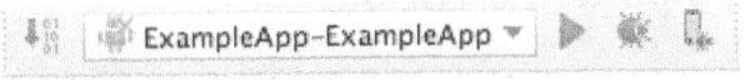

ExampleApp-ExampleApp

Figure 6-8. The toolbar run actions

To run an Android app on the currently connected device, select Run from the Run menu or press the Run button in the toolbar. This command will build the Android application and deploy it to the currently attached device.

To debug an Android app on the currently connected device, select Debug from the Run menu or click the debug icon in the toolbar. This command will build the Android app and deploy it to the currently attached device, and attach the debugger to it. At this point, if any breakpoints are set, Android Studio will stop execution so that you can inspect your runtime environment for debugging.

Another wildly useful tool is the "Attach Debugger to Android Process" command. This is mainly used when you need to start your app and navigate through a series of steps before attaching the debugger at a particular execution point (perhaps right before you click a button or before you navigate to a new screen). This tool allows you to quickly flow through your app and then set the breakpoint, instead of having the debugger running the entire time. To attach the debugger to your currently running app, install the app with the run command as outlined earlier and then select Run → Attach Debugger to Android Process or press the "Attach Debugger to Android Process" icon in the toolbar.

Creating New Android Components

A very common task during Android development is to create new components for the app. You can quickly accomplish this in Android Studio by right-clicking on the package name and selecting New → Android Component, as shown in Figure 6-9, or by pressing Command+N on Mac OS X, or Ctrl+N on Windows\Linux while your package name is highlighted in the *src* directory.

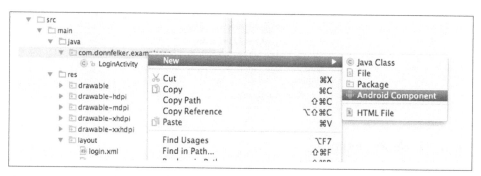

Figure 6-9. New Android component creation

Layout Designer and Layout Preview

Android Studio ships with two graphical tools to help you lay out your user interface: *Layout Designer* and *Layout Preview*. Layout Designer lets you arrange Views on the screen by dragging and dropping, while Layout Preview lets you see how your screen looks while you are editing your XML resources. I'll provide a brief introduction to both tools in this section.

Layout Designer

When you first open an Android layout file, you'll see the Android designer with the Design tab selected, as shown in Figure 6-10. The other tab is Text, which allows you to hop into the XML that defines the layout. I will cover that in the next section.

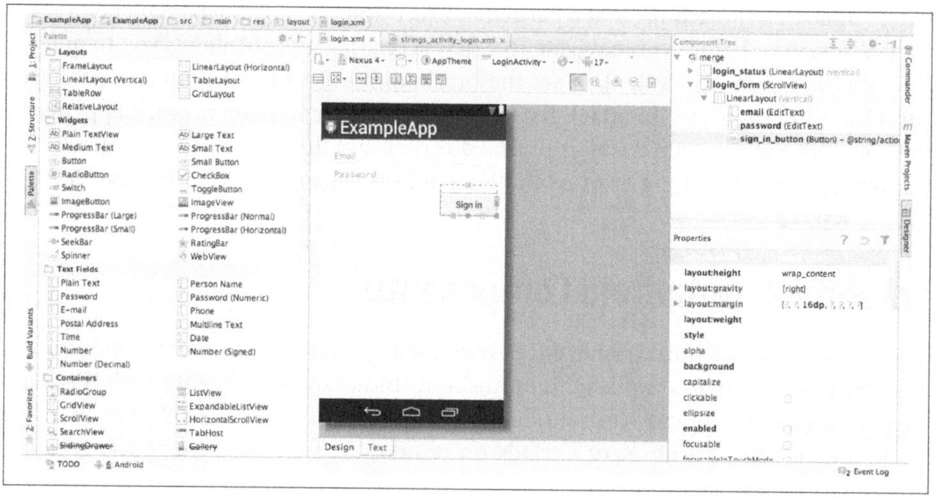

Figure 6-10. The Android Layout Designer

Android Studio's Layout Designer allows you to easily drag and drop controls onto the layout surface to quickly create a prototype of the layout that you need. Select one of the controls from the palette and drag it to the layout. Once the control is in place, you can edit the various properties of the control by selecting the control and editing the properties on the right, as shown in Figure 6-10. Layout Designer automatically creates the underlying XML code that represents the layout you created. The component tree shows you how the layout is organized in a hierarchical fashion.

To view the XML of a particular control, simply select it in the designer and click Command+B on Mac OS X, or Ctrl+B on Windows\Linux. You can also right-click and choose "Go To Definition." This will open the Text tab of the layout designer and you are navigated to the XML snippet that defines that control.

In Layout Designer, you can select various devices to emulate, themes, API levels, and orientations. I highly advise you to peruse the various options in the designer, as it is a very powerful tool.

If you love graphical editors, the Layout Designer is great for whipping up a user interface quickly. However, some of us love to get as close to the metal as possible, and in order to do that you need to edit the XML. To edit the XML, click the Text tab at the bottom of the Layout Designer.

Layout Preview

As soon as you enter the XML layout, you will notice that the control palette, component tree, property editor, and drag-and-drop designer are gone and replaced with a slew of XML code and a layout preview. This is shown in Figure 6-11. The preview shown here is the Layout Preview tool. You can turn this panel on and off by selecting the Preview button on the right side of the screen. This panel is shown only when the XML editor is in use.

The Layout Preview will update any time you make changes to the layout XML. As an example, if you change a TextView or Button to a bold font style, the Layout Preview will show the bolded text. If you like being closer to the XML, this is the view for you. I often hop back and forth between the Layout Designer and Layout Preview tools during my day-to-day Android development.

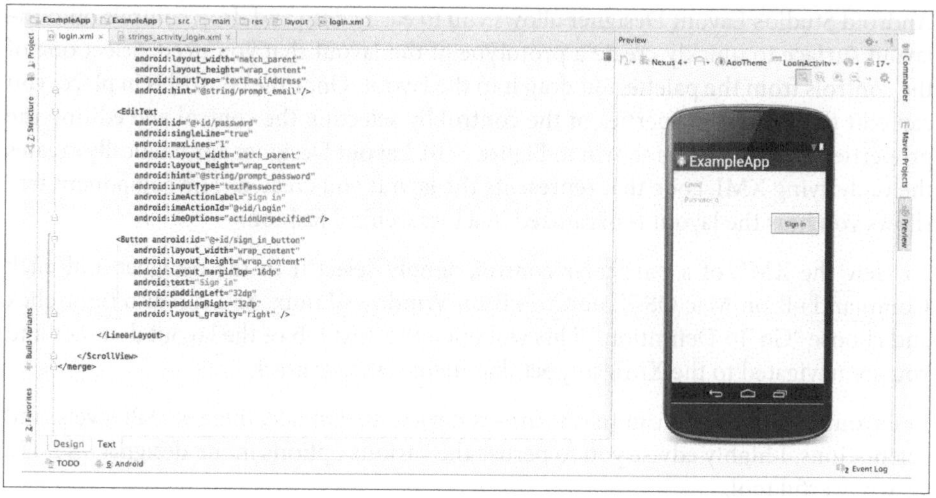

Figure 6-11. The Layout Preview with the XML layout editor

Generating an APK

Generating an APK in Android Studio is a snap. Follow these steps:

1. Select Generate Signed APK from the Build menu. This will display the Generate Signed APK Wizard.

2. Select your module and click Next.

3. Either supply the path to your keystore that you're currently using for your Android application, or create a new keystore.

4. (Optional) Once your keystore values are provided, click "Remember Password" and Android Studio will keep track of your entered password in a local password database so you don't have to enter it again. You will be required to provide a master password for this password database, so be sure you remember this password. Tools like LastPass.com are very useful for keeping track of numerous passwords safely. The remember password feature is very useful if you create or maintain a lot of Android applications.

5. Click Next.

6. At this point you can define the destination for your APK. You can also specify whether you'd like to run ProGuard (described in "ProGuard" on page 139), and where the ProGuard configuration file is located.

7. Click Finish and your APK will be generated in the destination folder.

Interacting with Maven and Gradle

Maven (see "Using the Maven Tools" on page 149) and Gradle (see "Gradle-Based Build Tools" on page 144) are build systems that are very popular within the Android community. Android Studio ships with support for Maven and Gradle right out of the box. This is great considering that in Eclipse you had to use a plug-in that was often buggy and not entirely reliable. Given that Android Studio ships with support for both tools, you can easily work with projects that use either technology via a panel in Android Studio.

Interacting with Maven

Projects that use Maven are easy to open in Android Studio. Simply start Android Studio and open the *pom.xml* file. Android Studio walks you through the Maven project import process. Once the import is complete, you can open *pom.xml* and edit it if needed for any reason, or you can open the Maven panel. The Maven panel is now populated with various options, as shown in Figure 6-12.

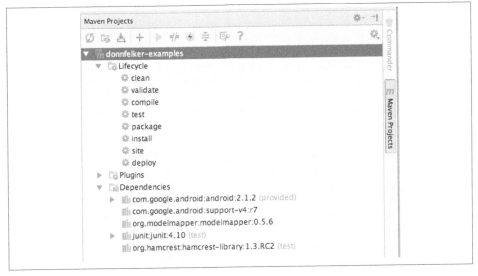

Figure 6-12. The Maven panel expanded

Once the Maven panel is expanded, you will be able to explore the lifecycle, various plug-ins, and dependencies. To refresh the Maven project, click the refresh icon in the top right of the panel. This loads all of the dependencies, plug-ins, etc., that are defined in the *pom.xml* file. To execute a lifecycle goal, simply select it and then press the play button in the top part of the panel. I recommend that you explore the panel and its options, because you can configure Maven and perform various other actions within it.

You can build a Maven project in Android Studio in a couple of ways. One way is to execute and build the task you want through the Maven panel. You can also set up a Maven build configuration (Run/Debug Configuration). Finally, you can build through the Build menu. I prefer to build through the Build menu because Android Studio caches the files and only builds off of changesets, so I'm not running through an entire Android Maven build every time (which can be very time consuming).

Interacting with Gradle

As with Maven, projects that use the Gradle build system are very easy to work with in Android Studio. There are a couple of panels that you should be familiar with. These panels include the Gradle panel and the Build Variants panel as shown in Figures 6-13 and 6-14. Once your project is loaded, you can open the Gradle panel and interact with the various tasks. You can also open the *build.gradle* file in the editor and edit anything necessary.

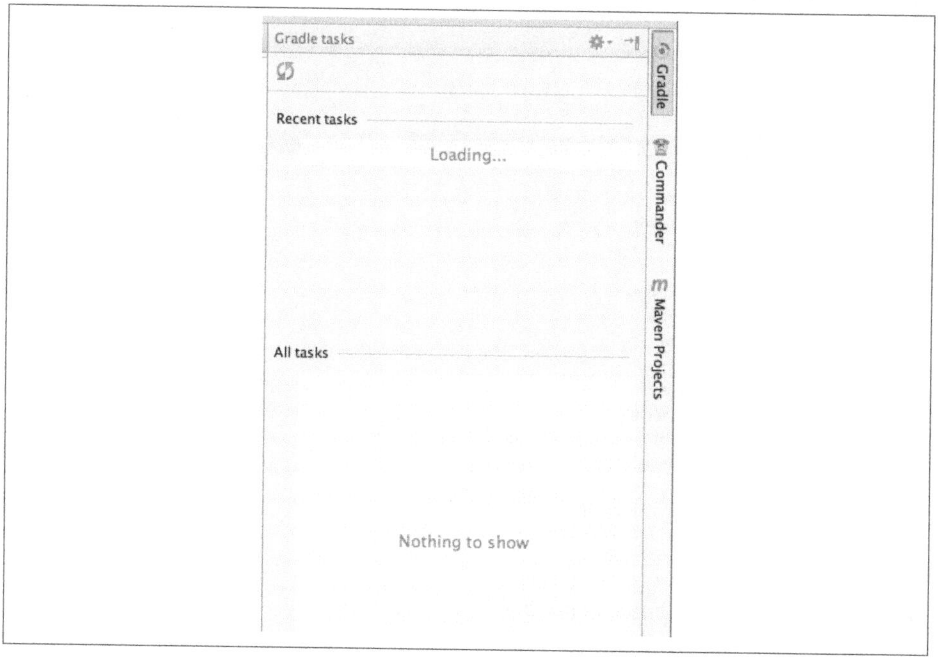

Figure 6-13. The Gradle task panel

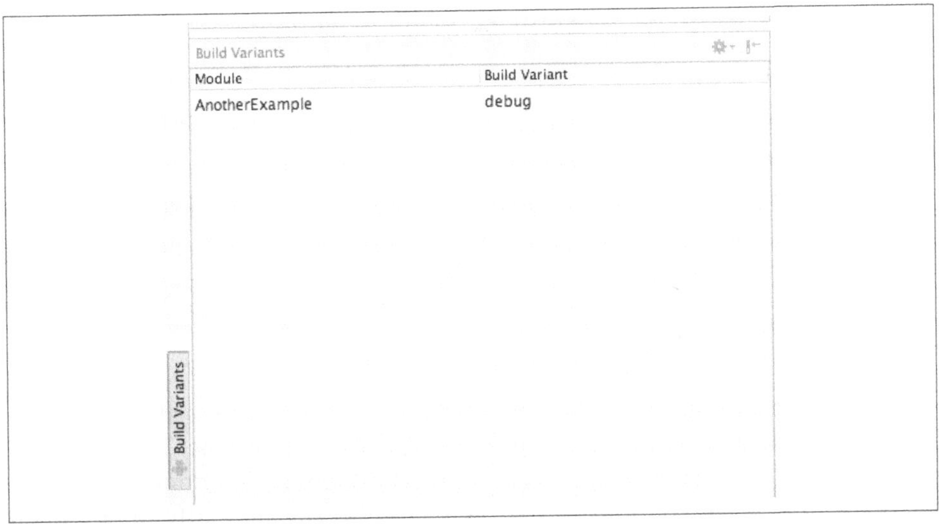

Figure 6-14. The Gradle Build Variants panel

Building your application is quite easy with Gradle. I recommend that you use the Build menu to build your application because it is the simplest way. If for any reason your application Gradle files become out of sync with your Android application, you can select the "Sync Project with Gradle Files" option from the toolbar, as shown in Figure 6-15. This will update your project with the settings defined in the Gradle file.

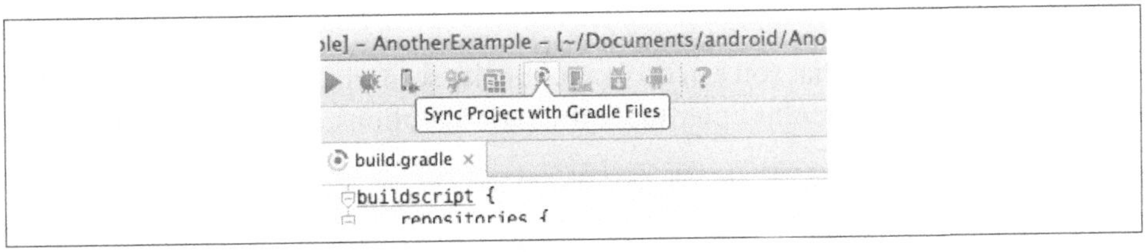

Figure 6-15. Sync Project with Gradle Files

Version Control Integration

Android Studio ships with numerous built-in Version Control System (VCS) integrations. These integrations allow you to perform VCS operations (commit, pull, push, update, etc.) within Android Studio:

Git
GitHub
Mercurial

SVN (Subversion)
CVS

If you're using something that is not listed here, plug-ins are available for various other VCS systems such as Team Foundation Server, Perforce, and others.

To configure your VCS system, select "Enable Version Control Integration" from the VCS menu and follow the steps. Once it is set up, you will be able to perform various VCS commands for all the files in Android Studio.

Migrating from Eclipse

Although Android Studio is not ready for prime time yet, it will be shortly and I'm sure a lot of folks are going to be moving to Android Studio from Eclipse. When the time comes for you to make the move, you can easily export your project from Eclipse using the Gradle export tool, and import it into Android Studio. The Android team has written an easy-to-follow guide (*http://bit.ly/14Cc5Bi*) on how to migrate from Eclipse.

Android Studio Tips and Tricks

Android Studio is packed with great keyboard shortcuts that allow you to be much more productive than previous Android development environments (except for IntelliJ, which is what Android Studio is based on). In this section, I'm going to show you some of the most common keyboard shortcuts that you'll use on a daily basis while developing Android applications.

When in doubt about what you can do in a particular scenario, place your cursor in the area of interest and press Alt + Enter to see the various options, as shown in Figure 6-16.

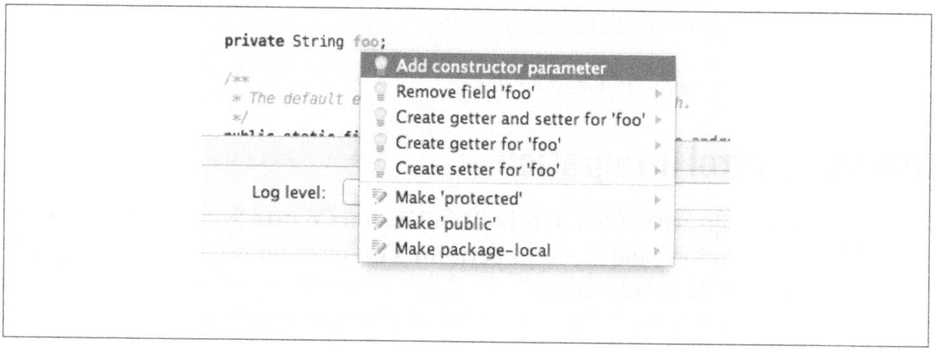

Figure 6-16. Context-specific options

Errors can also be refactored and edited. To do so, place your cursor on the error in the Android Studio file editor and press $\boxed{\text{Alt}}$+$\boxed{\text{Enter}}$ (on all platforms) to view the available options.

Refactoring and Code Generation

Many of the important code refactoring options available in Eclipse (see "Refactor Menu" on page 70) are also available in Android Studio. I advise you to review the "Refactor This …" option in Table 6-5 as well as the other options in the Refactor menu in Android Studio. Learning common refactorings, such as generating getters and setters, will save you valuable time and ensure the code you generate is standards-compliant.

Table 6-5. Refactoring options

Action	Shortcut on Mac OS X	Shortcut on Windows\Linux
Refactor This …	Ctrl + T (after placing cursor on area of interest)	Ctrl + T (after placing cursor on area of interest)
Rename	Shift + F6 (to rename files, resources, variables—anything)	Shift + F6 (to rename files, resources, variables—anything)
Generate: Create Constructor, New File, Layout, Getters/ Setters, Override Methods, Copyright	Command + N in a file	Ctrl + N in a file

Miscellaneous Shortcuts

Table 6-6 shows a few other miscellaneous shortcuts that I use day to day.

Table 6-6. Other useful shortcuts

Action	Shortcut on Mac OS X	Shortcut on Windows\Linux
Go to Line	Command + L	Ctrl + L
Reformat Code	Alt + Command + L	Alt + Ctrl + L
Run/Debug	Ctrl + R or D	Ctrl + R or D
Hiding Panels	Make sure the panel is active, then press Shift + Esc	Make sure the panel is active, then press Shift + Esc

Android Studio is packed with a ton of great features. Having used IntelliJ for Android for the last two years, I can honestly say I'm twice as fast at developing Android applications and I've become a better developer because of it. I believe that Android Studio will be an extension of that same strength and I hope you feel the same way about it after you use it for a while.

Additional training resources are available on my website, Donn Felker—Android Studio Training (*http://bit.ly/17cmdfQ*). I will update these tutorials as Android Studio evolves, so I encourage you to check it out if you would like to learn more.

## CHAPTER 7

Testing Your Code

Logcat

The Android platform provides a logging mechanism called logcat for collecting and viewing system information. Logs from the system and various apps are output to a series of buffers, which can then be filtered with the *logcat* command. If you have experience working with Log4J or the java.util.logging package, this will seem very familiar. You can review output from many different systems in a single location and filter it to view information relevant to your application. It is worth getting a good understanding of all the options, as this tool will make your life much easier.

Android logs pretty much everything in the system to a common log file. Information about garbage collection, various system activities, and app output are all sent to the same file. This provides a central location to gather a broad range of information in a single place. It is also important to note that this single file is shared by all apps installed on the device. Therefore, you should be careful not to output sensitive information to the logs. You can use the Proguard utility to obfuscate your code and hide certain details. It can also be used to remove log statements when packaging your app for release (details about using this tool can be found in "ProGuard" on page 139.

Viewing the Logcat File

To view the entire log file (without any filters), issue the command:

```
adb logcat
```

This outputs a very verbose log, which includes information about all processes on the system.

Anatomy of a Log Message

Each log message includes a variety of metadata that can be used to filter the output.

Log level
    Indicates the severity of the message being reported from the app's point of view.

Log tag
    Defines a process or ID associated with a message.

Log message
    The content being reported.

Reading logcat output

Each line in the logcat contains a variety of important information. I want to highlight what they mean, so you can understand where to find relevant information in the statement.

Here are a few lines from a logcat file:

```
E/PowerManagerService(  170): Excessive delay setting brightness: 101ms, mask=2
V/PhoneStatusBar(  308): setLightsOn(true)
I/ActivityManager(  170): No longer want com.android.contacts (pid 598): hidden
I/ActivityManager(  170): Displayed com.tools.demo/.LogcatDemoActivity: +955ms
D/UI      (  897): The user has pressed the button
D/UI      (  897): The user entered a value: value from the call is: 24324
```

Let's look at one statement to get an understanding of exactly what information it contains. The first statement we will look at is one generated from the system (remember both system and custom messages are output to the same file). This statement comes from the Android component that manages activity interaction with the core OS, and records how long the Activity Manager took to render the LogcatDemoActivity:

```
I/ActivityManager(  170): Displayed com.tools.demo/.LogcatDemoActivity: +955ms
```

This statement can be broken down to understand the exact information it contains:

I
    This is the severity level (see "Filtering Based on Logging Level" on page 91). This log statement was marked to be output when the Info level is being output.

ActivityManager
    This is the tag (see "Using Tags to Filter Output" on page 92) used when creating the log message. It tells us which system (in this case, Activity Manager) was responsible for generating this message.

(170)
    This is the "Process ID" of the application that originated this message. This is a unique identifier assigned to an application during runtime, and can be a great way to filter messages.

Displayed com.tools.demo/.LogcatDemoActivity: +955ms
    This is the custom content entered in the log statement. In this case, the message tells us that an activity was started, and how many milliseconds it took to be created.

To be clear, all this content was entered as custom text by the application that generated original log statement.

We can look at another statement; this time, it is output as a result of a statement I placed in my code. You can see the output from a custom statement looks exactly like a system message and contains the same information.

```
D/UI     (  897): The user entered a value: value from the call is: 24324
```

The information in a custom statement is exactly the same as the system messages:

D

Using the Debug severity level for this message.

UI

A tag I created to keep track of user interaction events.

(897)

The ID assigned to my application by the OS.

The user entered a value: value from the call is: 24324

Tracks that the user entered 24324 into a form field.

There is a lot of information in the logcat, which can be difficult to manage. Next I will discuss some strategies for generating and filtering logs that will make this easier.

Filtering Based on Logging Level

It is possible to filter logging output based on the severity of a message. Log messages are displayed based on their debug priority. You can specify a minimum level, and the output will be filtered to include only messages with that level or higher.

It is important to know the different log levels. You want to ensure that the level you are viewing is appropriate for the type of message you are looking for. Refer to Table 7-1 for a breakdown of the log levels.

Table 7-1. Logging levels shown by priority

Identifier (ID)	Name	Priority
V	Verbose (show everything)	1 (lowest)
D	Debug	2
I	Info	3
W	Warning	4
E	Error	5
F	Fatal	6
S	Silent (Show Nothing)	7

To view all of the messages with a certain level (and everything with a higher priority), enter:

```
adb logcat *:Identifier (ID)
```

As an example, if you wanted to see everything with a priority of Error or higher, enter:

```
adb logcat *:E
```

 It is a good idea to use the D level for most of your log statements. As the Android Log API states: "Debug logs are compiled in but stripped at runtime." This means that any logs you create with the D level will not be output in your production app. Therefore, it is safest to use this level for most of your log statements, in order to make sure that sensitive data doesn't accidentally get output into the field.

Using Tags to Filter Output

It is possible to apply filter expressions from logcat so you see only the messages that are most interesting to you. The filter expressions have the format *tag*:*level*. You can apply more than one filter at a time to isolate the specific information you need.

The procedure for finding messages of interest to you, therefore, is to create custom tags in your Java code and filter using these tags. The syntax for this follows:

```
Log.level("CustomTag", "Log message")
```

An example of this in use is:

```
Log.D("UI", "User entered a value: " + myEditText.getText());
```

You can then view only the specific messages you're interested in by typing:

```
adb logcat UI:D *:S
```

Getting the Most Out of Logcat

As you have seen, there are many ways to filter the logcat output, making it easy to ensure you are seeing the messages you need to see. You can apply as many different filter expressions to your logcat command as you need to fine-tune what is being displayed.

To apply multiple filter expressions, simply append them to your logcat command in the following format:

```
adb logcat    TAG1:level
              TAG2:level
              TAG3:level
```

For instance, if you want to see all statistics from the Activity Manager, use the `Activi tyManager:*` tag. To see only messages with a severity level of Error or higher from the Power Manager component, use the `PowerManagerService:E` tag. To see messages about the custom User Interface tag, use: `UI:*`. Don't forget to silence the other messages with the tag `*:s` (this means silence everything else). The combination of filters in this paragraph would look like this:

```
adb logcat ActivityManager:* PowerManagerService:E UI:D *:s
```

Viewing Alternative Log Buffers

The logging system keeps multiple buffers for log messages. For certain content (such as the radio or events), output will be left in an alternative buffer instead of the default one. To see the additional log messages, start logcat with the `-b` option and specify the alternate buffer you wish to view. For example, to view the radio buffer, enter:

```
adb logcat -b radio
```

Predefined Output Formats

Log messages include a variety of metadata fields, such as level, time, process ID, application, tag, and the error text. There are a variety of predefined output formats that can be specified in order to include the specific metadata field you want to see in the display. You can do this by including the `-v` option and one of these predefined output formats.

brief
    Displays the tag and the PID of process

raw
    Displays just the raw log message without other metadata

time
    Displays date, time information, tag, and the PID

long
    Displays all of the metadata fields and puts blank lines between messages.

For example, to generate output data in the time format, enter:

```
adb logcat -v time
```

Logcat Viewer in Eclipse

In the standard Java perspective in Eclipse, you will notice a logcat tab (▣) in the collection of tabs on the bottom of the screen (see Figure 7-1). This tool allows you to navigate the logcat of the currently connected device using some additional UI assistance.

There can be a lot of noise in the system log files. To make things easier, you can create an exclusion filter to exclude common system information that you don't want to see. To create a filter:

1. Select the plus icon (✚) icon to create a new filter.

2. Specify a "Filter Name."

3. Enter your filter value in the "by Log Tag" section: *^(?!exclude-term1|excludeterm2|excludeterm3).*$*.

4. I use the following filter as a good starting point: *^(?!dalvikvm|ActivityManager|SystemServer|BackupManagerService).*$*.

Level	Time	PID	TID	Application	Tag	Text
D	12-26 09:20:32.122	1646	1646	com.example.masterd	dalvikvm	Not late-enabling Chec
E	12-26 09:20:32.146	1646	1646	com.example.masterd	Trace	error opening trace fi
D	12-26 09:20:32.154	1646	1653	com.example.masterd	dalvikvm	Debugger has detached;
D	12-26 09:20:32.245	1646	1646	com.example.masterd	libEGL	loaded /system/lib/egl.
D	12-26 09:20:32.259	1646	1646	com.example.masterd		HostConnection::get() 1 id 1646
D	12-26 09:20:32.353	1646	1646	com.example.masterd	libEGL	loaded /system/lib/egl.
D	12-26 09:20:32.353	1646	1646	com.example.masterd	libEGL	loaded /system/lib/egl.
W	12-26 09:20:32.573	1646	1646	com.example.masterd	EGL_emulation	eglSurfaceAttrib not i
D	12-26 09:20:32.582	1646	1646	com.example.masterd	OpenGLRenderer	Enabling debug mode 0
W	12-26 09:20:42.833	1646	1646	com.example.masterd	EGL_emulation	eglSurfaceAttrib not i

Figure 7-1. The Logcat tool

Logcat Example

Logcat is a very powerful Android feature, but it can be hard to find what you need in it sometimes due to the amount of information that is output to the common log. Let's step through a simple example to demonstrate how to filter verbose system logs to find the information you want and get a better understanding of your code output.

For this example, I created code that takes an input value from the user in US dollars and sends this value to a web service, which returns the value in Euros. Finally, the value is converted to a custom formatted style and displayed on the user interface.

Determining areas to monitor

It is important to think about the specific characteristics of the code you are logging. You want to separate your logic into distinct areas (which will be represented with custom tags). This will make it easy to concentrate on specific areas because you will be able to isolate log statements based on functionality. In this case, there are a few particular functional areas, which should be tracked independently. The areas I want to monitor include:

User Interface

Check the values entered by the user, check the values actually displayed on the screen, monitor when the user presses a button, etc.

Network

Validate the URL I'm sending, monitor connectivity errors, display request/ response values, etc.

JSON Parsing

Output JSON values at various points during the parsing, etc.

Formatting

Check the algorithm I use to format the values for my application.

AsyncTasks

Track a call through the lifecycle of this code.

Creating log statements

After determining the categories I want to log, I create custom tags to represent each of them, in this case:

- UI
- NETWORK
- JSON
- FORMAT
- ASYNC

 I create a utility class with constants (e.g., `public static final String TAG_UI = "my_tag_ui";`) to represent common categories I use. Then I use this tag in my code (e.g., `Log.d(LogUtil.TAG_UI, "UI Log message");`). That way, I can easily look at a particular subsystem even across multiple activities, by filtering for that particular tag.

Then I put log statements in my code and use the custom tags as appropriate. The following code snippet shows how I used custom tags to track Web, JSON, and formatting functionality:

```
public static String ConvWebCall(String amount) {
    // To save space, I removed code not important to the example

    try {
```

```
        HttpClient client = new DefaultHttpClient();
        HttpGet request = new HttpGet();
        ...

        sb.append(amount);
        Log.d("NETWORK", "The URL we are sending is: " + sb.toString());

        request.setURI(new URI(sb.toString()));
        HttpResponse response = client.execute(request);
        Log.d("NETWORK", "Response received");
        ...

        Log.d("NETWORK", "The return String is: " + retStr.toString());
        String page = retStr.toString();
    } catch (URISyntaxException e) {
        Log.e("NETWORK", "URISyntaxException", e);
        e.printStackTrace();
    ...
    }
    Log.d("NETWORK", "Return value is: " + page);
    return page;
}

public static String parseConvedValue(String page) {
    String curr = "";
    try {
        JSONObject jso = new JSONObject(page);
        Log.d("JSON", "JSON Value: " + jso);
        curr = jso.optString("v");
    } catch (JSONException e) {
        Log.e("JSON", "Parsing exception: ", e);
    }
    Log.d("JSON", "JSON Value: currency element is " + curr);
    return curr;
}

private String formatEuroForDisplay(String amount, String name) {
    String euro = "Euro 00.00";
    Log.d("FORMAT", "Before formatEuroForDisplay: " + amount);
    if (amount != null) {
        int index = amount.indexOf(".");
        String euros = amount.substring(0, index + 3);
        Log.d("FORMAT", "Euros back from NETWORK: " + amount);
        euro = "Euro " + euros;
    }
    Log.d("FORMAT", "After formatEuroForDisplay: " + euro);
    String euroString = euro;
    return euroString;
}
```

Verbose logging

You can run the `logcat` tool without any filters (using the command `adb logcat`) to view the unfiltered output. As the following printout shows, this output can contain a lot of information and be difficult to understand. The following output is what you would see from a single execution of our currency conversion workflow. You can look at the tags to see how the process progresses: first the UI messages, then the FORMAT ones, then the NETWORK ones, and so on.

```
I/ActivityManager(   170): START {cmp=com.tools.demo/.LogcatDemoActivity u=0}
from pid 897
W/WindowManager(  170): Failure taking screenshot for (328x583) to layer 21010
D/dalvikvm(  170): WAIT_FOR_CONCURRENT_GC blocked 0ms
D/dalvikvm(  170): GC_EXPLICIT freed 114K, 39% free 13611K/22023K, paused 10ms
+9ms, total 267ms
I/Choreographer(   897): Skipped 35 frames!  The application may be doing too
much work on its main thread.
E/PowerManagerService(  170): Excessive delay setting brightness: 101ms, mask=2
V/PhoneStatusBar(  308): setLightsOn(true)
I/ActivityManager(  170): No longer want com.android.contacts (pid 598): hidden
I/ActivityManager(  170): Displayed com.tools.demo/.LogcatDemoActivity: +955ms
D/UI      (  897): The user has pressed the button
D/UI      (  897): The user entered a value: value from the call is: 24324
D/FORMAT  (  897): formatForWebcall() before: 24324
D/FORMAT  (  897): formatForWebcall() after: 243.24
D/ASYNC   (  897): onPreExecute()
D/NETWORK (   897): URL  to  send:  http://rate-exchange.appspot.com/currency?
from=USD&to=EUR&q=243.24
D/dalvikvm(  897): GC_CONCURRENT freed 121K, 2% free 11063K/11271K, paused 17ms
+32ms, total 78ms
D/NETWORK (  897): Response received
D/NETWORK (  897): The return String is: {"to": "EUR", "rate": 0.756258035,
"from": "USD", "v": 183.9522044334}
D/ASYNC   (  897): doInBackground(): {"to": "EUR", "rate": 0.756258035, "from":
"USD", "v": 183.9522044334}
D/JSON    (  897): Json Object is:
{"to":"EUR","v":183.9522044334,"from":"USD","rate":0.756258035}
D/JSON    (  897): Json parsed currency value: 183.9522044334
D/ASYNC   (  897): onPostExecute(): result is: 183.9522044334
D/FORMAT  (  897): Before formatEuroForDisplay: 183.9522044334
D/FORMAT  (  897): Euros back from call: 183.9522044334
D/FORMAT  (  897): After formatEuroForDisplay: Euro 183.95
D/UI      (  897): Setting value on screen to: Euro 183.95
I/ActivityManager(  170): START {act=android.intent.action.MAIN cat=[android.in-
tent.category.HOME] flg=0x10200000  cmp=com.android.launcher/com.android.launch-
er2.Launcher u=0} from pid 170
W/WindowManager(  170): Failure taking screenshot for (328x583) to layer 21015
W/IInputConnectionWrapper(  897): showStatusIcon on inactive InputConnection
I/Choreographer(   489): Skipped 42 frames!  The application may be doing too
much work on its main thread.
```

Filtering the logcat

I use the unfiltered view to get an overview of my entire process, but I often need to get a more granular view. To do this, I use the custom tags I created to view the specific categories I want to see. Because only the information I care about is displayed, it is much easier to understand the specific operations I am interested in.

For instance, if I wanted to see only information related to user interactions, I could filter based on the UI tag. In this case, I have an * next to the UI tag (specifying I want to see all messages), and an *:s to specify that I want to silence all other messages:

```
$ adb logcat UI:* *:s
D/UI       (  897): The user has pressed the button
D/UI       (  897): The user entered a value: value from the call is: 24324
D/UI       (  897): Setting value on screen to: Euro 183.95
```

Another example of something I need to track is the logic related to making the web call and parsing the response. For this, I use a combination of NETWORK and JSON categories to see the logic:

```
$ adb logcat JSON:* NETWORK:* *:s
D/NETWORK (     897): URL  to  send:  http://rate-exchange.appspot.com/currency?
from=USD&to=EUR&q=243.24-->
D/NETWORK (  897): Response received
D/NETWORK (  897): The return String is: {"to": "EUR", "rate": 0.756258035,
"from": "USD", "v": 183.9522044334}
D/JSON     (  897): Json Object is:
{"to":"EUR","v":183.9522044334,"from":"USD","rate":0.756258035}
D/JSON     (  897): Json parsed currency value: 183.9522044334
```

Debugging

Debugging is an important step in the development process, and can often take longer than actually writing the code. Debugging Android apps can be particularly difficult due to the various subsystems integrated into the OS. The ADT tools provide an integrated debug environment that makes this process easier.

A common method for debugging code is to create "breakpoints" that are triggered when code takes a certain execution path. The program execution pauses at that point, allowing you to inspect the state of the system (including current variable values and application status). You can use this information to analyze how code operates and locate errors.

Setting Your App to Debuggable

In order to debug an app, it is necessary to specify that your app is debuggable in the application manifest. If you are deploying your app using the ADT tools (from Eclipse or another IDE), this is done for you automatically. If you aren't building your project using those tools, you need to set this value manually. To specify that your app is debuggable, add the `android:debuggable="true"` attribute to the `application` element in your *AndroidManifest.xml* file. It should look similar to this:

```
<application
    android:icon="@drawable/ic_launcher"
    android:label="@string/app_name"
    android:debuggable="true">
```

If you set the debug flag manually, don't forget to remove it before releasing the app to production. You don't want this enabled in production, as it will negatively impact your performance. If you forget to remove it, there is a Lint checker (see "Lint" on page 107) that warns you that this is set when you are doing a release build.

Setting a Debug Point

The starting place in debugging is usually to set a breakpoint in the source code of your app. In Eclipse, this is done by clicking in the "alley" next to a code path and selecting "Toggle Breakpoint." You can also set the breakpoint by pressing Ctrl+Shift+B on Windows or Linux, or Command+Shift+B on a Mac. Either way, this triggers your IDE to show the "Debug perspective" when that particular code path is reached during execution. For example, in Figure 7-2, we set a breakpoint in the `onCreate()` method of the `LogcatDemoActivity`. The small caret next to line 12 shows the location of the breakpoint. During the execution of this code, when this code path is executed (in this example, when the `intializeView()` method is reached), the Debug perspective will automatically be launched, and the code execution will pause at this statement.

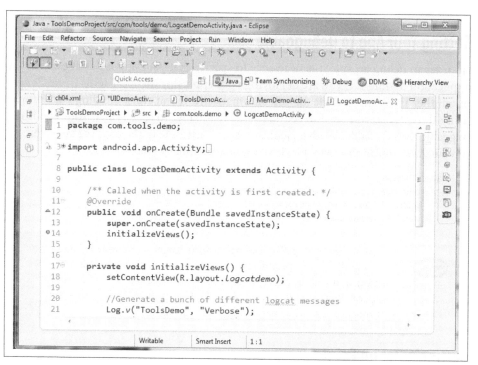

Figure 7-2. Setting a debug breakpoint

The Eclipse Debug Perspective

After you have successfully configured your environment and set a breakpoint, the Debug perspective will automatically be launched. It can also be launched manually by selecting Window → Open Perspective → Debug. The Debug perspective will look similar to Figure 7-3. Some sections on the screen are worth highlighting:

Debug
Shows the Android app that is being debugged and its currently running threads.

Variables
Shows the values of variables during code execution at the particular breakpoint.

Breakpoints
Contains a list of all breakpoints currently set in your app. In this view, you are able to control them, including enabling or disabling them.

Logcat
    Displays the system log messages.

Code and outline tabs
    Displays the currently executing source code, and an outline view.

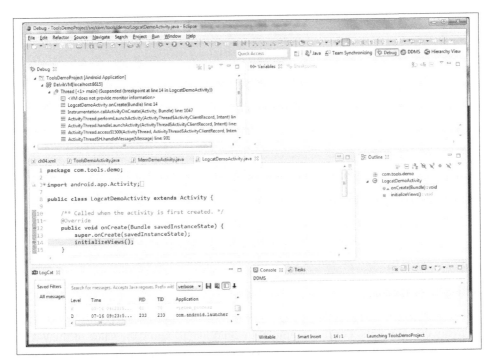

Figure 7-3. The Debug perspective

Debugging Example

Let me take you through an example to show you exactly how to debug a specific element of code. I created a very simple bit of code (see Figure 7-4) demonstrating how to use the debugger to inspect a value at different points in the execution cycle. The functionality of the code is simple. It takes a value input by the user, stores the value to an internal variable, and displays it back to the screen after a button has been pressed. Running the app will look similar to Figure 7-5.

```
  J DebugDemoActivity.java  ⊠                                    ⊟  ⊟
   1  package com.tools.demo;
   2
   3⊕ import android.app.Activity;⬚
   9
  10  public class DebugDemoActivity extends Activity {
  11      private TextView tv;
  12      private EditText et;
  13      private Button btn;
  14
  15      private String VALUE;
  16
 ▲17⊝     public void onCreate(Bundle savedInstanceState) {
  18          super.onCreate(savedInstanceState);
  19
  20          setContentView(R.layout.debug_layout);
  21          tv = (TextView) findViewById(R.id.debug_textview);
  22          et = (EditText) findViewById(R.id.debug_edittext);
  23          btn = (Button) findViewById(R.id.debug_button);
  24
  25⊝         btn.setOnClickListener(new View.OnClickListener() {
  26
 ▲27⊝             public void onClick(View v) {
 ●28                 String entered = et.getText().toString();
  29                 VALUE = entered;
 ●30                 tv.setText(VALUE);
  31             }
  32         });
  33      }
  34
  35  }
  36
```

Figure 7-4. Debug example source code

Setting the debug points

The first step in debugging the app is to determine the appropriate points in the code to create debug points. For this example, I would like to know the value of the VALUE variable at two execution points. The first is before the user has entered anything, which in this case is Line 28. I would also like to check the value after it has been set, so I'll set another debug point at Line 30. Remember, to set a breakpoint, just right-click on the line number and select "Toggle Breakpoint." Notice (in Figure 7-4) the little blue indicators next to each line number: these show that the debug points have been set.

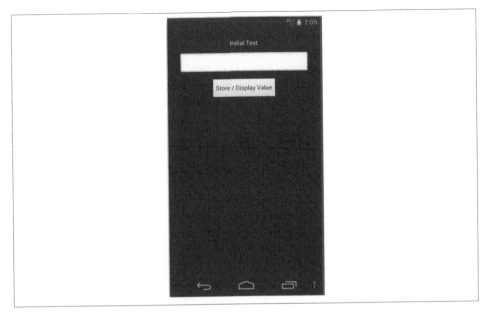

Figure 7-5. Running the debug example

Starting the debugger

After setting the debug points, I start the debugger by right-clicking on my project and selecting Debug As → Android Application (see Figure 7-6).

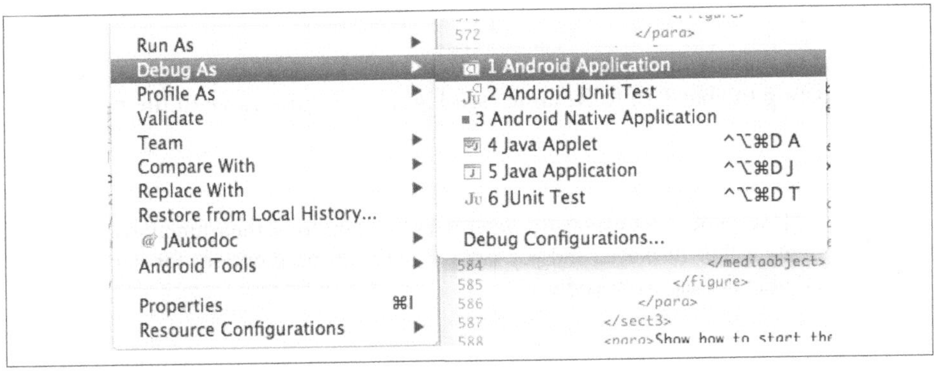

Run As	▶	572	</para>
Debug As	▶	📱 1 Android Application	
Profile As	▶	Jᵘ 2 Android JUnit Test	
Validate		▪ 3 Android Native Application	
Team	▶	📷 4 Java Applet	^⌥⌘D A
Compare With	▶	🗊 5 Java Application	^⌥⌘D J
Replace With	▶	Jᵤ 6 JUnit Test	^⌥⌘D T
Restore from Local History...			
@ JAutodoc	▶	Debug Configurations...	
Android Tools	▶	584	</mediaobject>
		585	</figure>
Properties	⌘I	586	</para>
Resource Configurations	▶	587	</sect3>
		588	<para>Show how to start the

Figure 7-6. Starting debugging with the right-click menu

This is basically the normal routine I use to run my app. I must select a device from the Android Device Chooser, and will navigate through my app to the point where I want to start debugging. At this point, I am presented with a dialog (see Figure 7-7) asking if it is OK to launch the Debug perspective. I click yes (and also select the checkbox on the bottom to authorize this for next time). This launches the Debug perspective.

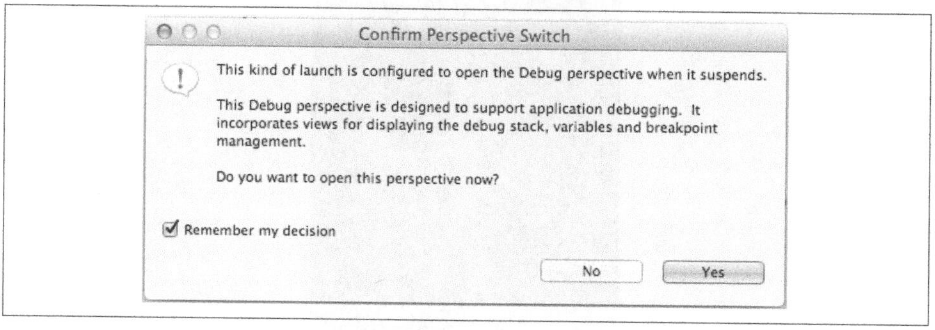

<figure>

Confirm Perspective Switch

! This kind of launch is configured to open the Debug perspective when it suspends.

This Debug perspective is designed to support application debugging. It incorporates views for displaying the debug stack, variables and breakpoint management.

Do you want to open this perspective now?

☑ Remember my decision

No   Yes

</figure>

Figure 7-7. Debug confirmation dialog

Stepping through the code

At this point, the Debug perspective is displayed, and the debugger has paused execution at my first breakpoint (see Figure 7-8). Notice the first debug point (Line 28) is highlighted. I can now use the other tools to learn more about my code at this point. In particular, I will use the Variables tab (on the top right) to determine the current state of my VALUE variable. At this point, it is null because I have not entered the value as a user.

To proceed to the next debug point, I need to tell the debugger to proceed. To do this, I use the debug toolbar (⇨) to Resume (see Figure 7-9) and move to the next debug point.

If you hover your mouse pointer over these buttons, their functionality will be displayed and you can discover advanced options for stepping through your code.

Figure 7-8. First debug point

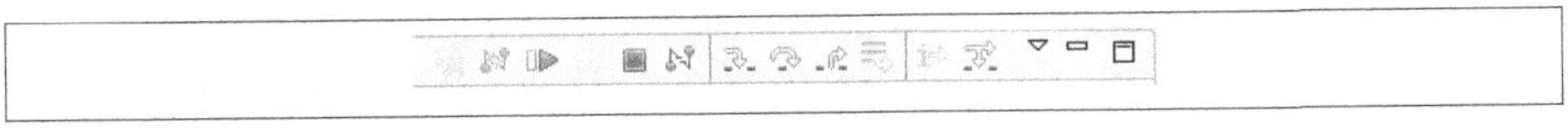

Figure 7-9. Debug toolbar

After I press the Resume button, the debugger executes the code and stops at the next debug point (in this case, Line 30). The view has changed (see Figure 7-10), because the code has executed to the next debug point. Execution stops at this point, and I can inspect my code again to determine how the values of my components have changed.

Looking at the Variables tab now, I see that the contents of the VALUE variable have changed, and it now has the value New Text Entered.

Figure 7-10. Second debug point

I can inspect other values at this point as well. If I click the "tv" component in the Variables tag (representing the TextView from our code), I can get a variety of information about this component (see Figure 7-11). I can get information about Android attributes (such as padding, animations, or formatting) or state information (such as the text content currently displayed). It is very useful to explore the various values at different execution points in order to understand detailed properties of your components.

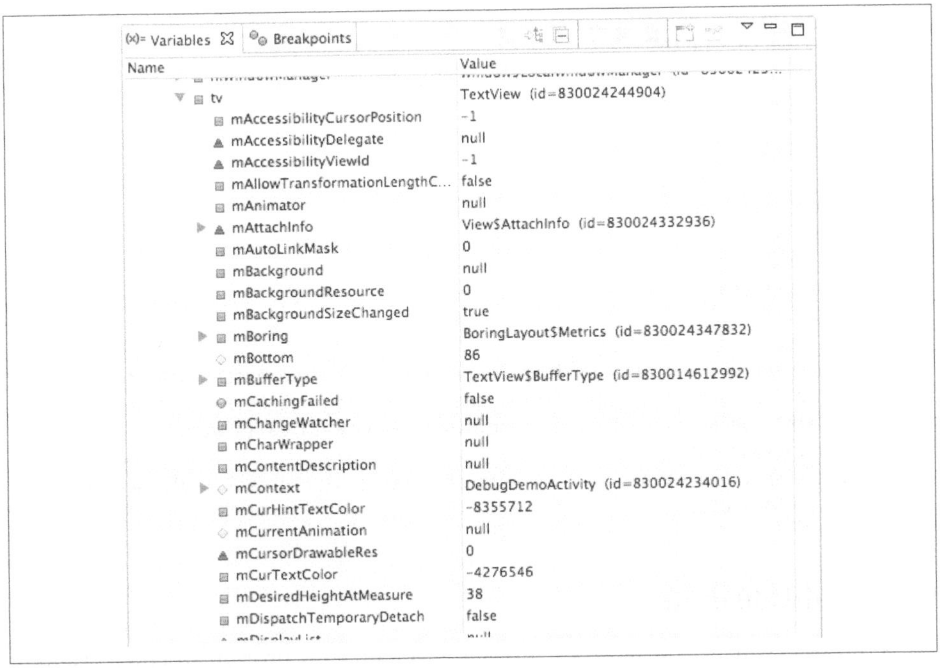

Figure 7-11. Inspect other values

Lint

Lint is a static analysis tool introduced in ADT 16 that scans your source code and identifies potential bugs. You can run it from the command line, use it directly with the Java or XML editors, and use it with your build tools. It is intended to identify potential issues based on established rules and patterns. Lint highlights these problems, and in many cases provides suggestions for remediation or quick fixes. It is a powerful tool and an easy way to improve the code quality with minimal effort.

Lint checks for a variety of different issues. Examples include:

- Accessibility and internationalization, such as missing translations
- User interface optimization, such as highlighting unused views
- Security, such as highlighting that you are not using HTTPS
- Code errors, such as inconsistent array sizes across classes
- Resource problems, such as missing densities for certain icons

You can get a list of every issue currently enabled by issuing the *lint --list* command. This outputs a list of the categories currently in use and a complete list of every issue with a short description of its purpose. It looks like this:

```
$ lint --list
Valid issue categories:
    Correctness
    Correctness:Messages
    Security
    Performance
    Usability:Typography
    Usability:Icons
    Usability
    Accessibility
    Internationalization

Valid issue id's:
"ContentDescription": Ensures that image widgets provide a contentDescription
"LabelFor": Ensures that text fields are marked with a labelFor attribute
"FloatMath": Suggests replacing android.util.FloatMath calls with
        java.lang.Math
"FieldGetter": Suggests replacing uses of getters with direct field access
        within a class
...
```

Command-Line Usage

The simplest way to get started with Lint is to run it on your project, and then examine all the errors it reports back to you. This gives you a good overview of the kind of errors Lint finds.

To run the tool, just execute the *lint* command, specifying the directory where you have the source code of an Android project. If you specify a directory that contains multiple projects, Lint will recursively check every project in the path.

Here's an excerpt from a sample Lint report I ran on a project of mine. You can get an idea of some of the items identified:

```
$ lint ./ToolsDemo

Scanning ToolsDemo: ..............................
Scanning ToolsDemo (Phase 2): .................
res/layout/gooduidemo.xml:15: Warning: Should use "sp" instead of "dp" for text
sizes [SpUsage]
        android:textSize="20dp" />
        ~~~~~~~~~~~~~~~~~~~~~~~~
res/layout/baduidemo.xml:167: Warning: [I18N] Hardcoded string "Text will go
here", should use @string resource [HardcodedText]
                android:hint="Text will go here"
                ~~~~~~~~~~~~~~~~~~~~~~~~~~~~~~~~~
res/layout/baduidemo.xml:120: Warning: Duplicate id @+id/imageView2, already
defined earlier in this layout [DuplicateIds]
                android:id="@+id/imageView2"
                ~~~~~~~~~~~~~~~~~~~~~~~~~~~~
```

```
res/layout/imagesdemo.xml:23: Warning: [Accessibility]
Missing contentDescription attribute on image [ContentDescription]
        >ImageView
        ^
res/layout/baduidemo.xml:89: Warning: This tag and its children can be replaced
by one >TextView/< and a compound drawable [UseCompoundDrawables]
        >LinearLayout
        ^
...
0 errors, 80 warnings
$
```

The example I've included is only an excerpt, and doesn't show every error Lint found on my project. You can see in the last line that Lint found 0 errors—but 80 warnings, and this project is pretty small. You should run Lint on your own project often, as you are likely to see a variety of things that will improve the quality of your code.

Excluding issues

You likely will want to omit certain errors from being checked (perhaps you don't support internationalization, so do not need to be warned about those issues). You can do this from the command line by including the --disable *list* argument. The list is a comma-separated list of issue IDs or categories you wish to exclude.

For example, I might want to eliminate any errors relating to the Internationalization category (perhaps my app uses English only), as well as the specific ContentDescription error (if I'm not worried if my images don't appear). When I run the same report as before, but with the --disable argument in my command, Lint produces fewer items: 26 warnings, which is much fewer than the 80 reported before. This practice allows you to narrow down the list of issues so you can concentrate on the particular ones that are most important to you.

```
$ lint ./ToolsDemo --disable Internationalization,ContentDescription

Scanning ToolsDemo: ...............................
Scanning ToolsDemo (Phase 2): ................
res/layout/gooduidemo.xml:15: Warning: Should use "sp" instead of "dp" for text
sizes [SpUsage]
        android:textSize="20dp" />
        ~~~~~~~~~~~~~~~~~~~~~~~
...
0 errors, 26 warnings
$
```

It is important to mention that the --disable command is permanent, and not per session. The issues will not be reported on your entire project, even when you test from within Eclipse, or start a new terminal session. If you intend to disable the options temporarily, make sure to enable them when you are finished. Simply issue the same command as before, but use the --enable option instead. This will rerun the Lint check and re-enable these issues for future tests. The output will look like:

```
$ lint ./ToolsDemo --enable Internationalization,ContentDescription

Scanning ToolsDemo: ...............................
Scanning ToolsDemo (Phase 2): .................
res/layout/gooduidemo.xml:15: Warning: Should use "sp" instead of "dp" for text
sizes [SpUsage]
        android:textSize="20dp" />
        ~~~~~~~~~~~~~~~~~~~~~~

res/layout/baduidemo.xml:167: Warning: [I18N] Hardcoded string "Text will go
here", should use @string resource [HardcodedText]
            android:hint="Text will go here"
            ~~~~~~~~~~~~~~~~~~~~~~~~~~~~~~

...
0 errors, 80 warnings
$
```

Running in Eclipse

Inside Eclipse, it is very easy to start Lint. Just right-click on your project folder, then
choose Android Tools → Run Lint: Check for Common Errors.

After launching Lint, you will notice a new tab named *Lint Warnings* (see Figure 7-12).
This is the Lint UI you will use to track and fix the errors. It contains a tree of errors,
organized by issue type. This makes it easy to concentrate on a specific category. The
toolbar has a variety of actions for manipulating the list and options for customizing
the display.

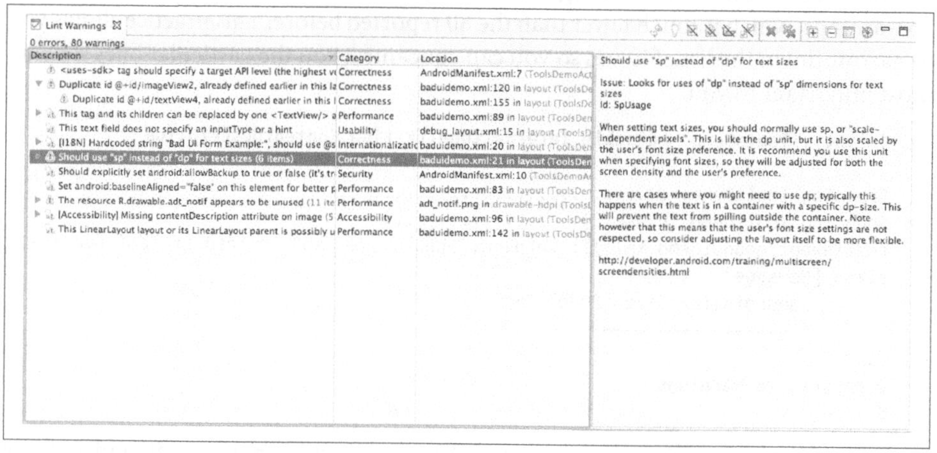

Figure 7-12. Lint Warnings tab

Lint toolbar menu

When you highlight an error, the toolbar (Figure 7-13) on the top of the tab becomes enabled. This is the Lint Warnings toolbar, which provides a central place to disable issues.

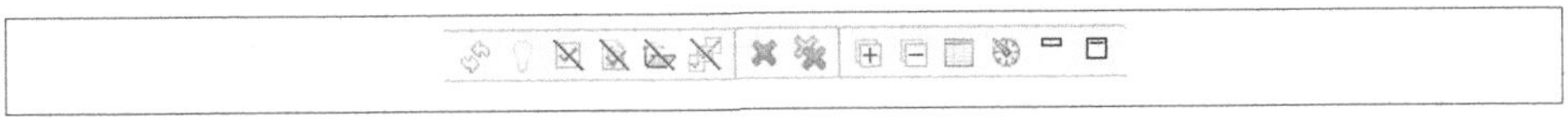

Figure 7-13. Lint Warnings toolbar

The buttons, from left to right, offer the following tasks:

Refresh
Reruns the Lint tests and displays new results.

Fix
Launches the XML or Java editor and modifies the source code to fix the issue.

Suppresses the selected error with an annotation/attribute
Suppresses the warning for the selected single instance, by placing the appropriate notation in the source file.

Ignore in this file
All instances of the selected issue will be suppressed for the entire file.

Ignore in this project
All instances of the selected issue will be suppressed for the entire project.

Always ignore
You will not see the selected error reported from any project or file.

Remove
Deletes the selected issue from this view, but does not disable the issue, so it will reappear the next time you run Lint.

Remove all
Deletes all issues from this view, but they will reappear the next time you run Lint.

Expand all
Expands every node in the issue tree so you can see every independent issue reported.

Collapse all
Collapses the issue tree so the items are grouped into categories.

Options

Launches a dialog (see Figure 7-14) that contains a few important options. This dialog provides another way to enable or disable issues and examine the issues that are enabled. This is also where you set your preferences for how and when Lint runs.

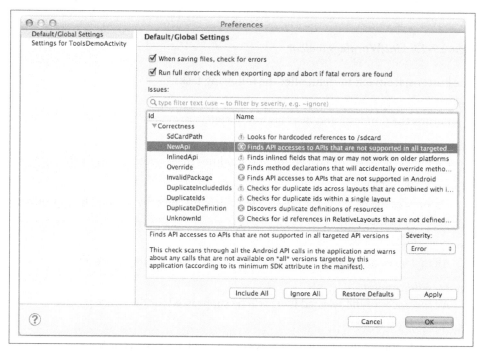

Figure 7-14. Lint options

Java and XML editor integration

By default, Lint runs automatically, so you have likely already seen the errors it flags. Depending on the option you specified, you will see the errors flagged when you are typing or when you save your file. When Lint encounters an error, it places a marker at the line of code with the problem. To learn more about the issue, hover your mouse over the warning icon, or the line of code (underlined in yellow) to learn more. Figures 7-15 and 7-16 show how this looks in both the XML and Java editors.

Figure 7-15. Lint warnings in XML file

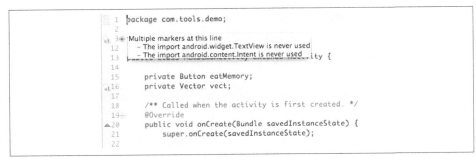

Figure 7-16. Lint warnings in Java file

Quick Fix tool

It is likely that you will want to do more than just learn about the errors in your code—you probably want to fix the problems! There is a "Quick Fix" tool that makes fixing errors very easy.

The best way to invoke this feature is to select the code with the error, and press Ctrl+1 on Windows or Linux, or Command+1 on Mac OS X.

After you launch the "Quick Fix" dialog, you will be prompted with a variety of options for handling the particular warning. These are the same options provided by the Lint toolbar (see "Lint toolbar menu" on page 111). The options will look like Figures 7-17 and 7-18 in Java, respectively.

It is possible that this functionality won't work for every issue you have. In cases where the system is unable to provide a "Quick Fix," you need to debug the code yourself and determine the way to fix your problem.

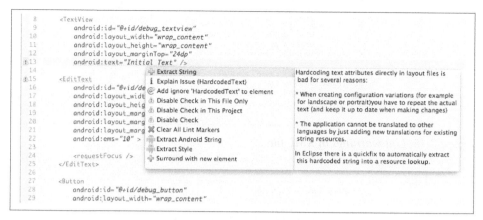

Figure 7-17. Lint Quick Fix in XML

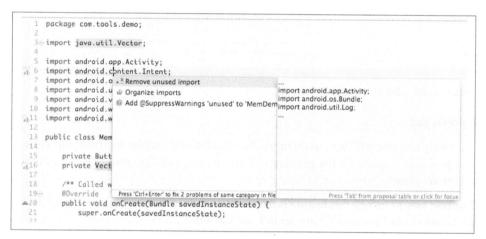

Figure 7-18. Lint Quick Fix in Java

## CHAPTER 8

Simulating Events

There are a variety of occurrences you will want to test that are difficult to replicate as they would happen in real life. In these cases, tools are available that will allow you to simulate events so you can test effectively.

Simulating Location and Routes

For instance, testing location can be challenging. It is impractical or impossible to travel to remote locations or simulate the exact same track over and over again. Fortunately, the DDMS tool provides a way to specify a location you would like your emulator to simulate (as latitude/longitude coordinates), or a path you would like to simulate (in the form of GPX or KML).

To simulate location, you need to open the DDMS tool (see "Launching the DDMS Perspective" on page 152). To launch the Eclipse perspective, select:Window → Open Perspective... → Other... → DDMS → OK.

Next, open the Emulator Control tab (which looks like Figure 8-1). In this tab, you can see a section marked Location Controls, where you can enter location attributes. When you are done entering your personalized data, hit the Send, Load GPX, or Load KML button (depending on which type of data you are working with). This causes your emulator to simulate the location you specified.

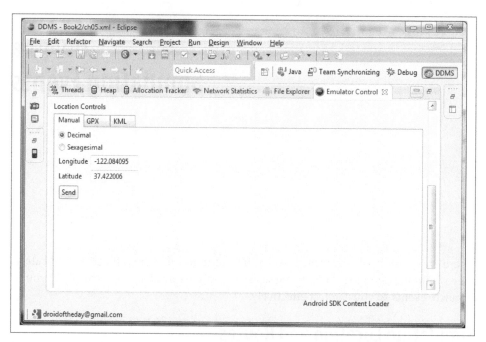

Figure 8-1. Simulating location with the emulator

The following steps demonstrate how to simulate a particular location on your device. The same process can be used to simulate a path using KML or GPX.

1. Launch the DDMS perspective in Eclipse.

2. Locate a device or emulator you want to work with, and highlight it in the Devices tab.

3. Select the Emulator Control tab in the right-side pane (as shown in Figure 8-2).

4. In the Telephony Actions section, scroll to the bottom section labeled Location Controls. In this section, select the Manual tab, and enter a valid latitude and longitude in the form. The default value (which is the default value that is set) is Mountain View, California.

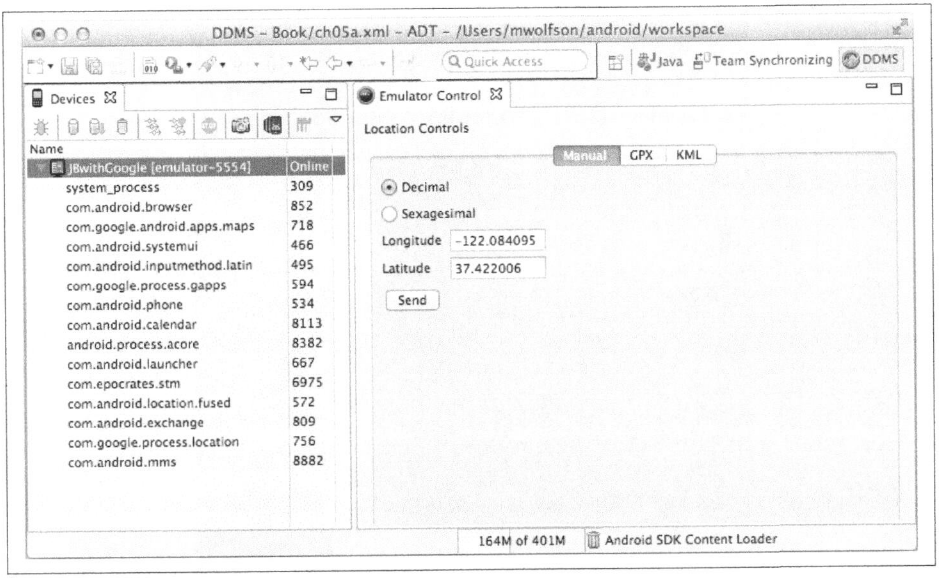

Figure 8-2. Setting up a location simulation

5. You might need to enable Location Settings on your device if it hasn't been done already (see Figure 8-3). You will be prompted the first time you try to access your location if you need to do it.

6. Press the Send button to simulate this location of your device. Your device now reflects this location.

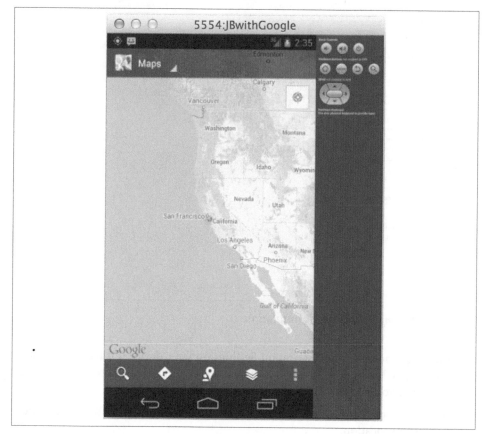

Figure 8-3. Viewing a location simulation

Simulating Telephony Operations

The Emulator Control tab has another section called Telephony Actions (see Figure 8-4), which can simulate telephone events and radio connectivity functionality. This is a useful way to interact with the emulator if you need to simulate phone calls or SMS messaging. It is also useful to adjust radio settings in order to learn your app's effectiveness in situations where connectivity is less than optimal. The top of the tab has a section titled Telephony Status. If you would like to simulate connectivity issues (such as latency or packet loss), you can adjust these settings. The other section, named Telephony Actions, is where you simulate phone calls or messages. To simulate either of these actions, enter a value for the return phone number, select the operation you want to perform (either phone call or SMS), enter your SMS message content (if appropriate), and click the Send button.

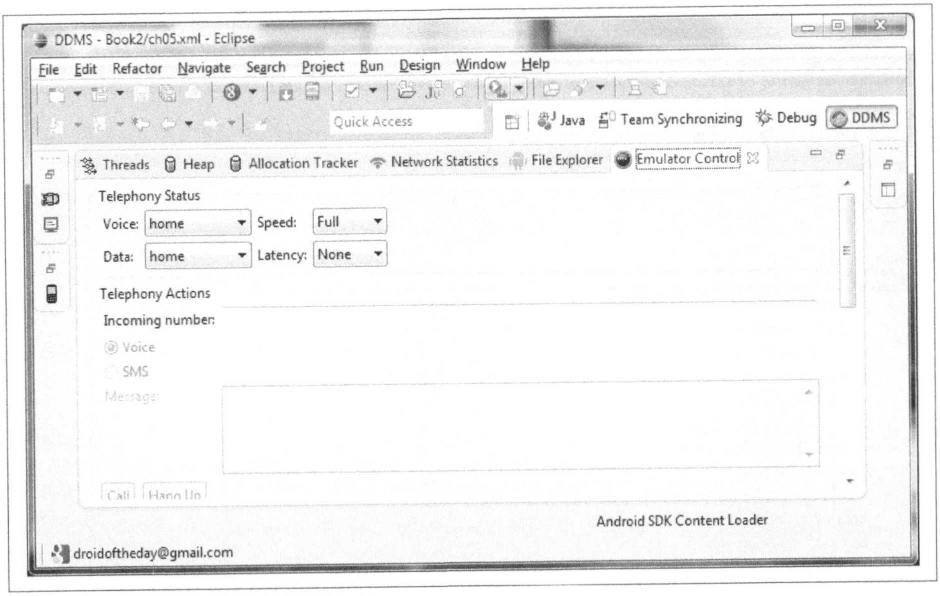

Figure 8-4. Emulator telephony simulation

The following steps demonstrate how to generate an SMS message. This is the same process used to simulate phone calls.

1. Launch the DDMS perspective in Eclipse.

2. Locate a device or emulator you want to work with, and highlight it in the Devices tab.

3. Select the Emulator Control tab in the right-side pane (Figure 8-5).

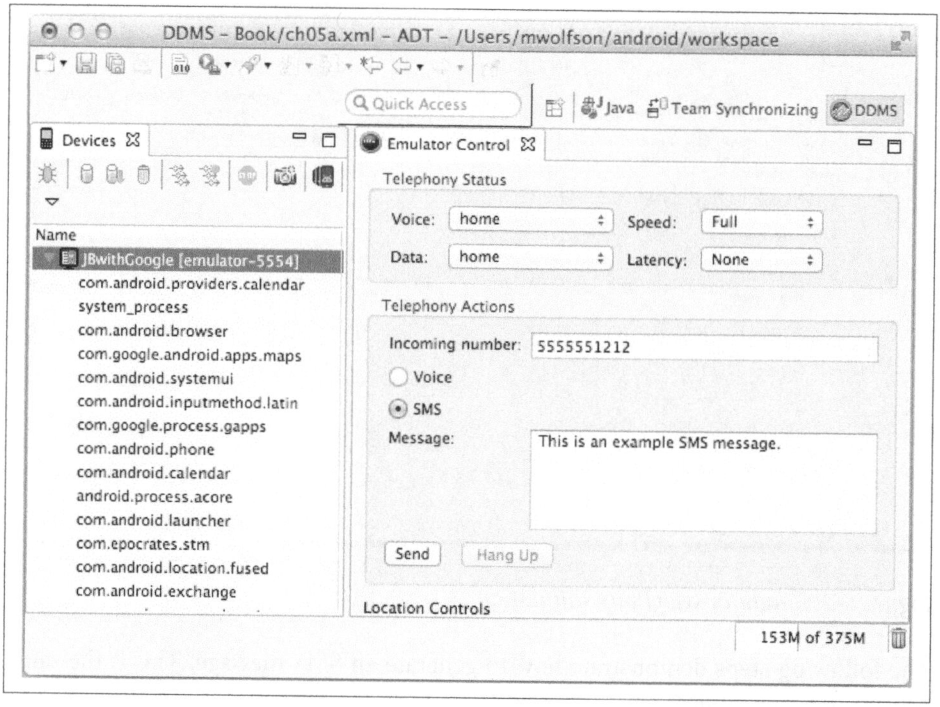

Figure 8-5. Setting up SMS simulation

4. (Optional) Adjust the Speed and Latency settings if you want to test how your app will perform with poor connectivity.

5. In the Telephony Actions section, enter a phone number (without dashes) and your example message text.

6. Press the Send button to send your simulated message, which will show up on your device or emulator. Your device shows an SMS has come into the system (as shown in Figure 8-6).

Figure 8-6. Viewing SMS simulation

Changing Networking Parameters

You likely will want to change the networking parameters of your device. This can be useful when you want to forward requests from your computer to your emulator or device (perhaps you want to test a configuration of the local network on the Android system).

It is pretty easy to do this using ADB. The syntax will look like this example:

```
adb forward tcp:9222 tcp:9333
```

Then, the next time you ping

```
localhost:9333
```

from your local desktop, your command will be forwarded directly to your Android device.

Using a Device with Sensor Emulation

It is difficult to simulate certain activities using the emulator, such as when simulating multi-touch or interacting with motion-based sensors such as the gyroscope. To work around this challenge, ADT provides the capability to connect a physical device to your emulator and use the sensors on that device to interact with your emulator. The app running on the emulator monitors changes in the device sensors, which are transmitted to the emulator and injected into the system image. This allows you to generate various sensor events using your physical device, and transmit them to your running emulator.

In order to use this feature, you need the system image for Android version 4.0, release 2 or greater running in your emulator.

The steps to enable sensor emulation are:

1. Edit the AVD you will be using. Add the hardware property "Multi-touch screen support," and set it to true. Chapter 3 describes how to do this.

2. Install the SdkControllerSensor application on the device. You can find the source code for this application in the *$SDK/tools/apps/SdkController* folder.

3. Enable "USB debugging" on your device, and connect it to your computer.

4. Run the SdkControllerSensor application on the device.

5. Select the particular sensors you wish to emulate using the application.

6. Enable port forwarding by running *adb forward tcp:1968 tcp:2068* from the device's shell command line.

7. Start the emulator that you plan to test with.

Port forwarding can be unreliable. If you are not seeing sensor events in the emulator, run the *adb forward tcp:1968 tcp:2068* command again to restore the connection.

Advanced Sensor Testing

If you are writing an app that makes extensive use of sensors, you will likely face many challenges when testing them. Testing different scenarios can be difficult, even impossible in many situations. It can be impractical to test extreme situations. For instance, if you need to test extreme temperatures, you can't put your phone in the oven or freezer. It is also difficult to test the exact precision of other sensors (try holding your phone still for a long period when testing the gyroscope for instance). SensorSimulator (*http://bit.ly/16zLVem*), an open source project managed by OpenIntents.org, makes sensor testing much more practical.

SensorSimulator is a series of applications, including a desktop component and multiple APKs. You can use the desktop component to send real-time sensor events to your device. Having the precise control and ability to reliably trigger sensor interactions is extremely valuable when writing apps that make use of sensors. This tool also provides the ability to record a series of sensor events that can be played back on a device. You can create a scenario (using the desktop app, or by recording events on your device), then save it to play back. This is an extremely valuable regression tool, as it allows you to trigger consistent sensor actions over and over.

Supported Sensors

The SensorSimulator project currently supports a variety of sensors including accelerometer, compass, orientation, temperature, light, proximity, pressure, gravity, linear acceleration, rotation vector, and gyroscope sensors. You can control how each of the sensors are being simulated using the Sensors tab (the right side of Figure 8-7 shows this). Sensors can be enabled or disabled in this window (they will be highlighted in blue when enabled). Only enable the sensors you are testing so you only see the particular data in which you're interested. If you want to modify the values of some of these sensors, you can do that in the Quick Settings and Sensors Parameters tabs.

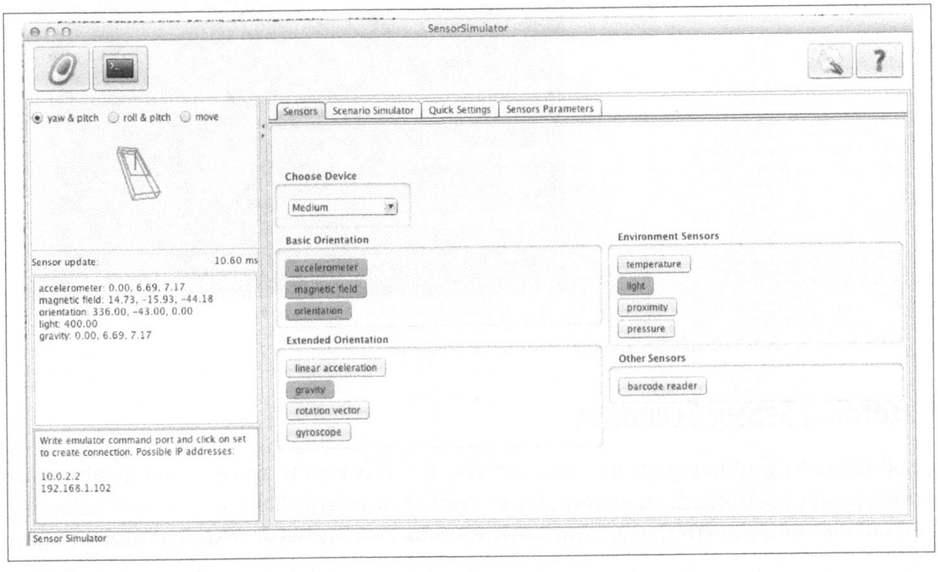

Figure 8-7. Optional sensors

Simulating Sensor Events in Real Time

You will download, install, and run this tool the same as any other native application (the simple instructions are on the project website). Run a desktop Java application (*bin/ SensorSimulator.jar*) on your computer, install, and run an APK on your device (*bin/ SensorSimulatorSettings-x.x.x.apk*), and then connect the two processes together using your WiFi connection. Once connected, use the desktop application to send sensor events and view them on your device. Figure 8-8 shows an example of what it would look like to use the accelerometer sensor to simulate moving the phone. You move the mouse in the desktop to "move" the phone, and can see these interactions on your device.

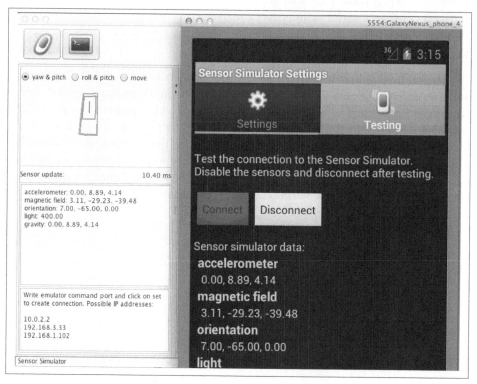

Figure 8-8. SensorSimulator accelerometer example

Recording Sensor Scenarios

In addition to simulating events, you can also use this tool to record a series of sensor events to play back on a device or emulator—called a scenario. This is extremely valuable, as it enables repeating the exact same sensor events over and over. This makes regression testing easier. For example, you could record the exact interactions required to pass a level of your gyroscope controlled game—then play it back against a build to validate it for production.

The easiest way to create scenarios is to use the Java app to generate them. The righthand section of Figure 8-9 has a Scenario Simulator tab. To create a scenario, create a sensor event representing a particular sensor state. You can then create more events, and string them together to play out a scenario (using the controls on the bottom of the tab).

Figure 8-9 shows how this would look if you were trying to simulate rotating the phone. You can use the simulator to set up your sensors, or modify the values directly by typing preferred values in the middle tab. After you create a scenario you like, save it, and load it later to play it back on any device.

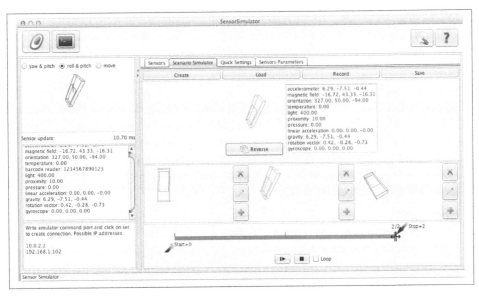

Figure 8-9. SensorSimulator recording scenarios

It is worth mentioning that you can record sensor interactions on a physical device. For complex scenarios, this is a simple way to record a series of UI actions that you can play back in the simulator later. Install and run an app on your device (*SensorRecordFrom Device.apk*, available in the *bin* directory) that allows you to record sensor activities. You can then play back the recorded scenario using the desktop application in the same manner as if it were created using the tool itself. This makes mapping a complex UI interaction pretty simple because you can simply record your interactions and reliably play them back over and over. For complex scenarios, this might be a more efficient way to record a series of events than creating them using the Java tool.

Developer Options Menu

The Android 4.0 release included a revamped Developer tool that introduced some very interesting features. The tool can be accessed by opening the Settings app on your phone, then selecting "Developer Options" (if you are on a version 4.1 or newer device, see Tip to enable this option). The app (see Figure 8-10) includes a variety of advanced options that can help you understand your UI and app performance on a deeper level. These options include:

Strict mode enabled

This flashes the screen when an app is doing a long operation on the UI thread. This is useful to help identify UI freezes and discover times when the UI is unresponsive. Mobile users perceive very small delays, so you need to minimize these whenever possible. This option makes pinpointing these long-running processes easier so they can be moved to the background and off the UI thread (where they won't cause your app to freeze).

Pointer location

Figure 8-11 shows how you can highlight a specific location on the screen. You can place your finger or mouse at any place on the screen to determine the exact location of that touch point. This is useful when you need to identify items that are hard to touch, determine optimal spacing between targets, or otherwise fine-tune touch interactivity. You can gather exact locations on your UI based on pixel measurements, which can be useful if you are trying to map your UI components to a very exact location on the screen (which can be critical in certain types of applications including games or other graphic-intensive apps).

Show screen updates

This feature flashes independent areas of the screen to highlight when different components of the screen are repainted. This is useful when trying to improve performance. You can identify large screen redraws and try to reduce them by selectively refreshing certain views instead of the entire screen.

Don't keep activities

Enabling this option forces the Android system to destroy activities as soon as the user leaves them (under the normal activity lifecycle, they probably would be moved to the background, but kept alive). This can be useful when trying to debug an issue that is isolated to a single activity. Normally, if you want to test an activity that is initialized to a new state, you would be required to quit your application completely (using the system menu). Using this option allows you to destroy your current activity, ensuring that when you start it again it is initialized from a clean state.

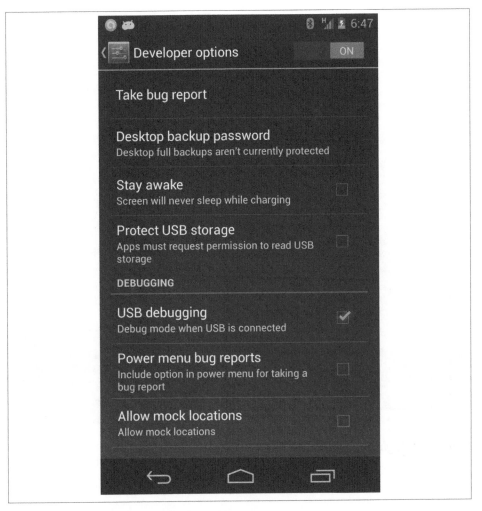

Figure 8-10. Viewing the Developer options

Force GPU rendering

This makes the system use hardware acceleration to render graphics. Enabling this option will offload graphics rendering to the GPU, which frees up the CPU for other operations. In many cases, this will improve your application performance, but in some cases this may cause issues. I suggest you enable this feature, and if your app performs as expected leave it enabled. If you are testing an app that makes extensive use of graphics, enabling this option should give you a better idea of how your app will perform on a modern device (that has a GPU).

Figure 8-11. Highlighting a specific location with the display pointer

## CHAPTER 9

Build Tools

When building apps, at some point it will be necessary to compile your code, and package it into a deployable artifact. This chapter outlines the tools used to do this.

The automated build tools can also package Android applications. There is support for a variety of tools, including Ant, Maven, and most recently Gradle (*http://www.gradle.org*). It is beyond the scope of this book to go into a lot of detail about using these tools, but let's go through some basic concepts to get you started.

Compiling Your Code

When writing computer applications, it is necessary to translate the computer language you are using (in our case Java) to a different computer language that the computer can understand (in this case, Dalvik Compatible executables, or DEX files). This process is called compiling. You will need to do this during the coding process in order to validate your code, and also when you are packaging your code for release.

If you are running the most current version of Java (or anything newer than version 1.6), it is necessary to set the compliance level of your project in order to get Android to build correctly. To do this:

1. Right-click on your Android project.
2. Select Properties → Java Compiler.
3. Check the "Enable project specific settings" option.
4. Choose either 1.5 or 1.6 from "Compiler compliance settings."

The code will then be compiled if you are using Eclipse and have the "Build Automatically" setting selected. To select it, make sure Project → Build Automatically is checked.

Packaging an APK for Release

In order to release your app to the Android market you need to create an Android application package file (APK). This is a specially formatted ZIP file that contains the various components of your app (including compiled code, static resources, library code, and the manifest file). To create an APK, source code is compiled into DEX files, which are packaged together with the other components, and then signed. The output of this process will be a file with the *.apk* extension. This file can then be deployed to your test devices, or uploaded to the Google Play Store for distribution.

Signing Your App

The Android system requires you to digitally sign all apps with a certificate before deploying them to the Google Play Store. Android uses the certificate to verify the identity of the developer, which is used to establish trust relationships between apps and the framework.

There are some important things to know about these certificates:

- You must sign your app to install it on an emulator or device.
- When you are developing your app, the build tools will sign your app with a debug key. This key cannot be used to sign an app for release to end users.
- Self-signed certificates are allowed. They do not need to be signed by a signing authority such as Verisign.
- It is important to ensure that your key is valid for the entire expected lifespan of your application. The Android docs specify that you should use 25 years for the validity term (it must expire after October 22, 2033 if you plan to deploy to the Play Store).

 It is extremely important to keep track of the key you are using to sign your app if you plan to deploy to the Play Store. You will need to use the same key for all updates to your app. If you are not able to sign your app with the same key, they will never allow you to update it.

You can take care of these tasks through either a wizard or the command line. I'll show the wizard first because it's easier.

An Export wizard in the tools can walk you through the process of creating a signed APK for deployment. It automates a variety of steps and is easy to use. Launch the wizard by right-clicking on your project and choosing Android Tools → Export Signed Application Package. You are presented with a series of screens that walk you through the process of creating a Java keystore, and building an APK for deployment.

1. *Project checks.* The wizard performs a variety of checks to ensure the project is valid and able to be exported. If the checks pass, the user is presented with the initial screen (see Figure 9-1).

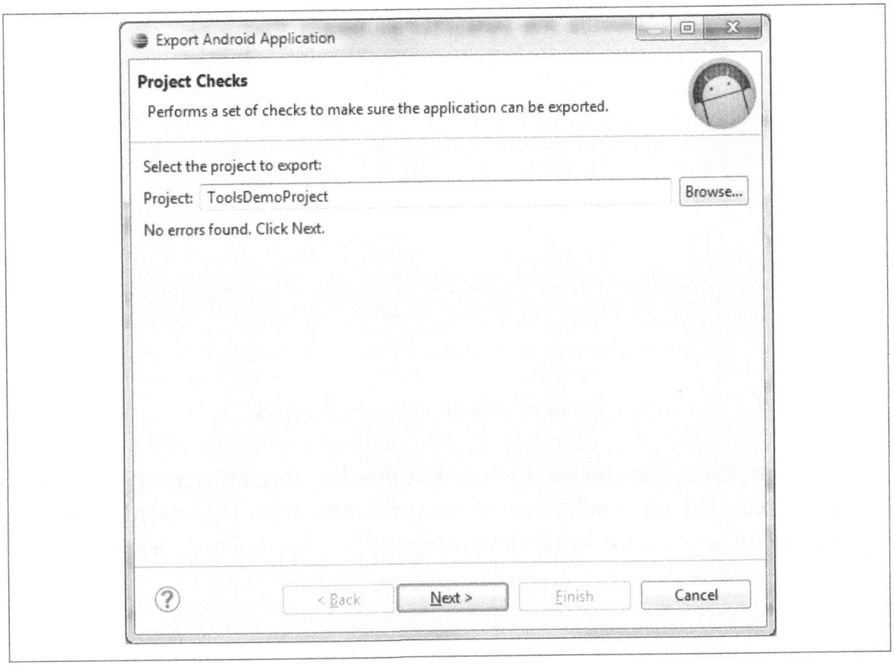

Figure 9-1. Launching the Build wizard

2. *Keystore selection.* This screen allows you to select a valid keystore to be used to sign the app. If a valid keystore doesn't already exist, you can choose the Create New Keystore selection to generate a new one (Figure 9-2).

Figure 9-2. Selecting a keystore and entering credentials

3. *Keystore creation.* If you want to create a new keystore for signing your app, enter all the required information into this form (Figure 9-3). The wizard then generates the key for you. This is easier than using the Java keytool to generate the key.

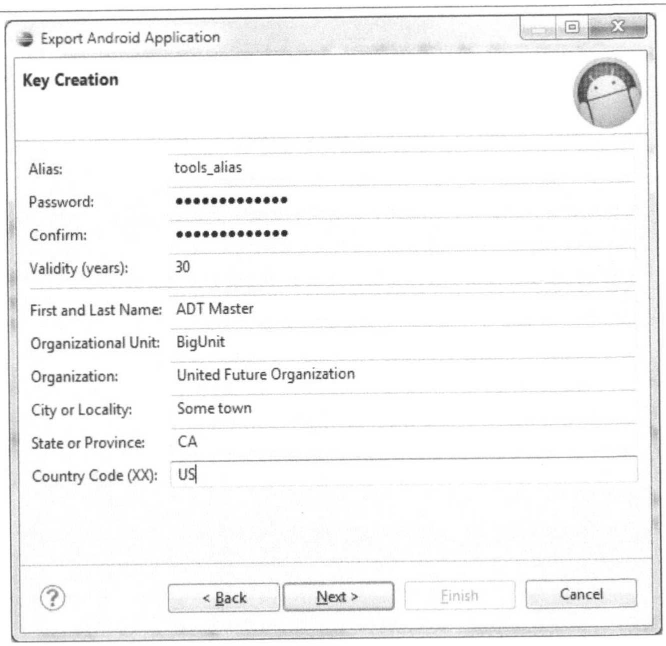

Figure 9-3. Confirming keystore information

4. *Keystore check.* The next step in the process is to validate the keystore to ensure it is valid for the amount of time necessary. If the keystore is valid, the APK is generated and placed in the location you specify (Figure 9-4).

At this point, you have successfully generated a signed APK that can be deployed to the Play Store or Android devices.

Instead of using the wizard, you can sign an APK using the standard Java tools, then use the command line to sign the app. To do this, first compile your project and generate an APK file (*yourApp.apk* in the example). Then enter the following command:

```
jarsigner -keystore your-key.keystore yourApp.apk alias_name
```

Building from the Command Line Using Ant

Ant is a standard Java build tool that Android uses to build projects under the covers. Although the ADT team is replacing Ant with Gradle (discussed later in this chapter), Ant is still the most full-featured build tool for Android. It includes a variety of scripts that can easily be modified to suit your individual needs. This build tool is very robust, and can be extended to do many useful things (such as running automated tests or static analysis tools). You can learn more about it at the Apache Ant home page (*http://ant.apache.org/*).

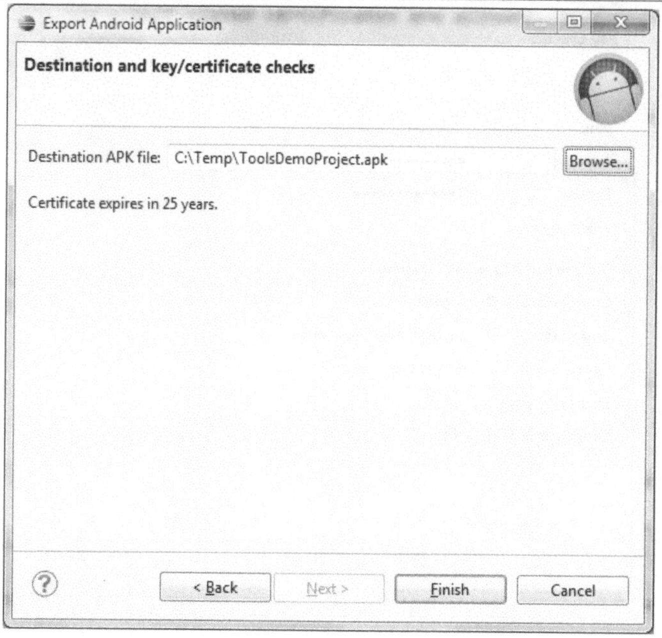

Figure 9-4. Defining destination location for APK

Ant comes preinstalled with ADT, and will automatically be available if you have correctly set your PATH (review "Setting your PATH variable" on page 5). There are two main types of builds you can do.

Debug mode
> Used for testing and debugging your app.

Release mode
> Used when creating a package for release.

Building an Android app (regardless of the type of build you are doing) involves the following steps:

1. Compiling the Java code into DEX bytecode.
2. Building the Android project into a deployable APK file.
3. Signing the APK, so it can be deployed to an emulator or device—remember, all apps must be signed before they can be deployed to a device.

If you are building from Eclipse, these steps are automatically performed by the tool. If you are using Ant to build from the command line, some of these steps need to be done manually.

Setting Up Your Project

In order to build, you need to create a *build.xml* file that provides Ant with the information it needs to build the project. This file is where we will set up information about signing our app, running Lint, or mapping project dependencies.

Creating the Ant build.xml file

Anyone who has experience with Ant knows that these build files aren't always the easiest to work with. Build files become large and disorganized quickly.

Fortunately, ADT provides a tool that creates *build.xml* automatically. To execute this command, open a command prompt at the base directory of your project, and execute the *Android update* command. Its syntax is:

```
android update project --name project_name --target target_api_id
--path path_to_project
```

Although you can omit some of the command-line options and leave as-is the command settings in the existing project files, it is often useful to override these settings in order to specify support for certain platforms, or to specify path values. For example:

```
android update project --name YourProject --target 17 --path /Users/yourUserId/
workspace/YourProject
```

If you don't want to specify custom values, and are working from the base directory of your project, you can simply enter:

```
android update project -path .
```

Building applications from multiple source libraries

It is very common to use open source libraries and other external sources of code when writing Android apps. In some cases, you can simply compile that library into a JAR file and include it directly in your project. In other cases, the library should be compiled as part of your build process. This is easy to accomplish using the Android tools if you follow some simple steps.

1. Define your project dependencies and target API. You should have a file in your project home directory named *project.properties*. This file contains the listing of each of the libraries you have as dependencies. A sample file follows.

```
# This file is automatically generated by Android Tools.
# Do not modify this file -- YOUR CHANGES WILL BE ERASED!
#
# This file must be checked in Version Control Systems.
#
# To customize properties used by the Ant build system edit
# "ant.properties", and override values to adapt the script to your
# project structure.
#
# To enable ProGuard to shrink and obfuscate your code, uncomment this
```

```
(available properties: sdk.dir, user.home):
# proguard.config=${sdk.dir}/tools/proguard/proguard-android.txt:
proguard-project.txt
# Project target.
target=android-17
android.library.reference.1=../shared/libs/android/ActionBarSherlock-4.2.0/
library
android.library.reference.2=../CustomLibrary/YourLibraryName
```

You will notice that the header mentions that this file is automatically generated. If you have used the Eclipse tools to create your project, this file should already have everything you need, but you may want to validate the dependencies or their order.

2. Run the *android update project* command, discussed in the previous section, in each folder you are including as a dependency.

3. Issue the *ant* command to start the build:

```
ant debug
```

This compiles each of the specified libraries, before compiling the application code or carrying out other build operations.

Building in Debug Mode

This method creates an APK for deployment, signed by the debug key. This app cannot be deployed to the Play Store, or other places. This mode can be used for quick debugging or testing when it is not necessary to create a real signing certificate.

The steps to building with this method are:

1. Open a command prompt, and navigate to the base directory of your project.

2. Issue the *ant* command to start the build:

```
ant debug
```

3. This creates an *.apk* file with the name of your project inside the *bin* directory of your project home. The file will be signed with a debug key that is automatically generated during the build process. This means that the key is different with each build, so it will restrict you from installing over old instances of your app (because the signing certificate will not always be the same).

Building an App to Release to the Play Store

The Release mode creates an APK that can be released to the Play Store and installed on other Android devices. This mode allows you to specify the keystore to use when signing your app. This is very similar to building in Debug mode, except that you use a real keystore during the signing process.

Signing an app with a custom keystore

In order to sign with a custom certificate, you need to specify the following information so the build system knows which parameters to use during the build.

1. Copy your keystore file to a location on your build machine and note the location. If you have not already created a custom certificate for signing, review "Signing Your App" on page 130 for instructions on how to create a valid certificate.

2. Create a new file in your project home directory named *build.properties.*

3. Insert the `key.store` and `key.alias` variables into this file to tell the build system about your custom keystore location and keystore alias. The contents of this file should look like:

   ```
   key.store=/path_to_location_of/my.keystore key.alias=my_key_alias
   ```

4. After creating this file and setting these values, issue the *ant release* command to start the process.

5. At the appropriate point in the build process, you will be prompted to enter your keystore and alias passwords. Enter the information to complete the build.

This creates an application file inside your *bin* directory. It will be signed properly and named *project_name-release.apk.* Because it is signed using a real certificate, you will be able to release this APK for public consumption.

Storing the password information

It is likely that you will want to store your password information so that your build can run automatically without requiring human intervention. In order to do this, you need to store your keystore and keystore alias password information.

You might be tempted to include this information in the *build.properties* file we already created. While this works technically, it's a bad idea. It is generally not suggested that you check secure information into source control. In fact, many corporate security policies prohibit doing so. You generally want to control access to these sensitive files by storing them locally on the build system, and ensuring read permissions are secured on the file.

1. Create a new file named *secure.properties.* This will be used to store the password information, and thus should be stored someplace secure where the information is not available publicly. The name and location of this file are completely up to you. Keep track of this information because we will use it in the following steps.

2. Insert two variables into this file to tell the build system about your keystore and alias passwords. You will use the `key.store` and `key.alias` variables for this. The contents of this file should look like:

```
key.store.password=keystore_password
key.alias.password=keystore_alias_password
```

3. Now you need to create yet another file to tie this all together, and inform the build system where it can get the password information. The new file is named *custom_rules.xml* and will be discovered automatically during the build. It should look like:

```
<?xml version="1.0" encoding="UTF-8"?>
<project name="custom_rules" default="help"/>
<property file="/path_to_secure_location/secure.properties"/>
</project>
```

4. At this point, you can issue the

```
ant release
```

command again. This time however, instead of stopping to wait for the password information to be entered, the build finishes without interruption.

5. This application file inside the *bin* subdirectory of our project home directory will be signed with your custom key, and named *project_name-release.apk*. It is signed, and thus can be released to the public.

Additional Ant Commands

There are a variety of things you can do with Ant. The documentation (*http://bit.ly/ 13615Lt*) does a great job of explaining them. I highlight some of the more useful options here, but I suggest checking the documentation to learn more about the advanced options available. Many of these tags can be combined to perform multiple operations in a single build.

ant emma debug
   Builds a test project with instrumentation turned on. This is designed to generate code coverage information during a run.

ant installd
   Installs an already compiled debug package to a running device or emulator.

ant test
   Runs the tests in your project. This works only if the test *.apk* files are already installed.

ant emma debug install test
   This is an example of running multiple operations in a single operation. The command shown will build a test project, install *.apk* files, and run the tests with code coverage enabled.

Advanced Packaging Steps

At some point, it will be necessary to do some additional things to prepare your artifact to be released to the public. These things include obfuscating your code, minimizing the size of the artifact, and signing the app with a correct certificate. The steps to accomplish these tasks are outlined in the following sections.

ProGuard

ProGuard is a free Java tool that shrinks, optimizes, and obfuscates your code in preparation for deployment. It does this by removing unused code, replacing class or method names with semantically distinct ones, and optimizing bytecode. This makes your application smaller, more efficient, and harder to reverse engineer. The process protects against reuse of your code and protects your confidential data.

Enabling Proguard

It is very easy to run this tool, and mostly automatic, especially if you package your APK using the Export Signed Application Package wizard shown in "Signing Your App" on page 130. If your build target is higher than 2.3, this tool is automatically run as part of the packaging process. A default configuration file is placed in the root directory of your project, and looks similar to the following example. It is placed at the root level of your project home and named *proguard-project.txt*.

```
# To enable ProGuard in your project, edit project.properties
# to define the proguard.config property as described in that file.
# # Add project specific ProGuard rules here.
# By default, the flags in this file are appended to flags specified
# in ${sdk.dir}/tools/proguard/proguard-android.txt
# You can edit the include path and order by changing the ProGuard
# include property in project.properties.
#
# For more details, see
# http://developer.android.com/guide/developing/tools/proguard.html
# Add any project specific keep options here:
# If your project uses WebView with JS, uncomment the following
# and specify the fully qualified class name to the JavaScript interface
# class:
# -keepclassmembers class fqcn.of.javascript.interface.for.webview {
# public *;
# }
```

You can enter specific configurations and rules for your project in this file. To enable ProGuard to run automatically as part of a build, modify the file to remove the # comment symbol before the following statement:

```
proguard.config=${sdk.dir}/tools/proguard/proguard-android.txt:
proguard-project.txt
```

Your file should then look like:

```
# This file is automatically generated by Android Tools.
# Do not modify this file -- YOUR CHANGES WILL BE ERASED!
#
# This file must be checked in Version Control Systems.
#
# To customize properties used by the Ant build system edit
# "ant.properties", and override values to adapt the script to your
# project structure.
#
# To enable ProGuard to shrink and obfuscate your code, uncomment this
(available properties: sdk.dir, user.home):
proguard.config=${sdk.dir}\tools\proguard\proguard-android.txt:
proguard-project.txt
# Project target.
target=android-10
```

Next time you do a release build, Proguard will automatically be run, and your code will be obfuscated. This means all your error reports (including reports you receive through the Play Store) will be modified to a format that is hard to read.

Configuring ProGuard

Default ProGuard rules are defined in a file that is external to your project (*${an droid.home}/tools/proguard/proguard-android.txt*). These standard rules are defined by the Android tools team, and should work for most cases. The standard rules include basic configurations designed to accommodate most users. You may need to override these defaults. You should not do this by modifying this file directly, as it will get updated with the rest of the tools and your changes will not persist. Instead, if you need to define custom rules, define them in the *proguard-project.txt* file mentioned in the previous section, as they will be persisted and won't be overwritten.

There are many different possible rule combinations. The following listing includes a good starting point. It provides a "safe" configuration that should not break your code execution, but will still allow you to get the other benefits of ProGuard (including packaging optimization and code obfuscation).

```
#Does a 5 step optimization
-optimizationpasses 5

#Support for systems - such as Windows that don't care about capitalization
-dontusemixedcaseclassnames

#Don't ignore non-public library classes. Is default on newer ADT builds
-dontskipnonpubliclibraryclasses

# The Dex tool does its own optimizations, so we shouldn't do them with Proguard
-dontoptimize
-dontpreverify
```

```
-dontwarn android.support.**

#Verbose option - will print stacktrace if build fails
-verbose

#To repackage classes on a single package
#-repackageclasses ''

#Keep annotations (if this is uncommented)
#-keepattributes *Annotation*

#Keep classes with references from the AndroidManifest
-keep public class * extends android.app.Activity
-keep public class * extends android.app.Application
-keep public class * extends android.app.Service
-keep public class * extends android.content.BroadcastReceiver
-keep public class * extends android.content.ContentProvider
-keep public class * extends android.app.backup.BackupAgentHelper
-keep public class * extends android.preference.Preference
-keep public class com.google.vending.licensing.ILicensingService
-keep public class com.android.vending.licensing.ILicensingService

#Keep classes from the Support library
-keep public class * extends android.support.v4.app.Fragment
-keep public class * extends android.app.Fragment

#To maintain custom components names that are used on layouts XML.
#Uncomment if having any problem with the approach below
#-keep public class custom.components.package.and.name.**

# In Views, keep getters and setters so that animations still work.
-keepclassmembers public class * extends android.view.View {
  void set*(***);
  *** get*();
}

#To not obfuscate names of methods invoked in a layout's onClick method.
# Uncomment and add specific method names if using onClick on layouts
#-keepclassmembers class * {
# public void onClickButton(android.view.View);
#}

#Remove debug, verbose, and warning error messages from Logcat
-assumenosideeffects class android.util.Log {
    public static *** d(...);
    public static *** v(...);
    public static *** w(...);
}

#Keep native Java methods
-keepclasseswithmembernames class * {
    native <methods>;
```

```
}

#Keep custom components names layouts
-keep public class * extends android.view.View {
    public <init>(android.content.Context);
}
-keep public class * extends android.view.View {
    public <init>(android.content.Context, android.util.AttributeSet);
}
-keep public class * extends android.view.View {
    public <init>(android.content.Context, android.util.AttributeSet, int);
}

#Keep enums
-keepclassmembers enum * {
    public static **[] values();
    public static ** valueOf(java.lang.String);
}

#Keep parcelable classes (when used to serialize objects sent through Intents)
-keep class * implements android.os.Parcelable {
  public static final android.os.Parcelable$Creator *;
}

#Keep the R
-keepclassmembers class **.R$* {
    public static <fields>;
}

#Uncomment if using Serializable
#-keepclassmembers class * implements java.io.Serializable {
#    private static final java.io.ObjectStreamField[] serialPersistentFields;
#    private void writeObject(java.io.ObjectOutputStream);
#    private void readObject(java.io.ObjectInputStream);
#    java.lang.Object writeReplace();
#    java.lang.Object readResolve();
#}
```

Viewing obfuscated code

The ProGuard technique of renaming variables makes it very difficult to read and debug
your code. This is great when you are trying to keep other people from viewing your
code, but presents challenges if you need to read the code yourself (from a stacktrace
or logs). ProGuard provides a tool named *retrace* that allows you to switch the non-
sensical names back the real ones.

After ProGuard runs, you will notice some new files in the *proguard* subdirectory of
your project home directory. These files manage the obfuscation process and the con-
sequent restoration of meaningful names. The files contain:

dump.txt
> Includes information relating to the internal structure of the class files in your project.

mapping.txt
> Maps the original names to the obfuscated names. This file will be used to decode obfuscated messages back into readable format (as described in the following section).

seeds.txt
> Contains a list of all the classes and members that were not obfuscated.

usage.txt
> Contains a list of all classes that were stripped from the APK.

In particular, you can use the *mapping.txt* file to de-obfuscate a stacktrace and read the output. To decode a stacktrace, run the *retrace* script with two arguments: the name of the mapping file, and the name of the text file containing the stacktrace. On Windows, for example, enter:

```
{$android.sdk}/tools/proguard/retrace.bat mapping.txt obfuscated_stacktrace.txt
```

On a Mac or Linux, the command is slightly different:

```
{$android.sdk}/tools/proguard/retrace.sh mapping.txt obfuscated_stacktrace.txt
```

As an example, the following error comes from the logcat file of an APK that has been built using Proguard.

```
E/AndroidRuntime( 1655): FATAL EXCEPTION: main
E/AndroidRuntime( 1655): java.lang.NullPointerException
E/AndroidRuntime( 1655):    at com.tools.demo.f.onClick(Unknown Source)
E/AndroidRuntime( 1655):    at android.view.View.performClick(View.java:4084)
E/AndroidRuntime( 1655):        at android.view.View$PerformClick.run(View.java:
16966)
...
```

Notice on the third line that the location in the code that encountered the null pointer is not shown. It has been obfuscated to look like com.tools.demo.f.onClick(Unknown Source). We are not able to see the name of the file or the line number where the error is being reported.

Use the *mapping.txt* file to restore the correct information through a command like:

```
{$android.sdk}/tools/proguard/bin/retrace.sh
{$project.root}/proguard/mapping.txt proguarded_log.txt
```

After running this command, you will be able to read the output and determine exactly where your error is. The output from this command looks like:

```
E/AndroidRuntime( 1584): FATAL EXCEPTION: main
E/AndroidRuntime( 1584): java.lang.NullPointerException
```

```
E/AndroidRuntime( 1584):      at com.tools.demo.ToolsDemoActivity
$1.onClick(ToolsDemoActivity.java:36)
E/AndroidRuntime( 1584):      at android.view.View.performClick(View.java:4084)
E/AndroidRuntime( 1584):        at android.view.View$PerformClick.run(View.java:
16966)
...
```

Zipalign

Zipalign is a tool that optimizes APK archives by aligning all uncompressed data within the archive relative to the start of a file. This allows the app to consume less RAM when running. The tool should be run on all APKs before releasing them to the end user. If you are using the Export wizard to package your code, Zipalign will be run automatically.

It is also possible to run it on the command line. It should only be run after the *.apk* file has been signed with your private key. Otherwise, the signing will mess up the alignment.

```
zipalign inFile.apk alignedFile.apk
```

Gradle-Based Build Tools

Official support has recently been added in ADT for Gradle, a build tool that many developers are using to replace such classic utilities as Ant (the original build tool used in ADT) and Maven (which was never officially supported by the Android team). The ADT team chose Gradle as the foundation of a new tool set because it embodied many principles to meet their goals of supporting the reuse of code and resources, creating multiple specialized variants of applications, and ensuring that the build system is extensible. The Gradle project works hard to create high-quality documentation (*http://www.gradle.org/documentation*). Documentation about its integration with ADT can be found at the ADT project site (*http://bit.ly/1983q7L*).

The Ant build system will be deprecated in Android, and the Tools team has stated that Gradle is their build tool of choice moving forward. It is strongly suggested that developers migrate their builds to this tool.

Installing Gradle

In order to use this tool, make you have the proper version downloaded and installed.

You need version 1.6, which you can get from here: Gradle download site (*http://www.gradle.org/downloads*). Put Gradle in your PATH (see "Setting your PATH variable" on page 5) and you will be ready to go.

Key Concepts and Terms

There are a few definitions you need to know to understand building with Gradle.

Product flavor

This specifies a customized version of the application build by the project. The concept helps manage small variations, such as changing SDK support, version number, or release signing information.

Build type

This determines how an application is packaged. It's where you do things such as specify debug flags, enable ProGuard, or specify native compilation settings. The system provides two default build types, debug and release, but you can create your own as well.

Build variant

This is combination of a product flavor and a build type. In fact, this is the only way to define the output of a build.

Flavor group

This allows you to add even more dimensions to your build. You would use this if you wanted to package differently for different target environments, such as different GL texture formats based on the chipset you are targeting.

Sourceset

This term is used to define the different source folders you will create for each build type or product flavor.

Task

This represents an atomic element of work performed during a build. This might be packaging an APK, signing a JAR, or publishing an archive to a repository.

Creating Multiple Build Variations

The concept of Gradle is that you will put files (Java class files, image resources, XML, etc.) in a particular folder designed to represent a particular "Product Flavor." The different source folders (known as *sourcesets*) represent different build variations.

Gradle follows the concept of *convention over configuration*, which means that if you don't explicitly override something, the system defaults to a standard configuration. This means it is only necessary to include the particular item that is specific to your build and let the system handle the defaults.

Example

I will show a few examples that demonstrate how easy it is to customize build types in Gradle by putting unique files in appropriate directories.

Let's say you want to change the flavor1 build to contain custom icons and translations for the app you plan to distribute only to Mexico. You need to replace the *launch er_icon.png*, and the *strings.xml* file (containing my translations), and use the rest of the defaults from the "main" build. This would look like this:

```
src/
    main/  - standard Android Project files
        AndroidManifest.xml
        aidl/ - ex. my_interface.aidl
        assets/ - ex. database_preload.db
        java/ - ex. com.project.SomeActivity
        jni/ - ex. jni_file.c
        res/ - ic_launcher.png, main_layout.xml, strings.xml
    flavor1/ - files specific to 'flavor1' build
        res/ic_launcher.png - (custom icon for Mexico)
        res/strings.xml - Spanish translations
    ...
```

As another example, you could provide a unique function that would be available only for a certain user base (such as to enable an advanced feature available only in a "Pro" build.). To do this, place your unique activity and its appropriate manifest entry in the correct sourcesets, which look like this:

```
src/
    main/  - standard Android Project files
        AndroidManifest.xml
        aidl/
        assets/
        java/
        jni/
        res/
    proVersion/ - files specific to 'Pro' build
        AndroidManifest.xml - contain entry for Activity
        source/com/myapp/pro/ProActivity.java - class for 'Pro' function
        res/pro_activity.xml - the layout file for ProActivity.java
    ...
```

One final example is if you wanted to preload different database data (perhaps to support different default datasets for different target audiences). To handle this, you would place specific database resources in each folder, which looks like:

```
src/
    main/  - standard Android Project files
        AndroidManifest.xml
        aidl/
        assets/db_preload.db - default database file
        java/
```

```
    jni/
    res/
dev/ - files specific to 'Developer' build
    assets/db_preload.db - database for 'Developer' release
qa/ - files specific to 'Developer' build
    assets/db_preload.db - database for 'Quality Assurance' release
prod/ - files specific to 'Developer' build
    assets/db_preload.db - contains for 'Production' release
  ...
```

Build File

To use the build tool, you need to configure it in a file called *build.gradle* in the root folder of the project. The build file is written using the Groovy syntax.

As I mentioned, Gradle is designed to use convention over configuration. This is why the basic *gradle.build* file is actually very simple and provides sensible default options. The most basic file defines:

- Repositories used to hold build artifacts and dependencies
- Dependencies within your project
- Basic information (API level, etc.) specific to your Android build
- Optional parameters specific to your Android build

The most basic build file looks like:

```
buildscript {
    repositories {
      mavenCentral()
    }

    dependencies {
      classpath 'com.android.tools.build:gradle:0.3'
      }
}

apply plugin: 'android'   // Note: do not also use the Java Plug-in
                    // which will break the build


android {
   compileSdkVersion 18

//Optional: Set parameters for a particular buildType
buildTypes {
      release {
        runProguard true
          proguardFile getDefaultProguardFile('proguard-android.txt')
        }
      }
}
```

```
        //Optional: Define specific parameters for a flavor
        productFlavors {
            flavor1 {
                proguardFile 'flavor1_rules.txt'
            }

        }
    }
```

Build Tasks

You can execute Gradle tasks from the command line, similar to how you would run an Ant task. Enter the *gradle* command followed by the task you wish to execute, such as:

```
gradle build
```

You can define your own task, or use one of the common default ones:

assemble
Create the output of a project.

check
Run the tests to ensure the validity of the build.

build
Performs both the *check* and *assemble* tasks.

clean
Removes files created by a build.

To see a list of all possible tasks and their dependencies, run:

```
gradle tasks --all
```

Just as with Ant, you can issue multiple tasks in a single command and they will be executed in order:

```
gradle clean build
```

Generating a Gradle Build from Eclipse

It is possible to generate a Gradle build from your existing Eclipse project. This will not change your existing project, but will add the appropriate Gradle build files. The steps to do this are:

If you use the new Android Studio IDE, you can import a project without generating the Gradle build file. It will successfully build and run within Android Studio, but you will not be able to use build variants or other advanced features in the future. It is strongly suggested that you generate a Gradle build file (or write your own) if you plan to use Android Studio.

1. Update your ADT Plug-in to version 22.0 or higher.
2. Select File → Export.
3. In the next dialog, select Android → Generate Gradle build files.
4. Select the projects you want to export, and click Finish.

Using the Maven Tools

As with most things Android, the developer is not stuck using the supported tools. There is good support for using other build tools, including Maven.

To learn more about Maven integration, I suggest checking out the great free resources at Sonatype, and in particular, the Android-specific chapter: Android Application Development with Maven (*http://bit.ly/14CcuDy*).

## CHAPTER 10

Monitoring System Resources

It is important to monitor resource usage on mobile devices because memory is limited. In this chapter, I show how to use the profiling tools to help you understand your application's memory usage.

Memory Usage in Android

Android programmers don't explicitly allocate free memory, as they do in other languages like C++. It is still possible to create a "memory leak." This is when code keeps a reference to an object that is no longer used, which can prevent a large set of objects from being garbage-collected. This can be a result of improper scoping of variables, not closing handles to system resources after using them, or long-running processes that may not expire.

The Dalvik runtime is garbage-collected, which means that unused memory is automatically recovered by the system at certain intervals. This might lead you to think that you can ignore memory usage entirely because the system will eventually take care of it. This is not true, as memory issues can manifest in many different ways. Some may be obvious, such as getting an *OutOfMemory* exception due to not recycling your bitmaps correctly.

There are other issues related to memory usage that are far more difficult to debug and that can impact performance more significantly. These are issues related to inefficient garbage collection as a result of frequent or large collections that manifest themselves in ways that aren't as obvious. Instead of your app force closing with an *OutOfMemory* exception, your app continues to run, but with degraded performance, pauses, continues, or stutters. Garbage collection is an expensive operation for the system to run. It is best to manage memory efficiently in your code so the process runs less frequently.

Memory issues are very common in Android, so you will likely encounter a variety of issues throughout your development.

Dalvik Debug Monitor Server (DDMS)

The main tool you will use to analyze memory is called the Dalvik Debug Monitor Server (DDMS). This tool is used to analyze memory consumption over a given time period. You will use this tool to understand how the footprint of your app grows over time (in particular relating to memory and thread usage). It offers fine-grained information about your app in relation to performance by providing statistics about memory and thread usage. The tool itself will likely look familiar to you by this point, as we already covered some of its usage earlier in the book (see "The Devices Tool" on page 48). I am going highlight some of the other tools you might not have used that are particularly useful for diagnosing resource issues and eliminating performance problems.

Launching the DDMS Perspective

It is useful to have a single view of all the DDMS tools in one place. Fortunately, ADT has already created this for us. The DDMS perspective organizes the most important device tools into a single view, which is useful when analyzing performance and device functionality. To launch this perspective, select: Window → Open Perspective... → Other... → DDMS → OK.

 There is also a version of the tool that can be run from the command line without Eclipse. This is particularly useful for team members that might not have the full development suite installed, but could still benefit from using these tools. The tool is named Android Debug Monitor and can be started with the following command:

```
{$android.sdk}\tools $   monitor
```

After launching the DDMS or the Device Monitor (see Figure 10-1), you will see a screen with a few important tools:

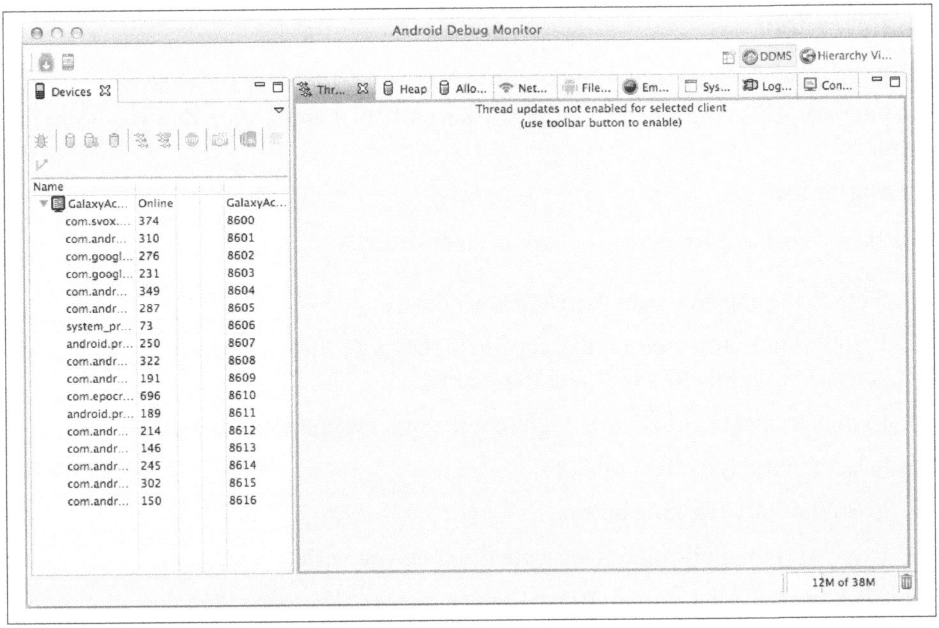

Figure 10-1. Android Debug Monitor

Analyzer Tool

Used primarily to track memory over a specific time period. You will be able to track allocation order, size, where the allocation occurred, and a stacktrace showing the specific classes associated with the memory allocation.

Threads

Offers information about thread usage within your process. You can get information about current status, utime, name, and a stacktrace listing all the classes being accessed by that thread.

Heap

Used to track general information about your heap usage, including its size, how much space is used, and the number of objects allocated.

Traceview

Tool for tracing method calls, including timing and resource allocation.

Each of these tools serves a unique purpose and has its own usage nuances. I will describe details about each one.

Analyzer Tool

This tool allows you to track individual memory allocations in an Android app. This can be extremely useful when analyzing how a particular application flow is consuming memory.

Running the tool

The steps to run the Analyzer Tool are straightforward:

1. Launch the app you want to profile on a device.
2. If you want to test a particular code path, navigate through your UI until you are at the point just before the code is executed.
3. In the Devices tab of DDMS, highlight the process you want to track.
4. Select the Analyzer Tool tab (🔋).
5. Press the Start Tracking button.
6. Exercise your application to execute the code you wish to analyze.
7. Click the Get Allocation button to gather metrics. This generates allocation information based on that time. You can press this button as many times as you want, to refresh the allocation information.
8. Click the Stop Tracking button when you are done to finish the process.

Viewing the results of Analyzer Tool

After running the tool, you will see details about the memory allocations that occurred (see Figure 10-2). This shows the objects that were allocated and a variety of information about them. The information includes the allocation order, the amount of memory allocated, and the type of object created. If you select one of the elements in the list, you can see the stacktrace containing the names of the classes that were allocated.

If you would like to find a specific class in the list, you can type the name into the Filter box. The search will happen as you are typing.

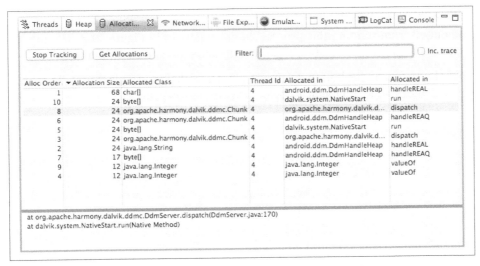

Figure 10-2. Viewing output from the Analyzer Tool

To see even more detail about a particular object, highlight it to display a stacktrace in the second table. This view has more details about the object, including the file, object, and method where it was created and the stacktrace that led to the allocation.

Threads

When you start an application, the Android system launches a new Linux process with a single thread of execution. In general, all components of an app run within the same process and thread, which is commonly called the *UI Thread*. Because everything runs off this single process, it is important to identify particular processes that are blocking execution (and thus locking up the rest of the app). Fortunately, the *Threads tool* makes it easy to track a variety of statistics about thread usage.

Running the Threads tool

To run the Threads tool:

1. Launch the application you want to profile on a device.

2. In the Devices tab, highlight the process you would like to track.

3. Click the Update Threads icon (🐾) to enable profiling (you will click this again after you are done to stop tracking).

4. Select the Threads tab (🐾) on the right.

5. Click the Refresh (⬛) button once to ensure that you are viewing current threads.

Viewing thread information

The output from running this process should appear as in Figure 10-3. The top tab includes a variety of information regarding thread status and execution time.

The information on the bottom tab is a *stacktrace* related to a single thread. To see this detailed information, highlight a single thread in the top pane.

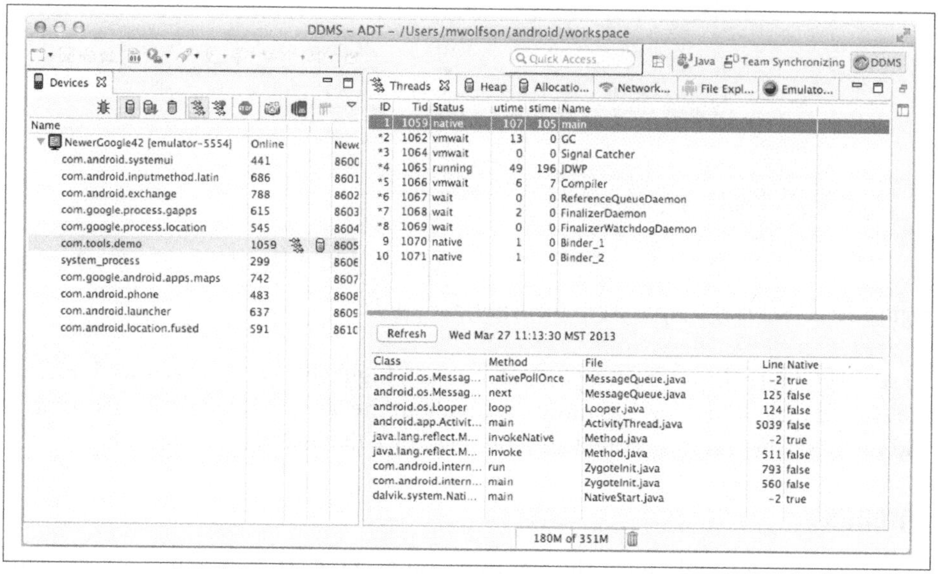

Figure 10-3. Viewing information about Heap execution

Heap

The Heap tool makes it easy to view how much heap memory a process is using. This is useful to track memory usage at certain execution points.

Running the Heap tool

To run the Heap tool:

1. Launch the application you would like to profile on a device.

2. In the Devices tab, navigate to your application and highlight the process you plan to track.

3. Click the Update Heap icon (🐾) to enable profiling (you will click this again after you are done to stop tracking).

4. Click the Cause GC button (🗑) to collect the current heap information.

5. Select the Heap tab (🗑) on the right.

Viewing heap information

The output from running this process should look like Figure 10-4.

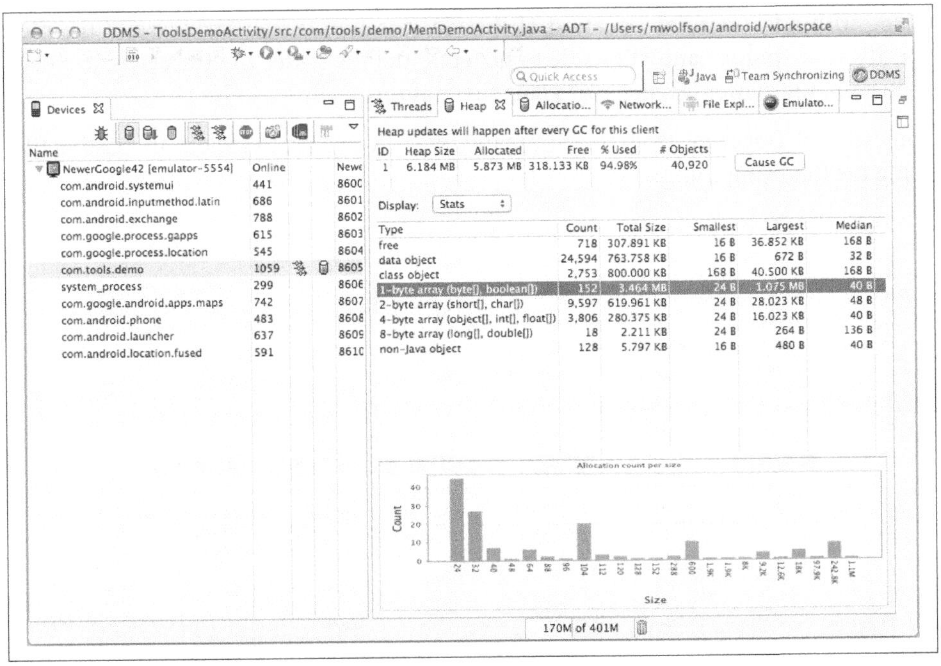

Figure 10-4. Heap view

The heap information is displayed in three sections:

- The top section contains overview information about the heap, including size and how much memory is allocated.
- The center section contains more detail about the objects that are in the heap, including details about how much memory they are consuming.
- The bottom panel, "Allocation count per size," is a graphical representation that shows when specific objects were created in relation to the overall size of the heap.

Traceview

Traceview is a tool that gives very fine details about the execution path of an application, including when a method or thread was started, what methods or threads were accessed while it was running, and when it stopped. This can be useful if you are working on optimizing particular code paths, as it allows you to track very fine details about your performance (and understand if your optimizations are effective). The tool includes support for saving the files it creates, which makes it possible to track optimizations over time because it is easy to keep a historical record.

To generate a traceview, press the button (⬛) in the Devices tab. You will be shown a dialog with a few options (location of the file, duration to run, max size of the file). Specify your options and click OK to generate the file. After the traceview has been generated, the viewer (Figure 10-5) launches automatically.

You can start Traceview from the command line (if you wish to look at an existing file) using the following command:

```
traceview filename.trace
```

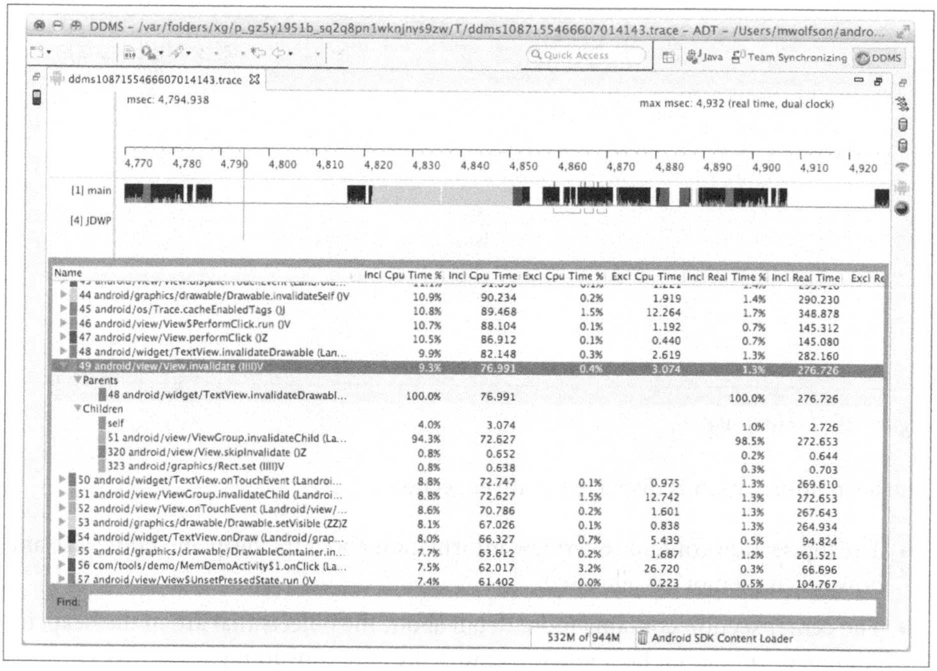

Figure 10-5. Example output from Traceview

Traceview output—timeline panel (top section)

The timeline panel (see Figure 10-5) allows you to see detailed information about the execution path and order of methods within your app. It shows the threads and resources the app consumes across the time period you were tracking. This includes the classes and methods that are being used, how often, and how much time is spent in each call. You can get finely grained detail about parent/child relationships and CPU utilization metrics. There are two sections of the view, showing different types of information.

The timeline is color coded to coordinate with specific process names in the lower pane. Each method is displayed in its own color-coded column. You can look at this chart and quickly determine which methods are taking the most time to execute by looking for areas in the graph with the most color (which represents more time spent in that method). You might notice some small lines beneath these columns. These are designed to show the extent (entry to exit) of the calls to the method being tracked.

Profile panel

This panel is designed to show more detailed information about the time spent in a method, so that you can get fine details about the timing of your method execution. You can track entry and exit times and the time actually spent in the method. It is even possible to track executions between methods by clicking on the triangle (▼) next to the method to expand and see its children.

This table includes a few different columns including information about CPU time, and actual time spent in a method. You can gather exact times (in milliseconds) or percentages (%, which indicates the ratio of time spent in relation to total execution time.) There are a few different columns representing different data. The tool shows the data in two distinct ways:

Exclusive time (Excl)
    Time spent within the method

Inclusive time (Incl)
    Time spent in the method *and* time spent in any functions called by that method

The Traceview tool is useful for determining nuanced details about the execution order of your app, which is useful when debugging applications with complex execution paths. It is also a great tool for tracking your application performance over time, since you can easily archive the output files to compare historical data.

Memory Analyzer Tool (MAT)

Another great way to analyze memory is to generate snapshots of the application's heap at certain points in time. The Android tooling will generate these files into a common format named *HPROF*. The file contains binary data that can be used to find performance problems that result from inefficient memory usage in your application. There are tools available (such as *MAT*) that allow you to browse the allocated objects when you supply a valid HPROF file. Having a collection of these files makes it easy to analyze them, track trends, and identify issues.

Generating an HPROF File

There are two primary ways to generate a new HPROF file.

1. Include the code `android.os.Debug.dumpHprofData()` in your application to trigger a dump at a specific execution point.

2. Use the "Dump HPROF file" button (📥), which generates a dump file when you press it.

HPROF File

Both of these methods generate a file that is slightly different than what the Android tooling requires. It is necessary to convert the file before it can be analyzed.

To convert it, use the provided conversion tool from the command line. For instance:

```
hprof-conv dump.hprof dump-converted.hprof
```

After completing the conversion, you will be able to analyze the dump file in any of the applications designed to handle this kind of file—like jhat (*http://bit.ly/12TiQXD*), or MAT, the Eclipse Memory Analyzer Tool (*http://www.eclipse.org/mat/*).

Installing MAT into Eclipse

MAT is not available by default and needs to be installed separately. The MAT update site (*http://bit.ly/18pq4rZ*) includes directions on how to install it into Eclipse.

> You might see a "Duplicate Location Exists" warning when you enter the update site URL. In this case, you will find the MAT update site as a subcategory to your main update site. To install MAT, in the *Work With:* box, select your main update site (for instance "Eclipse Indigo Update Site"). Then find "Memory Analyzer" in the list. Place a checkmark next to it here, and proceed to install as normal.

Launching MAT from Within Eclipse

If you are using Eclipse, there is a DDMS preference that automatically converts the HPROF file and starts the MAT tool (if it is installed). This happens automatically when you press the "Dump HPROF file" button (📥). If you want to set this as the default behavior, go to Window → Preferences → Android → DDMS.

If you would like to view historical heap data, you can maintain copies of the HPROF files (which could be triggered during automated testing or manually).

Using MAT to Analyze HRPOF Files

Using the MAT tool can be somewhat complicated. It is very feature rich and provides many ways to identify memory problems. I will discuss the three most commonly used options. If you would like to learn about other options, the official site (*http://www.eclipse.org/mat/*) is a great resource.

When you launch the MAT wizard, the first screen to appear looks like Figure 10-6. It provides you three options for viewing your data:

Leak Suspects Report
>   Analyzes your file to detect leaks automatically. It also reports which objects are kept alive, and what is stopping them from being garbage-collected.

Component Report
>   Allows you to analyze certain objects, and to find duplicate strings, unused collections, weak references, and other memory issues.

Reopen previously run reports
>   Use the tools to review previously run reports.

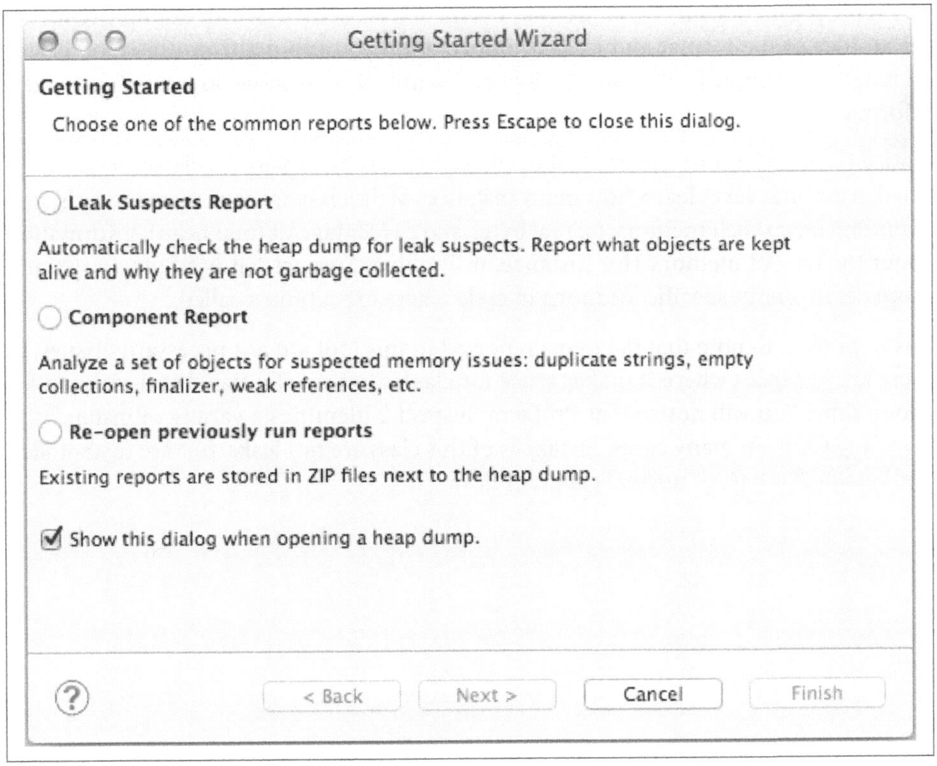

Figure 10-6. Launching the MAT wizard

If you would like to learn more details about using MAT, the documentation for the tool does a great job. It details different memory scenarios and describes ways to use MAT to find them. It is available at Eclipsepedia (*http://bit.ly/15SeyVv*).

There is also a great Android-specific write-up (*http://bit.ly/15RuIwc*) on the developers blog. It is worthwhile reading.

The MAT Overview Screen

The first screen (see Figure 10-7) that appears provides an overview of the memory footprint of your app, and links to other tools (like Histogram or Top Consumers) that allows you to learn more about your memory usage. You can get some general information about your heap from this screen such as total size, and how many objects and classes are allocated. This is a great way to get a general overview of your heap, which you can then use to learn more about specific areas.

Viewing a Report

The reports generated by MAT are very detailed. It is useful to see an example report to get an idea of the format and kind of information you can get from this tool. I have included an example Leak Suspects Report (Figure 10-8) to show how easy it is to view information.

Notice the tool lists information about each of the Problem Suspect classes it has identified. It outlines very clearly how many instances of the class are causing memory issues, including how much memory (actual bytes and percentage of total heap), information about the type of memory (for instance, in Problem Suspect 1 it is a byte array), and more details about specific locations in code where execution is called.

It is important to note that the items reported in this tool are not necessarily issues, as there are instances where it makes sense for classes to be instantiated and retained for a long time. You will notice that Problem Suspect 2 identifies a variety of instances of *java.lang.Class*. In many cases, instances of this class are not leaks, but are instantiated and retained as part of normal program flow.

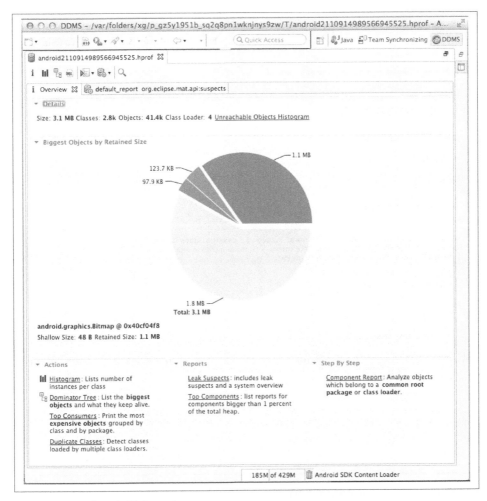

Figure 10-7. The MAT Overview screen

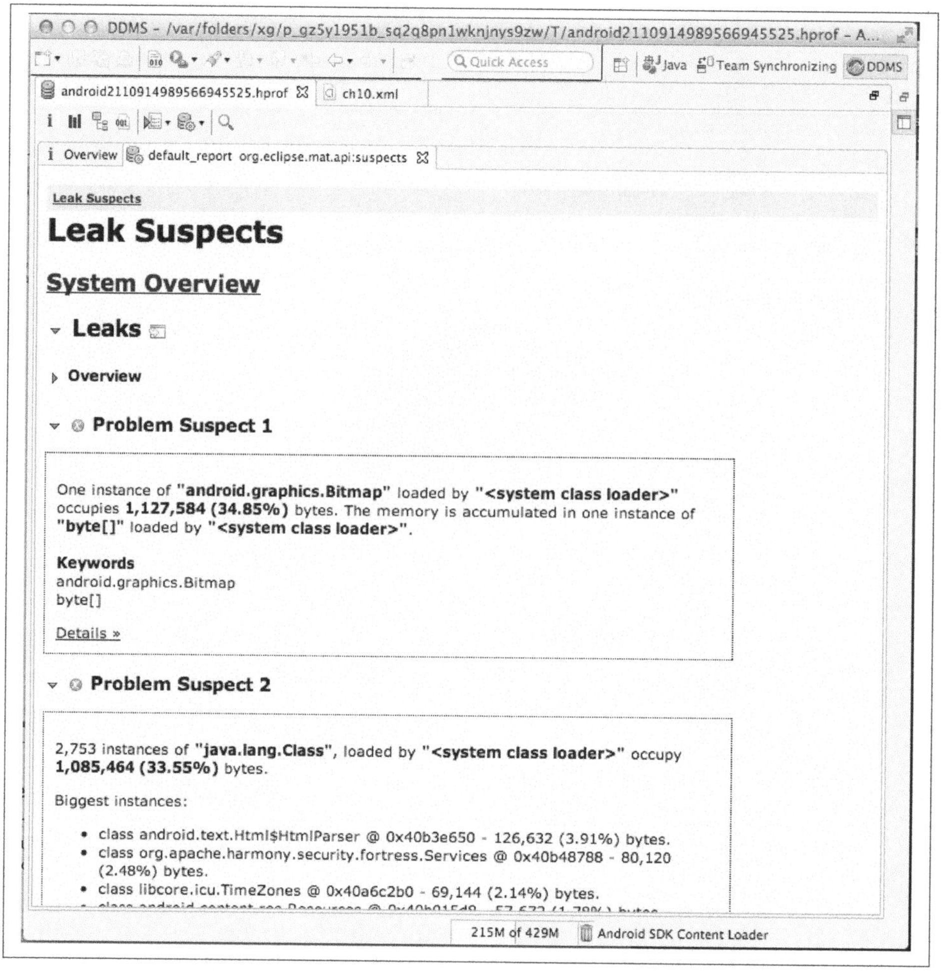

Figure 10-8. MAT Leak Suspects Report

## CHAPTER 11

Working with the User Interface

The user interface (UI) of any mobile application is important, and Android's widespread use requires that your software run well on a variety of different target devices. Generally, the wider range of devices you can support, the larger your potential customer base.

In almost all mobile applications, the elegance and usability of the user interface are more important than anything else. Your app has to look good to succeed in today's market. However, creating an attractive UI is made more difficult by the vast profusion of screen sizes and resolutions in Android. You can't finesse the problem by restricting your app to work on only one or a small range of devices; at least, you can't do that without giving up a very large number of potential customers.

This is where the Android framework comes to the rescue. From the beginning, Android was designed to support various devices and has thus offered simple ways for the developer to support them. The developer tools are also designed to make supporting multiple devices easier.

Android Layout Basic Concepts

In order to leverage all the features of the UI, it is important to understand the fundamental concepts of the framework.

Defining Layouts Using XML

Android layouts are conventionally created using XML syntax to define the user interface (UI) of an app. These XML files contain descriptions of various interface widgets, which could be TextViews, Buttons, or ImageViews (don't confuse these with "Desktop Widgets," which are a different thing). The files contain information defining the widgets you wish to display and detailed information about them (for example, orientation, spacing, or the specific location of an element on the screen).

The advantage of placing the layout into XML is that it separates the presentation of your application from the business logic. Your layout definitions are separate from your application code, so you can modify the layout without needing to change your source code or recompile. You can create different layouts for multiple device orientations, screen sizes, or locations.

It is worth noting that almost everything you do in XML can also be done in Java code, or by using a combination of both. For instance, you might define the placement and size of a button in XML and then use Java to set the text at runtime, depending on a particular code path execution.

Terminology

There are a few definitions you need to know to follow the next few chapters.

Widgets
> Native controls available to be used by the developer. These include a variety of elements, such as TextViews, ListViews, Buttons, and other UI components you will use to create layouts. These built-in components are commonly found in the `android.widget` package and are frequently subclasses of the class an `droid.view.View`. If the native controls don't provide the capabilities you need, it is possible to use custom components imported from libraries or developed as part of your codebase.

Layout Files
> XML files that describe the widgets making up your UI. These are located in the *res* folder of your project.

Layout
> A class whose primary purpose is to contain other controls. These classes (such as `LinearLayout`, `TableLayout`, and `FrameLayout`) organize widgets (such as Text-Views, Buttons, etc.) on the screen.

Attributes
> Control specific behavior in your components. They have the format (`name space:name=value`), which allows you to specify characteristics of your components. Some examples of these with which you are probably familiar include `android:width="48dp"`, `android:color="@colors/text_color"`, and `android: text="Text Value"`.

Themes and Styles
> Allow the developer to define the specific look and feel of a layout in external files. This is a common way to apply color or text attributes in a single file to apply them to multiple widgets, and also make changes to multiple screens from a single file.

Views and ViewGroups

Layouts in Android are constructed by combining these two base objects into
hierarchies.

Views
    This is the base class for many widgets (such as TextView or Button). It is the
    base class (`classes.android.view.View`) for almost all UI components in
    `android.classes.android.view.View`.

ViewGroups
    This is a view that contains other views. The ViewGroup class (`android.view.View
    Group`) is the base class for many layouts in Android or other specialized compo-
    nents such as ListView and WebView.

The first step in visualizing your layout is to define a simple hierarchy. This might look
like Figure 11-1.

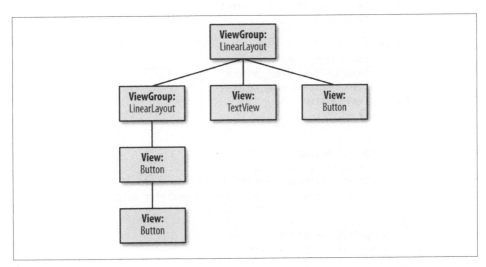

Figure 11-1. Layout basics: view hierarchy

The next step in creating a layout is to describe your hierarchy in code. To do this, create a layout file and insert the appropriate XML tags describing your Views and View-Groups. The following XML file below shows a basic layout. It contains two View-Groups, (the LinearLayout elements) that contain other Views (in this case the Buttons and a TextView). The order in the XML file matters: it lays out two buttons side-by-side, with text below them, and then another button below that. The screenshot (see Figure 11-2) shows how this would look on a device.

Example 11-1. XML file that produces screen in Figure 11-2

```
<?xml version="1.0" encoding="utf-8"?>
< Layout xmlns:android="http://schemas.android.com/apk/res/android" ❶
    android:layout_width="match_parent"
    android:layout_height="match_parent"
    android:orientation="vertical" > ❷

    <LinearLayout ❸
        android:id="@+id/button_linear"
        android:layout_width="wrap_content"
        android:layout_height="wrap_content"
        android:orientation="horizontal" > ❹

        <Button ❺
            android:id="@+id/button1"
            android:layout_width="wrap_content"
            android:layout_height="wrap_content"
            android:text="Button1" />

        <Button ❻
            android:id="@+id/button2"
            android:layout_width="wrap_content"
            android:layout_height="wrap_content"
            android:text="Button2" />
    </LinearLayout> ❼

    <TextView ❽
        android:id="@+id/textView1"
        android:layout_width="wrap_content"
        android:layout_height="wrap_content"
        android:text="Lorem ipsum dolor sit amet, consectetur adipisicing elit" />

    <Button ❾
        android:id="@+id/button3"
        android:layout_width="wrap_content"
        android:layout_height="wrap_content"
        android:text="Button3" />

</LinearLayout> ❿
```

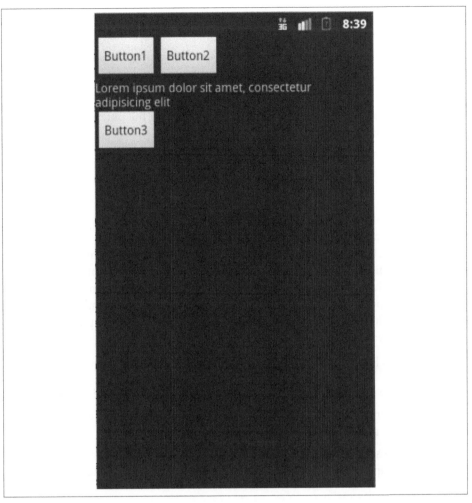

Figure 11-2. Layout basics: rendered UI

❶ The outermost layout, filling the screen. The other layout, the TextView, and the final button are nested inside it.

❷ The vertical orientation ensures that the other layout, the TextView, and the final button are stacked up in the order in which they are specified from the top down.

❸ We include a second layout, nested in the first, so that we can arrange some things horizontally in it.

❹ This orientation specifies that the buttons will be side-by-side.

❺ The first button, at the top left of the screen. This is within the second, innermost layout.

⑥ The second button, to the right of the first. This also is within the second, innermost layout.

⑦ This line ends the innermost layout, the one containing two buttons.

⑧ The TextView, which is within the outermost layout but outside the innermost layout. It is therefore oriented vertically under the first two buttons.

⑨ The third button, which like the TextView is within the outermost layout and therefore oriented vertically.

⑩ This line ends the outermost layout.

Resources

An Android application consists of much more that just Java files. A variety of other files (such as images, videos, and colors) are also used to create your interface. These are known collectively as *resources* and *resource files*. The Android framework supports an easy way to tie different versions of a resource (a different resolution image, or a different size of icon, or text in a different natural language) to different configurations on the device (no keyboard, French locale, hi-res screen). For example, in order to support different screen resolutions, it is necessary to include multiple copies of the same image, in various resolutions.

Using resources has many advantages, including:

- Source code is separate from resources, which makes customization easier.
- Resources are static and compiled into the application, which means they can be checked for availability before runtime.
- It is easy to support additional functionality (localization, for instance) by simply adding the appropriate resources without requiring modification to existing source code.

Android specifies that you put these items in the *res* folder at the base level of your project (see Figure 11-3). You will put resources in unique folders that are determined by the features you want to support. At compile time, Android scans the folders and uses the appropriate resource. For instance, when your app is run, the system will know to use the appropriately sized image and retrieve it from the *res* folder.

Figure 11-3 shows how to supply a graphic resource that supports different resolutions. To do this, put a resource with the same name (in this case, *ic_launcher.png*) in the folder appropriate for each resolution you support (mdpi for medium resolution, hdpi for high resolution, etc.). When your app is run, that image will be used by the system automatically.

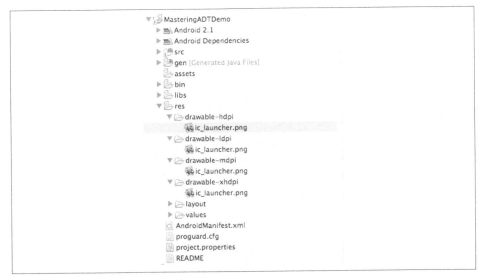

Figure 11-3. Using multiple graphic resources

In the same way that you provide alternate image resources, you can supply layouts, strings, colors, dimensions, and much more to support specific device configurations.

There are many nuances to externalizing application resources, and understanding them can really help the development process. The official documentation (*http://bit.ly/1361xt8*) describes all the different ways you can customize your application using alternative resources and is worth reading.

Leveraging ADT to Build Great UIs

Generating Android applications that support multiple devices is one of the more challenging aspects of working with the platform. Fortunately, ADT provides a robust set of tools to aid the developer (or designer) in creating the UI layer. There are tools to create layouts using a drag-and-drop editor, generate code templates, extract resources, refactor XML, and much more. This chapter (and the next few) will highlight all the great tools available, and show how you can leverage them to make responsive interfaces that work well and look good on a variety of devices.

The documentation describing how to handle multiple devices (*http://bit.ly/17CeIhq*) does an excellent job of explaining what the different resolution formats are, as well as specific strategies for making the most of this feature. I suggest reading it.

Editing XML Files Directly

In "Code Templates" on page 59, we discussed using the tools to generate code. There are also a lot of templates you can use to generate XML files. There is support for creating a variety of different XML files, which makes creating them simple.

Using Templates

The XML templates can be accessed by choosing File → New → Other → Android → Android XML File. You will be presented with a menu (similar to Figure 11-4) showing a list of XML files available. There is support for a variety of file types, so it is worthwhile to know which ones the system can create for you.

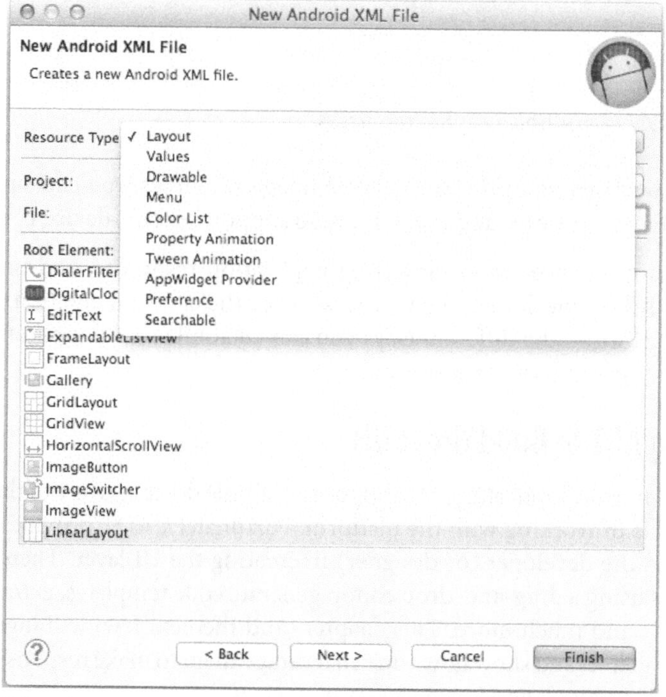

Figure 11-4. XML editor: code templates

Editing XML Directly

Editing XML files can be challenging. You have to be careful to match tags, and always use correct attribute values. Many times, errors don't show up until compile time or runtime, which makes the debug cycle long and inefficient. The XML editor that is built into the tools includes functionality to simplify manually editing layout files. Using these features makes it easy to write valid XML, use correct attributes, and refactor layouts without syntax errors.

Code completion

You have probably already used the code completion facilities available when editing Java files. ADT provides similar capabilities when editing layout XML files. You will be able to use this functionality to insert UI widget definitions, look up attribute values, and identify resources (such as drawables, layout elements, string values, or style definitions). These tools make it much easier to generate XML layout files correctly, so you won't spent time fixing syntax errors or searching APIs to find acceptable values.

The key combination that launches code completion is the same one you use in Java and the same on all platforms: Ctrl+Space. It provides different options depending on the code you have highlighted.

Inserting new layouts or widgets

If you place your cursor on a blank line or outside an existing tag, when you press this key combination, you will be provided with a list of elements you can insert (like in Figure 11-5). Selecting one of the items from the list as shown will create a stubbed item, which you can extend with your own custom attribute values.

Figure 11-5. XML editor: inserting new element

Attribute values

If you place your cursor inside an XML attribute definition (i.e., between the quotation marks), you will be provided with a list of appropriate entries. There are two different possibilities for these values, depending on the particular attribute you are defining.

The first allows you to fill in API options to define elements from the system (such as width attributes or buffer). For example, in Figure 11-6 I am using code completion to define the width attribute for a TextView.

Figure 11-6. XML editor: adding a new element

The second allows you to locate local or system resources for your UI. These things might include color definitions, string values, style definitions, or other layout elements. The example in Figure 11-7 shows how the tool provides you with a list of values available.

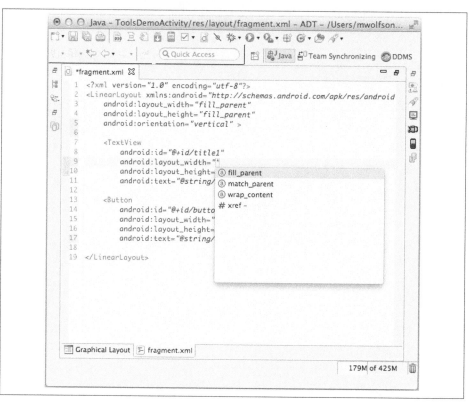

Figure 11-7. XML editor: adding a new API attribute

Refactor menu

This tool allows you to quickly complete refactoring operations. These include removing layout elements, wrapping multiple widgets in a container, or extracting XML to be shared by multiple resources. To launch this menu, highlight the starting tag of the element you want to refactor, then select the Refactor menu from the top menu bar. It offers a variety of options, some of which we already covered in the IDE section ("Refactor Menu" on page 70). It is worth discussing the layout-specific options here:

Change layout

This lets you change the layout and then re-renders the canvas automatically. You might need this if you need to convert to another container type because of a limitation with your current type (for instance, you needed finer control over placement than a LinearLayout provides).

Change widget

This allows you to change the type of one or more widgets. It automatically removes incompatible attribute types, and includes default values for any new ones that are required.

Extract as include

This allows you to extract views into a separate layout file. It creates the new external layout file and includes the appropriate reference in your XML. This is a simple way to reuse common view components, which avoids duplications and creates cleaner code.

Wrap in container

You can use this menu to select one of more siblings and wrap them in a new layout container. The tool transfers layout attributes from the sibling to the new parent container. This can be useful if you need to group UI components, perhaps to apply common gravity.

You can use the Quick Assistant if you aren't sure which refactor you need to use. This is a great way to allow the system to provide suggestions depending on the current context. In either editor (Java or XML), highlight a field and press Ctrl+1 on Windows\Linux or Command+1 on Mac OS X. This will bring up a list of refactor possibilities, and is the quickest way to access these common options.

The example in Figure 11-8 shows how you would use the Refactor menu to remove a layout container. After highlighting the LinearLayout to remove, select the Remove Container menu item and a screen appears (Figure 11-9) allowing you to review the changes before clicking OK to commit them.

Figure 11-8. Accessing the refactor menu from the XML editor

XML formatting

Layout files can get complicated fast. You will likely use many different attributes to specify unique parameters for your different UI elements. The XML files can become particularly difficult to follow when attributes are not spaced uniformly or when they are out of order. You can use the following keys to quickly format your code: Ctrl+Shift+F on Windows\Linux or Command+Shift+F on Mac OS X.

It automatically adjusts tab spacing and organizes the attributes into a specific predefined order. Having correctly formatted XML makes it easier to understand element relationships and find particular attributes you may need to modify.

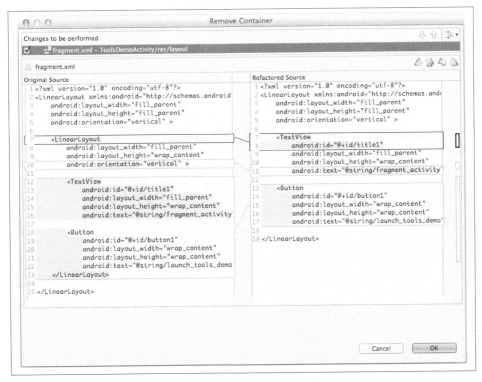

Figure 11-9. XML editor: options shown by Refactor menu

The default formatting style matches the conventions used in official Android documentation, tutorials, and source code, so your code will match standards. The system automatically applies custom formatting rules depending on which type of file is being edited. This means that custom formatting rules will be applied to standard layout files, resource definition files (such as *strings.xml*), or *AndroidManifest.xml*. This makes a big difference in the readability (and maintainability of your code). The XML files can become particularly difficult to follow when attributes are not spaced uniformly or when they are out of order (as seen in Figure 11-10).

Figure 11-10. XML editor: before reformat

Having correctly formatted XML (like that shown in Figure 11-11) makes it easier to understand element relationships and find particular attributes you may need to modify.

Figure 11-11. XML editor: after reformat

Editor Preferences menu

The Editor Preferences menu, shown in Figure 11-12, allows you to change the format that the editor uses. This is valuable, for instance, if your company has unique coding standards. Another important setting causes the system to automatically format your code when you save it. I recommend you set this value, so you can ensure you are performing the formatting operations on all of your files.

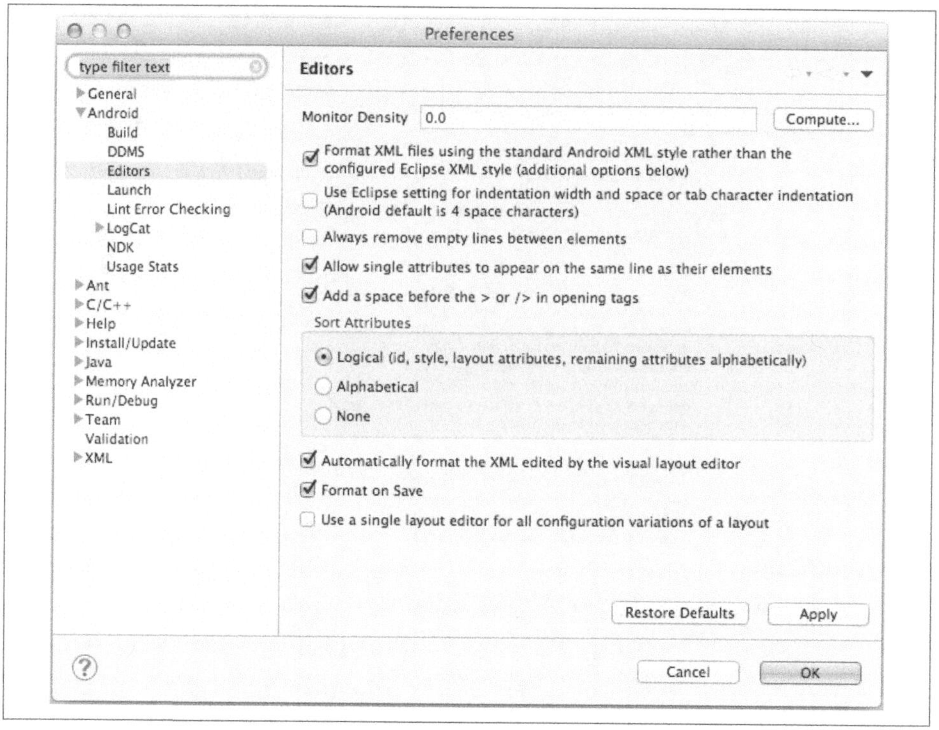

Figure 11-12. XML editor: preferences

There are two preferences worth highlighting. You can access them from Window →
Preference → Android → Editor on Windows and Linux, and from ADT → Preference → Android → Editor on Mac OS X.

This menu contains a variety of useful options that allow you to customize Editor functionality further. Some of the more useful ones include:

- Configure style (spacing, line wrapping, etc.) of formatting
- Modify the default order of the attributes (there are a few alternate options, and
  you can create a custom sort order as well)
- Specify if you would like the format operation to be run on every save

Working with Graphics

In the beginning of the chapter, I described how Android uses multiple resources to
support different device resolutions. Supplying each of the proper resolution images is
one of the most important ways to ensure that your app looks good everywhere. If the
system is not able to find an image resource matching its preferred resolution, it will

find the next closest resolution and scale it to fit. This can result in unexpected visual artifacts, and can significantly effect the responsiveness of your app, as image rescaling can be memory and CPU intensive.

It can be difficult to understand what size each of the images can be, the names of the folders, and other information associated with this way of doing things. In my experience, this is one of the bigger frustrations for designers and developers.

There are two great ways of dealing with the complexities of manipulating image resources: the Android Asset tool, and the use of Nine-patch images.

The Asset Tool

The Asset tool automatically creates the appropriate resolution resources and places them in your project. Launch it by entering Ctrl+N on Windows or Linux and Command+N on Mac OS X.

From the New wizard launcher, expand the Android section and select Android Icon Set, as shown in Figure 11-13.

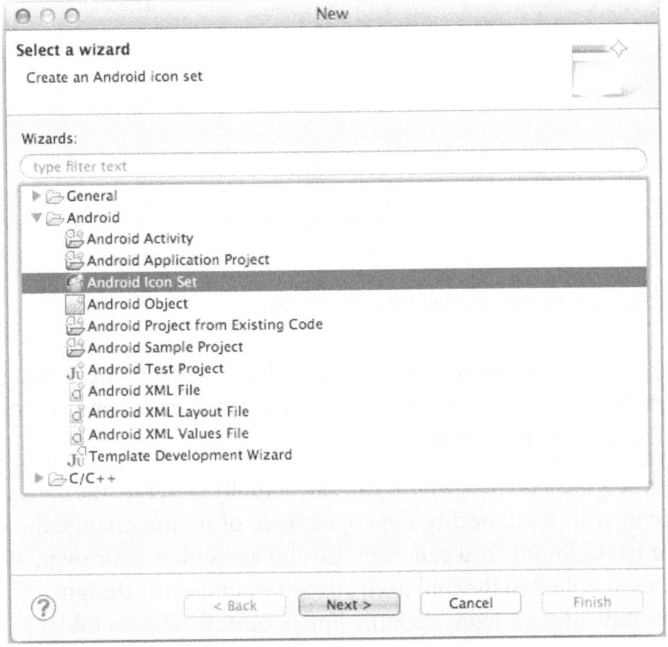

Figure 11-13. Launching the Android Icon Set generator

A screen (Figure 11-14) prompts you to specify the type of resource you want to generate. There are different sizes for images, depending on whether they are intended to be used in notifications, on the Action Bar, or elsewhere on the screen. You will need to specify the type of icon that should be created.

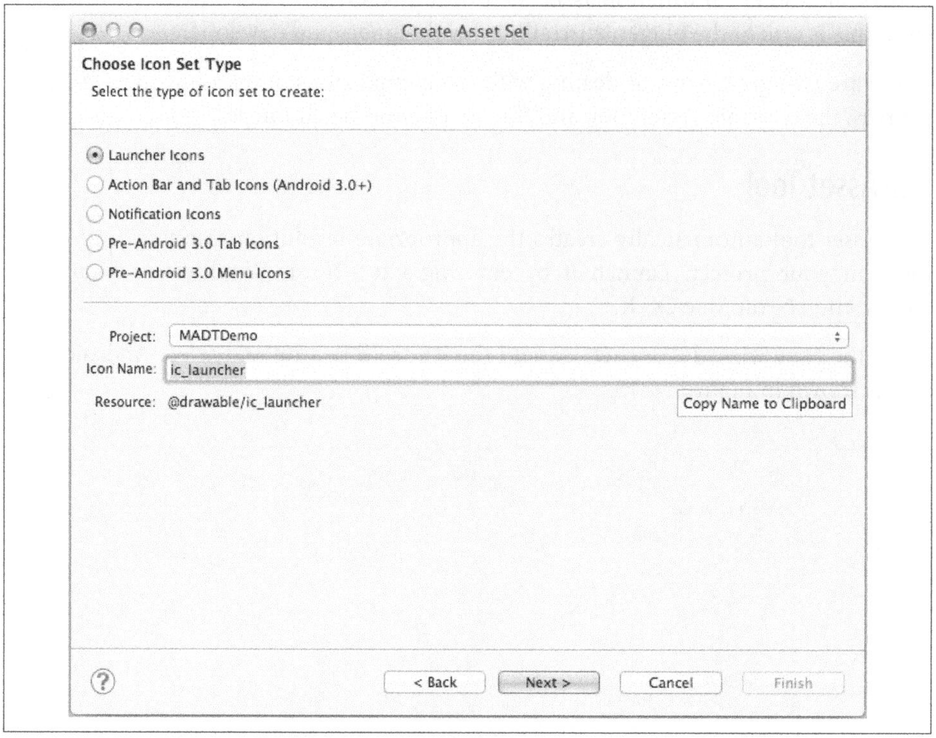

Figure 11-14. Specifying options to customize icons

Next, you will specify the name of the icon, and the project where you would like it created. When the tool is done, it will create all the appropriate images and place them in the correct folders in this project.

The last screen (Figure 11-15) is where you can actually generate the icon asset. You can generate an icon with text, modify the appearance of it, and change the colors of the foreground or background. You can even use clip art (either your own, which you can import, or icons supplied in the tool itself) to generate specific designs. When you have configured the look of your icon, click the Finish button. The *res* folder in your project will now have PNG files with your design at the correct resolution.

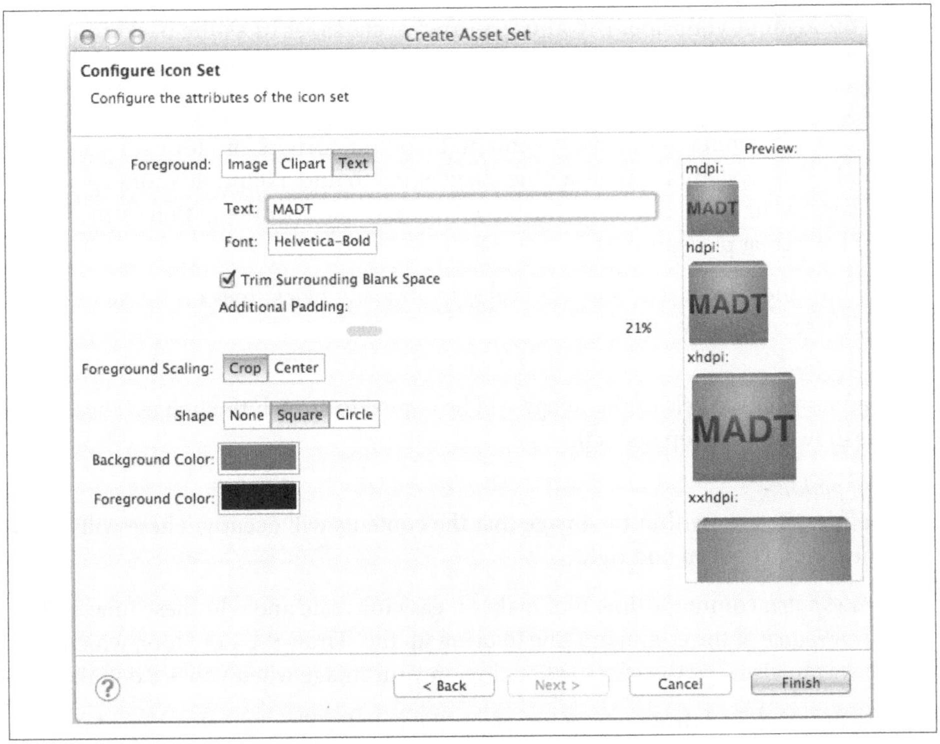

Configure Icon Set

Configure the attributes of the icon set

Foreground:	Image	Clipart	Text
Text:	MADT
Font:	Helvetica–Bold
	☑ Trim Surrounding Blank Space
	Additional Padding:
	21%
Foreground Scaling:	Crop	Center
Shape	None	Square	Circle
Background Color:	
Foreground Color:	

Preview:

mdpi:

MADT

hdpi:

MADT

xhdpi:

MADT

xxhdpi:

MADT

(?)   < Back   Next >   Cancel   Finish

Figure 11-15. Creating an icon set

I have found an excellent way to work with my design team. When I create my source code, I use the Asset Studio to create sample icons. Then, when I request real icons from the graphic artists, I just copy the *res* folder out of my projects and give it to them. I ask them to replace the sample images with their own. Since they know the names and sizes of each of the resources they need to supply, this eliminates communication errors. The best part is that, when it is time to integrate the real images back into the project, all I have to do is copy the *res* folder with the correct resources back into my code, and I'm done!

Using Nine-Patch Images

Android lets you supply your image assets as Nine-patch images. This format allows you to define lines along the edges of an image, which control how it is scaled by the system. The placement of black lines informs the framework whether that section of the image will be grown/shrunk by zooming it, or should be kept unchanged. A good example of when it's useful to provide this type of image is when creating a styled button to use throughout your app. If you use a `NinePatchDrawable` as the background for your buttons, it will stretch and scale to look uniform across all of them.

To use a `NinePatchDrawable`, you must slice your image resource into nine regions. There is a center container for your content, then four corners and four sides that will be scaled by the system. It can be a little challenging to understand this concept at first so if you would like to brush up on the topic, the drawable documentation (*http://bit.ly/13oIJzY*) is a great place to start.

Specify how the Nine-patch image is scaled by drawing black lines on the sides of the image. These specify two things:

Stretch regions
> Defines which pixels of the image will be copied to stretch the image. These lines are drawn on the top and left.

Content padding
> Defines the area within the image that the contents will occupy. These will be the lines on the bottom and right.

The *draw9patch* command-line tool makes it easy to create and edit these images. Just type *draw9patch* at the command line to bring up the "Draw 9-patch" tool, which provides a way to visualize the effects of scaling on your image when you are defining it.

Start by dragging and dropping an image on the palette. This launches the editor (see Figure 11-16).

Then use the mouse to draw the lines that specify the various regions. Check the "Show patches" and "Show content" options at the bottom of the screen to visualize exactly how the system will scale your image. You can change the black lines to show:

Stretch regions
> Shown by the pink box in the center of the pane on the left.

Content padding
> Shows how much space is available for your content, via the purple box in the right side pane.

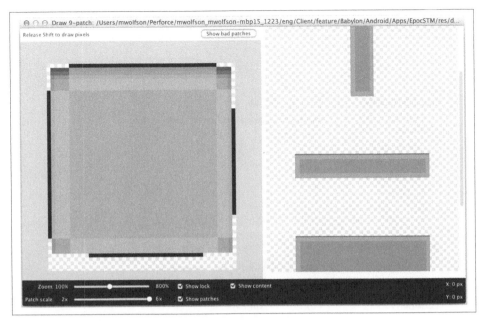

Figure 11-16. Editing Nine-patch drawables using the visual editor

Asset Studio Website

It is worth noting an excellent open source project called Asset Studio (*http://bit.ly/ 14sqRrh*) that automates many of the procedures we discussed in this section. The home page (shown in Figure 11-17) shows some of the things you can do. This site automates many of the things the tools do, including generating multiple image resources, editing Nine-patch images, and others. It also has some additional functionality not available elsewhere, including generating screenshots such as device frames for marketing, or generating styles for commonly used resources—specifically the Action Bar.

Figure 11-17. Android Asset Studio website

## CHAPTER 12

Using the Graphical Editor

By far the easiest and most productive way to design a user interface (UI) in Android apps is to use the Graphical Layout tools. In the past, these have been difficult to use, sometimes creating code that was hard to understand and had other practical limitations. But the tools have improved over successive releases. They are getting close to the standard set used by GUI builders for Windows or iOS, and now work better than the Android alternative (manually editing XML files). They make it easy to generate the user interface, refactor existing layouts, visualize your UI on multiple environments, and much more. They can make development more efficient and ensure that you are creating well-formed layout code.

Generating Layouts Using the Graphical Layout Editor

If editing XML isn't your thing, there is a graphical tool that allows you to drag and drop UI components to construct a layout. You will use this to create your basic layouts, then modify the XML to fine-tune your layouts.

The Graphical Layout editor (see Figure 12-1) can be accessed by selecting the appropriate tab (on the bottom left) of any Android *layout.xml* file. Selecting this tab presents you with a perspective containing the tools you can use to construct your interface. Switch back to the XML view by selecting the tab showing the layout filename. The two views are kept in sync when you save the file.

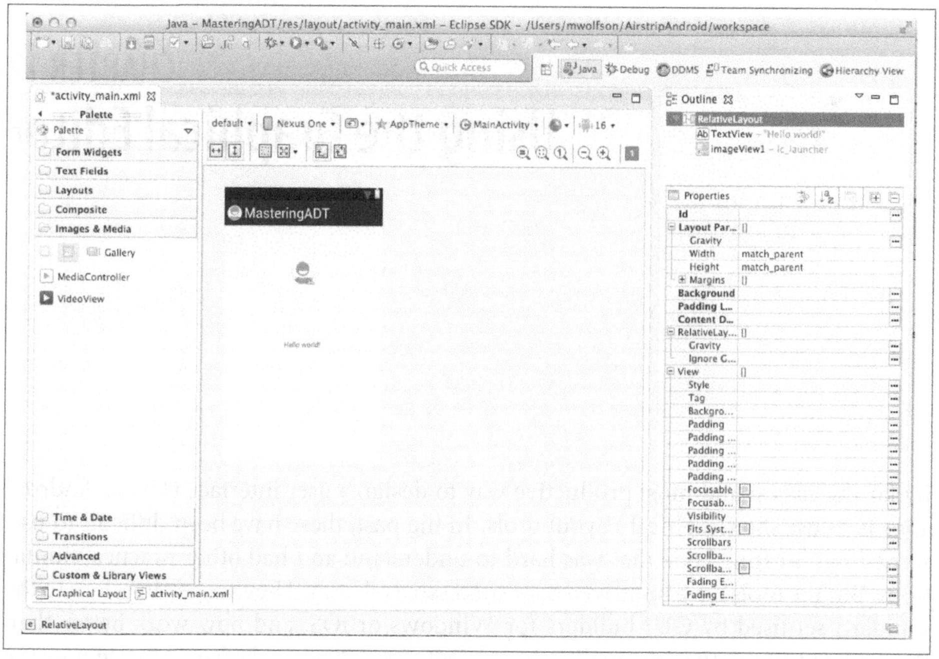

Figure 12-1. Visual editor, full view

This tool has a few different components that work together to provide a comprehensive visual editing environment. We will discuss each in detail in this chapter.

Palette

On the left is the panel that contains the widgets you can drag onto the canvas. The palette contains rendered views of the components available, making it easy to find the component you want.

Canvas

This is the component in the middle of the screen. When you drag elements onto this canvas, a view will be rendered to show how it will look. There are many different options available in this tool that allow you to determine how your UI will look on different devices. XREF discusses these in detail.

Outline

This panel (on the top right) provides a hierarchical view of your layout, displayed as an ordered list.

Properties editor

This window (on the bottom right) allows you to modify attributes of your widgets.

Configuration chooser

The list of menus on the top of the canvas allow you to configure how the view is rendered. These allow you to render different views of your UI, right in the tool. This is easier and quicker than trying to duplicate UI in different configurations using emulators.

Palette

On the left side of the tool is the palette. It contains categories of widgets and UI components that are available to drag onto the canvas. You can select a category heading to display the view types in that group.

You will notice that the widgets are rendered according to the currently defined style. The dark bottom part contains any custom views you have defined in your project (see Figure 12-2). ADT automatically makes them available via this tool (you may have to press the Refresh button if they don't display automatically).

Figure 12-2. Palette

The palette contains a large variety of components that are preconfigured to perform certain actions. Find the appropriate component and drag it to your canvas to place a properly configured UI component on your interface. For example, if you wanted to add a Password field to a form, you would locate the component from the Text Fields category (see Figure 12-3) and drag it onto your canvas. When you look at the XML, you will see that a default value is defined for ems (which is a property used to control text size), and the inputType is set to textPassword (which masks the values the user enters).

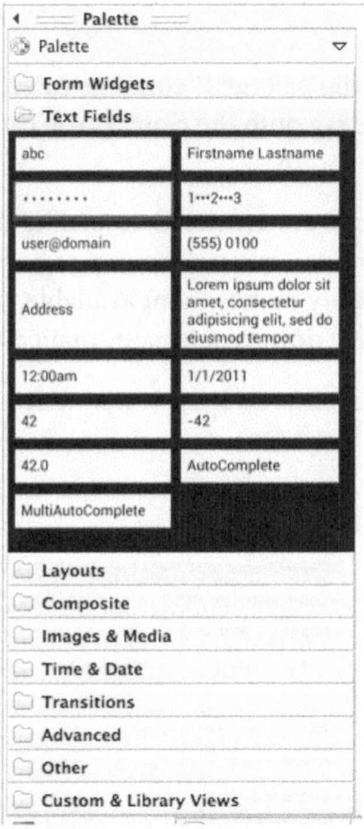

Figure 12-3. Graphical editor: password example

Canvas

This is where you can drag widgets from the palette and drop them to create your UI. The canvas renders a preview of your app in real time based on the widgets you add. You can then modify the preview to visualize your app on multiple screen sizes, orientations, and other ways using the configuration chooser (see "Configuration Chooser" on page 197).

To add a view to your UI, find it in the palette and drag it onto the canvas. You can also add Views to other Views (see "Views and ViewGroups" on page 167) by dropping them onto the Outline part of the screen. After a component is placed on the canvas, you can drag it around to reposition it, assuming the Parent view supports the move.

Just as when you are editing the XML directly, you can use Ctrl/Command+Z to undo your last operation. You can do the same thing from the Edit → Undo menu. Because it is easy to undo any operations, you can be comfortable that any changes you make are not permanent (so feel free to experiment a little).

When you drag and drop a component from the palette onto the canvas, indicators appear that show you the alignment and approximate location of the widget on your UI. This allows you to control how the view is placed in the parent. Depending on the type of parent container, you can control the alignment and placement of the view you are creating. In Figure 12-4, for instance, you are placing a Button into a RelativeLayout. A pop-up in the figure shows the alignment (in this case, centerHorizontal="true") with an arrow tying the component to its parent. Understanding the relationships among views helps you a great deal in controlling layouts, and getting this feedback visually is much easier than trying to decipher XML files.

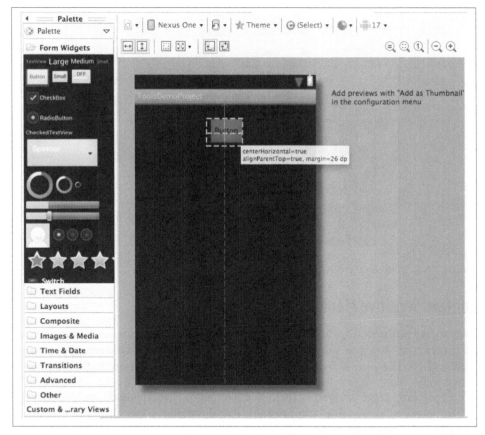

Figure 12-4. Viewing extents while dragging items onto the canvas

Layout Actions

At the top of the canvas are two rows of buttons. The top one is the configuration chooser (see "Configuration Chooser" on page 197), and the bottom one is the layout actions bar (see Figure 12-5). This bar offers context-sensitive options (meaning they will change based on what you currently have selected) relating to the currently selected view and its parent.

Some of the common options available here include changing the `gravity`, `lay` `out_width`, and `layout_margins`. For example, in Figure 12-5 I selected a Button in a LinearLayout. The bar shows actions related to the LinearLayout, such as a toggle to change the orientation from vertical to horizontal. Some other available options might include a control to specify how children are aligned, actions to control the child's layout attributes (like `layout_width`), or a button to change the layout's margins.

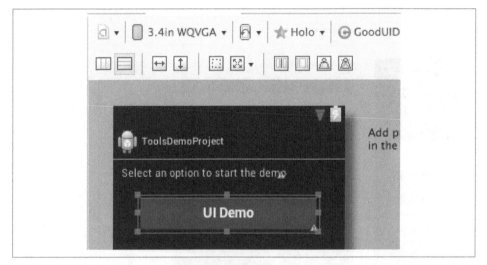

Figure 12-5. Viewing the layout options available

Context-Sensitive Menu

You might be surprised by the functionality hiding when you right-click on any element in the canvas. You are presented with a menu of context-sensitive options (see Figure 12-6). These provide a variety of shortcuts to useful functionality, including:

- Changing widget properties, including a menu to navigate based on Java package structure within Android source code (as an alternative to the full-blown properties editor, "Properties Editor" on page 196).

- Creating or previewing animations. If you have enabled animation on a component, this allows you to view it from the canvas.

- Performing most of the refactor operations we discussed in "Refactor menu" on page 176.
- Exporting a screenshot that contains a preview of your app, rendered to appear on the device you are currently showing.

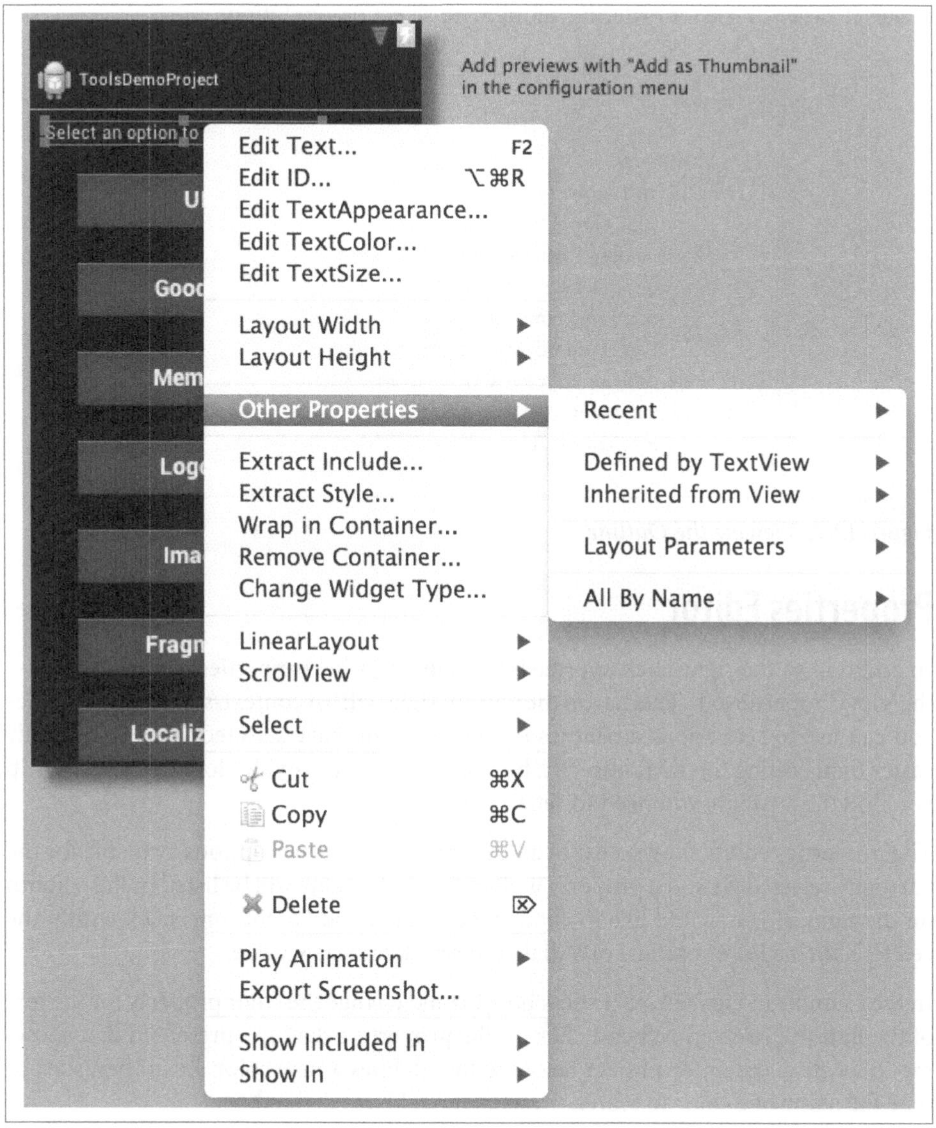

Figure 12-6. Launching the context-sensitive menu

Outline View

This tool (shown in Figure 12-7) provides a visual representation of your layout elements. It organizes them into a clear hierarchy that is easy to navigate. This view offers additional functionality that allows you to drag and drop the elements within the outline. It has a lot of the same functionality as the canvas, but provides a different view that makes it easier to use for ordering, along with selection operations.

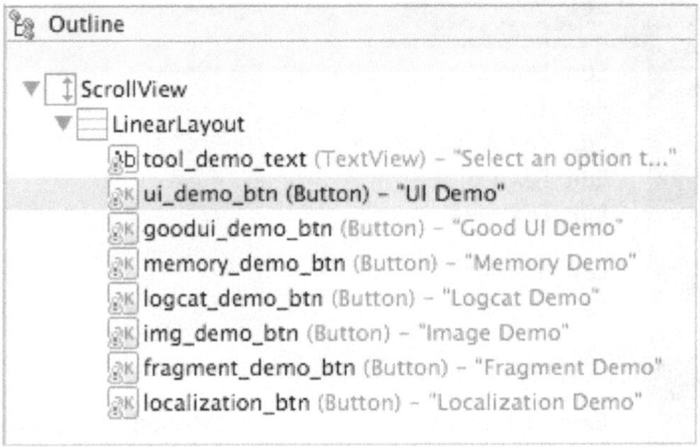

Figure 12-7. Viewing the Outline

Properties Editor

In addition to the right-click approach to changing view properties, you can also use the View Properties tab. This tab on the bottom right will list context-sensitive properties you can use to set various attributes on the view you have selected. This is generally easier than editing the XML directly, because the editor provides lookup tools to help you find the attribute you need to set.

The properties editor shows a list of all the various properties options available for the currently selected view. If a property is already set, the value will be listed in the column on the right. If you would like to change the value, or add a new one, click within the cell to launch a list of options or a dialog to select your new value.

In the example in Figure 12-8, I show how I could change the color property for the text of the Button I selected. When I click on the property, a dialog is presented that allows me to locate a system or project resource that defines a new color. I can then start to type the name of a color to search for a resource I have defined.

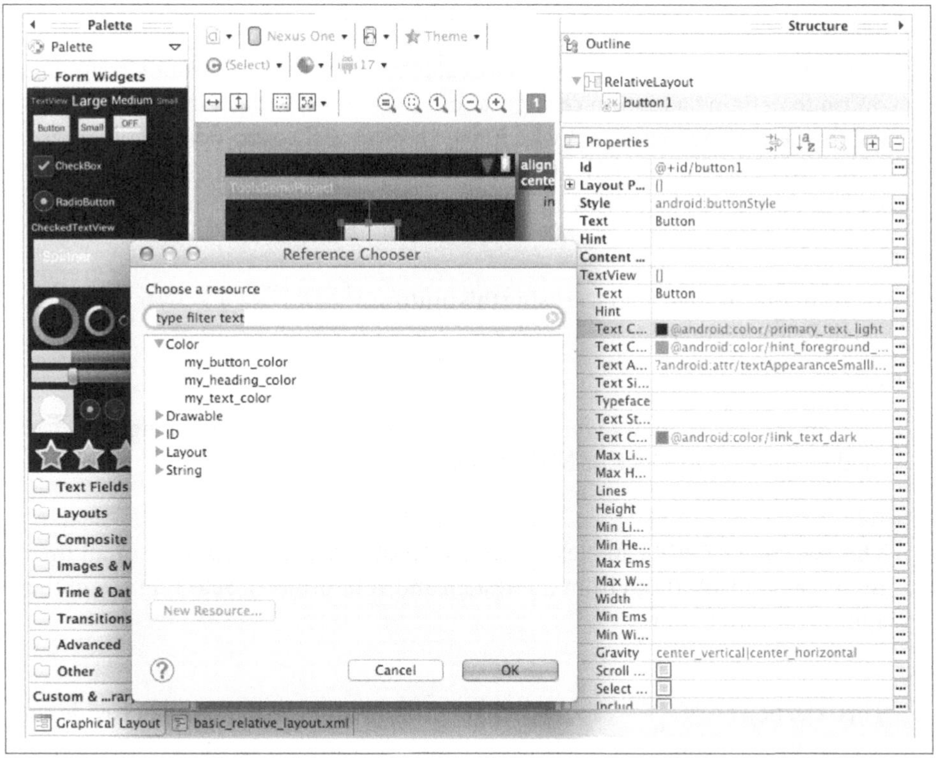

Figure 12-8. Viewing the Properties editor

Configuration Chooser

This set of tools (Figure 12-9), which appears at the top of the editor, allows you to see a visual rendering of your layout in various configurations. This is a great way to test your layouts against a variety of different configurations, and is much easier that creating emulators or finding devices for each of these options. While this won't replace real testing across different devices, it's a great way to get instant feedback about your UI while you are creating it.

Figure 12-9. Viewing the Configuration chooser

There are a variety of options for changing the way your UI is rendered. It is worth exploring each of the options, as there are a lot of different ways to customize your canvas.

Configuration menu

This button (🔲 ▾) lets you save a particular configuration of the tool itself. In addition to defining a custom configuration, there are existing configurations, such as "Preview All Screen Sizes," which will show how the screen will look on every device you have configured, and "Preview All Locales," which shows how it will look in the various languages and local settings you have configured.

Screen

You can control the screen size using this button (📱 3.4in WQVGA ▾). I cover this in more detail following this list.

Orientation

This option (🔲 ▾) allows you to change screen orientation, or change to special modes (such as Car Dock or Night Mode).

Theme

This selection (☆ Holo ▾) applies a theme to your UI. It presents a list of all theme resources available (both from the system and your project). Selecting any of them applies the styling to your UI.

Activity

This selection (⊕ GoodUIDemoActivity ▾) changes the Activity class that would provide context for your layout.

Localization

This option (🌐 ▾) applies any changes supported by your project for internationalization. If you have alternative resources (strings in *strings.xml*, images, etc.) for multiple countries, you will be provided with a list of these and be able to switch between them.

SDK

This selection (📱 17 ▾) show how your app looks on devices with different versions of the Android OS. This option is important to test because the UI changes a lot with each release. The SDK you select does not need to be the one you are targeting.

The option for changing the screen size is a great example of how useful this tool can be. As you know, Android applications need to run on a large variety of different devices, and it can be challenging to test each of these configurations. This tool provides the capability to check multiple resolutions of your layout. You can quickly switch between different device configurations, and instantly see how your UI will render.

To change the screen size and resolution in the visual editor, use the option in the top bar (see Figure 12-10) that allows you to view your layout on a variety of preset screen sizes. The list includes any AVDs you've created at the top, then a variety of other devices below. You can select any of the devices from the list, and the rendering of your UI will be updated to show how it would appear in that configuration.

GalaxyAce_mdpi_g8
GalaxyNexus_xhdpi_g16
Galaxys3_xhdpi_16
Nexus7_tvdpi_g17
NexusOne_hdpi_g10

Nexus 7 (7.27", 800 × 1280: tvdpi)
Galaxy Nexus (4.65", 720 × 1280: xhdpi)
Nexus S (4.0", 480 × 800: hdpi)
Nexus One (3.7", 480 × 800: hdpi)

10.1" WXGA (Tablet) (1280 × 800: mdpi)
7.0" WSVGA (Tablet) (1024 × 600: mdpi)
5.4" FWVGA (480 × 854: mdpi)
5.1" WVGA (480 × 800: mdpi)
4.7" WXGA (1280 × 720: xhdpi)
4.65" 720p (720 × 1280: xhdpi)
4.0" WVGA (480 × 800: hdpi)
3.7" FWVGA slider (480 × 854: hdpi)
✓ 3.7" WVGA (480 × 800: hdpi)
3.4" WQVGA (240 × 432: ldpi)
3.3" WQVGA (240 × 400: ldpi)
3.2" QVGA (ADP2) (320 × 480: mdpi)
3.2" HVGA slider (ADP1) (320 × 480: mdpi)
2.7" QVGA slider (240 × 320: ldpi)
2.7" QVGA (240 × 320: ldpi)

Preview All Screens

Figure 12-10. Setting screen resolution in the visual editor

I already mentioned the option at the bottom named Preview All Screens. It renders, in one view, your UI the way it will look on a variety of different devices (Figure 12-11). The tool actually updates each of the various views in real time, which means that you can see the impact of any changes you make on a variety of different screen sizes at the same time. In the example below, I adjusted the top Button to move it to the left. You will notice that the smaller screens on the right are updated to reflect this UI change.

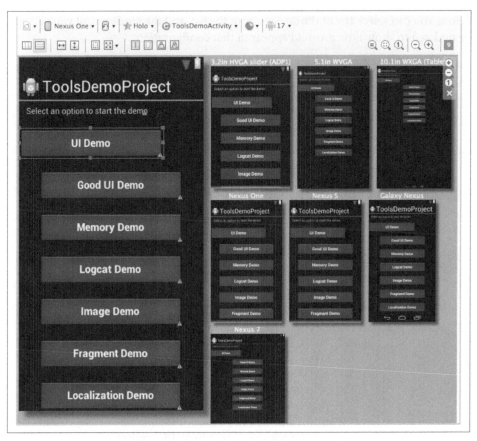

Figure 12-11. Previewing all screen sizes

If you are using resource qualifiers (see "Resources" on page 170) to enable different layouts (for size or orientation-specific UIs), you need to modify each one independently. The changes you make in this tool will take effect only on the *layout.xml* file you are currently editing. You need to edit each of your alternate layouts independently and make your changes in each of those files.

## CHAPTER 13

Optimizing the User Interface

Earlier chapters presented aids for creating dynamic and efficient layouts. The tools can make your UI good, but you'll probably need to do some additional work to make your UI great. This chapter discusses the various tools that help you improve the efficiency of your interface code. I will show you how to use the tools to eliminate:

- Slow or jittery redraw rates
- A nonresponsive, poorly performing UI

Introduction to UI Performance

In addition to the content covered in Chapter 11, there are a few concepts relating to how Android builds user interfaces that are important to understand.

How Android Draws Views, and How It Affects UI Performance

When an activity gets started, it asks the framework to draw its UI from its layout definitions. The UI is drawn by walking the View tree and rendering each ViewGroup. Then each ViewGroup requests each of its children to be drawn until all Views in the hierarchy have been rendered. The tree is traversed in order, which means that parents are drawn before their children, with the final order determined by where they appear in the tree.

Two-pass layout

The runtime draws the layout through a two-pass process via the View tree, visualized in Figure 13-1. For each View rendering, the system must perform two operations: a *measure pass* and a *layout pass*. The measure pass collects dimension specifications and the layout pass positions the Views on the screen.

Measure pass

> This pass traverses the entire View tree to determine dimension specifications for each View. The size and position of a ViewGroup depends on the number and size of the Views it contains. The measure pass calculates sizes based on the relationships between a ViewGroup and its related Views. The system will do a series of measurement passes. At the end, the system knows the size required for each View, and validates that they can be placed on the layout.

Layout Pass

> After the system has determined the proper dimensions for a requested layout, it renders the items to the screen.

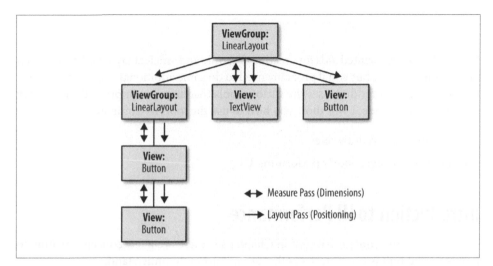

Figure 13-1. Two-pass layout process

Nested layouts reduce performance

Nested layouts can be a big source of performance issues. Overhead is involved with each redraw of a ViewGroup. When Android redraws a component on the screen, it must redraw every component and hierarchy it contains. The OS does a variety of complicated measurement and placement calculations for each screen draw. Complex nested components and unnecessary items impact performance and diminish the user experience with a slow response.

There are a few tools designed to help isolate Views with inefficient hierarchies. You can use the Developer Tools (see "Developer Tools Application" on page 52) to visualize problems, Lint (see "Lint" on page 107) to find and fix the errors in XML or Java, or the Hierarchy Viewer (see "Hierarchy Viewer" on page 203) to visualize your View organization and determine possible optimizations.

Hierarchy Viewer

It is important to have a good understanding of the View elements in your application. Fortunately, ADT provides a collection of tools called the Hierarchy Viewer that allows the developer to visualize these elements and quickly identify problems.

Dealing with complicated layouts can be very challenging. It can be hard to understand deeply nested layouts, or find and remove unused layouts. We will use these tools to create a diagram of the View hierarchy of a layout, which allows us to get a clearer understanding of the nature of all the components in our layouts and how their relationships might be optimized. We optimize the layouts by removing unused layouts and flattening the View hierarchy (which has a positive impact on performance). These tools are also useful when debugging slow UIs, as you can navigate to a specific point in your UI and get measurements about the actual render times of the individual widgets in your apps.

Starting the Hierarchy Viewer

To start the tool, you first need to deploy your application to a running device. Then use the preconfigured Eclipse perspective that organizes a collection of tools into a single dashboard. Start it from the menu through: Window → Open Perspective → Other → Hierarchy View. You will see something that looks like Figure 13-2.

Loading the View Hierarchy into the Tools

To begin analyzing your UI, navigate in your test app to the specific view you want to inspect. Then:

1. Highlight the Window tab (▯) on the top left.
2. Find your app activity in the list and highlight it.
3. If your app is not showing up, press the Refresh button (↻) to renew the list of views.
4. Generate the View by pressing Tree View button (⊞).

A progress dialog on the bottom right corner will indicate that the View is being generated. When complete, your view will look similar to Figure 13-3.

Navigating the Tree Hierarchy

Notice that the two tabs on the right side of Figure 13-3 now have content in them. There are two different ways to navigate using these tools:

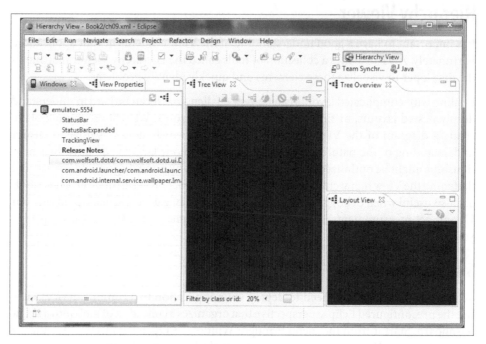

Figure 13-2. Initial Hierarchy View perspective

Tree Overview ( )

> You might remember from "Nested layouts reduce performance" on page 202 that unused views can be detrimental to performance. Figure 13-3 shows a high-level overview of how each View in the UI is being rendered. This is a good place to identify unnecessary components, because you can look for instances where a component has only one descendant (and hence you can drop the container, and just use the View directly). I highlight how to find these in the example at the end of this section.

Layout View ( )

> This section shows a wire-frame rendering of your Views. You can click any individual component in this display to highlight it in the center Tree View.

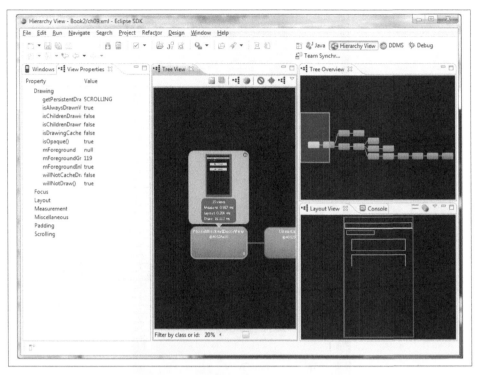

Figure 13-3. Hierarchy loaded into tools

Gathering View Information

The center column named Tree View () is the main tool used to gather detailed information about your UI. To start getting details, click on any View within your hierarchy to bring up the detailed information about the View, which will look like Figure 13-4. We will dig into each of the things you can do here.

The information displayed when you click on the node contains a variety of details about the View's rendering characteristics (and its children when appropriate). This display contains a lot of great information, so I want to take a moment to explain what the values mean.

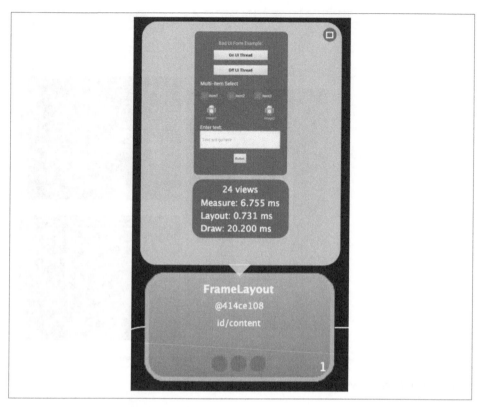

Figure 13-4. Hierarchy View: Tree View

Measurement information

The middle section (see Figure 13-5) has two important items:

- The number of Views in this container. This example shows 24, which is a lot because this happens to be the main node in the tree.
- Measure, Layout, and Draw times for this node (and all of its children). Keep in mind that high times are not necessarily evidence of an issue, especially for screens with a lot of objects, which naturally take longer to render.

Identification and performance indicators

The bottom part of the node information display (see Figure 13-6) has some other useful information that you can use to quickly identify objects within your hierarchy. It also includes performance indicators that you can scan to quickly understand how the View performs (in relation to all other Views in the same layout). Information you can find here includes:

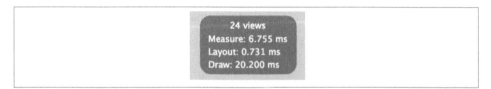

Figure 13-5. Hierarchy View: node measurements

- Class type of this view (in this case, the component is FrameLayout).
- The internal ID (i.e., how this View is referenced in the R class) for this View.
- The android:id used when the element was created in the XML.
- The three colored balls indicate the rendering speed of this View relative to other objects in the tree. The left ball shows the measure time, the middle one shows the layout time, and the right ball represents the draw time. If the ball is red, it means that View is the slowest one in the tree; if the ball is yellow, that View is slower than 50% of the other Views. If the ball is green, it means that the View renders faster than 50% of the other Views on the screen. You should use these indicators to quickly scan your UI to identify the problems you should look at first.
- The number on the bottom right indicates the index of this View within its parent. In this case, the node has one parent, so its index is one (if this were the top node in the hierarchy, it would be zero).

Figure 13-6. Hierarchy View: node identification and performance indicators

Gathering View Rendering Details

The Tree View contains detailed information about exact rendering times. You will see the exact times (in milliseconds) it takes to measure, lay out, and draw a component.

Notice the three colored balls at the bottom of the screen. This is a quick way to identify particular view groups that may not be rendering efficiently. The balls represent the same cycles (Measure, Layout, and Draw, in order) as detailed in the Tree View in the previous section. A ball will be green if everything looks good, yellow if there might be reason for concern, and red if there is definitely something to fix.

In addition to gathering metrics about rendering, there are a variety of operations you can do on a selected component:

- Save as a PNG (▦).
- Capture window layers as a Photoshop document (▦).
- Reload the View Hierarchy (⋅⊣).
- Display the selected View image in a new window (◉).
- Invalidate the View layout for the current window (◎). This marks the View as invalid, and it will be redrawn the next time the layout view is refreshed.
- Request the View to lay out (✳). This marks the View and its children as invalid, so they will be redrawn the next time the layout view is refreshed.
- Request the View to output its display list to logcat (⋅⊣).

Example: Debugging a UI Using the Hierarchy Viewer

Examples in this section show how to find common problems, reveal a poorly implemented UI, and identify issues. This section compares two different screens that achieve the exact same UI result. They look exactly the same, but have significantly different performance characteristics due to some design decisions. I am going to step through how you would use the Hierarchy Viewer to analyze their performance and identify issues.

Different ways to design a UI

As an example, I have created two different XML layouts. They have the exact same output on the screen, but one of them performs significantly worse than the other due to implementation differences. The key difference is:

- The "bad" layout nests many different LinearLayouts. It is not unusual for developers to use LinearLayouts for complex layouts, but this often creates overly complex layout files and poorly performing UIs.
- The "good" layout was written using a single RelativeLayout, and all the other Views are laid out within this single container. This creates simpler layouts, and makes them perform better.

Let's use the Outline tool to show the format of the code. This is a good way to show that the bad outline has a much more complex and deeply nested structure than the good outline.

The "bad" layout nests many different LinearLayouts. It is not unusual for developers to use LinearLayouts for complex layouts, but this often creates overly complex layout files and poorly performing UIs. You can see this complexity in the Outline view (Figure 13-7).

Figure 13-7. Hierarchy View: bad outline

Figure 13-8 shows the result of creating simpler layouts and making them perform better: a much cleaner Outline view.

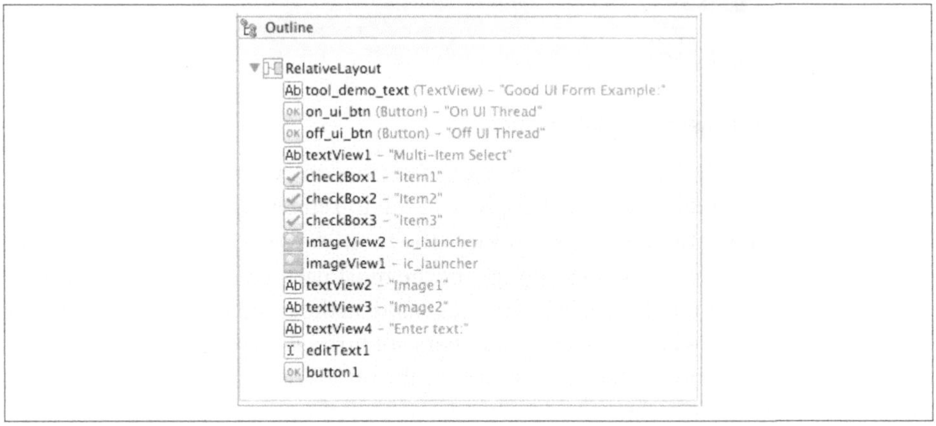

Figure 13-8. Hierarchy View: good outline

Despite the big difference in design, the "bad" screen (see Figure 13-9) and the "good" screen (see Figure 13-10) look and operate in exactly the same way.

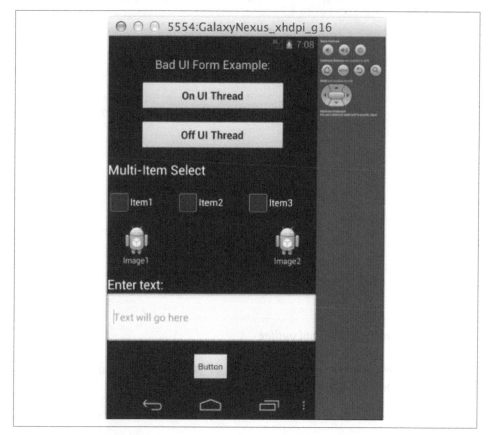

Figure 13-9. Hierarchy View: bad layout

Using the Tree View to get timing information

To understand the UI, let's use the Tree View described in "Gathering View Information" on page 205 to discover how long it is taking to render our View. Use the steps described in "Loading the View Hierarchy into the Tools" on page 203 to load the display and determine how the UI is performing. For the most part, you need to get a feel for the optimal performance number, which varies based on the complexity of the particular screen. You will learn what the optimal numbers are through experience, and you generally will want to compare the layout times for the same layout, before and after optimizations (to determine whether your changes are beneficial).

In our example, it is easy to see that the "bad" layout is a poor performer. We select the top element in the Tree View and look at the measurement on the bottom. This shows

Figure 13-10. Hierarchy View: good layout

the time it takes to draw this View. In this case, it takes 24.483 ms for the bad UI (see Figure 13-11), and only 19.640 ms for the good one (see Figure 13-12). There is a 20% difference between the two, and they both look exactly the same.

It is worth getting multiple measurements, as they will vary each time you generate the Hierarchy View.

Reviewing the structure with the Tree Overview

So now that we have identified the poor performance of the UI, let's next take a look at its general structure. Tree Overview makes it easy to look at a high-level overview of the tree hierarchy, and understand when a View has a complicated structure. The more complicated structures take longer to render. You will also use this View to identify when a hierarchy is too deep. Having deep hierarchies causes significant performance impact, as it increases the time it takes the system to measure the components before laying them out.

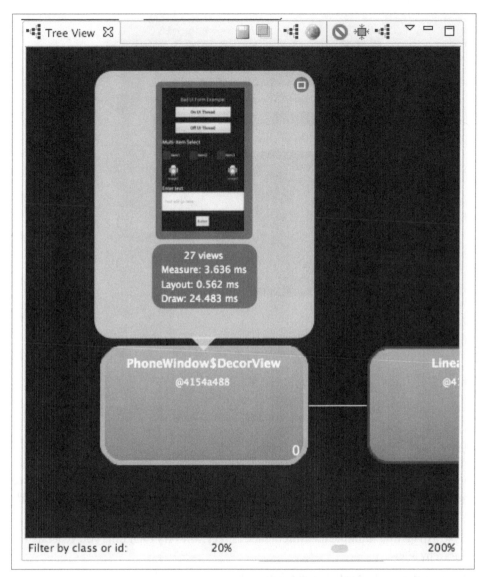

Figure 13-11. Hierarchy View: bad timing

Looking at the two different structures, it is easy to see why one might perform better than the other. The "good" layout is basically completely flat (see Figure 13-13), without any deep hierarchies. The "bad" layout (see Figure 13-14) has a lot of different hierarchies, and some of them are even a few levels deep. You will use this View to quickly identify overly complicated structures by looking at how organized they appear.

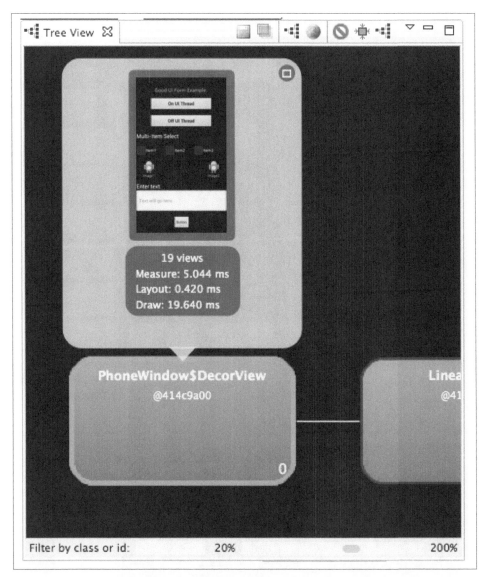

Figure 13-12. Hierarchy View: good timing

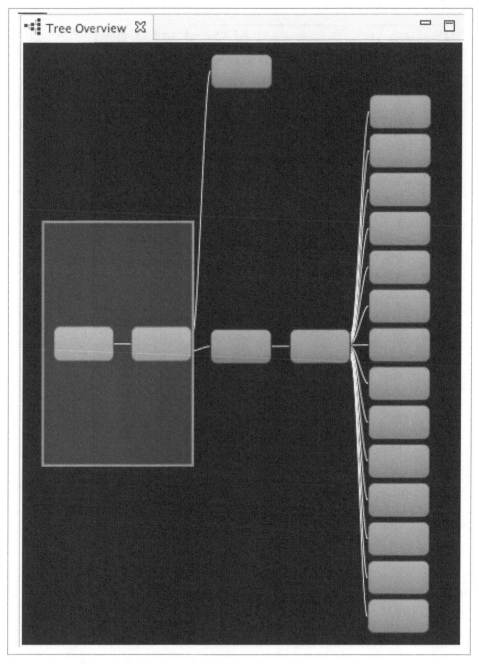

Figure 13-13. Hierarchy View: good tree

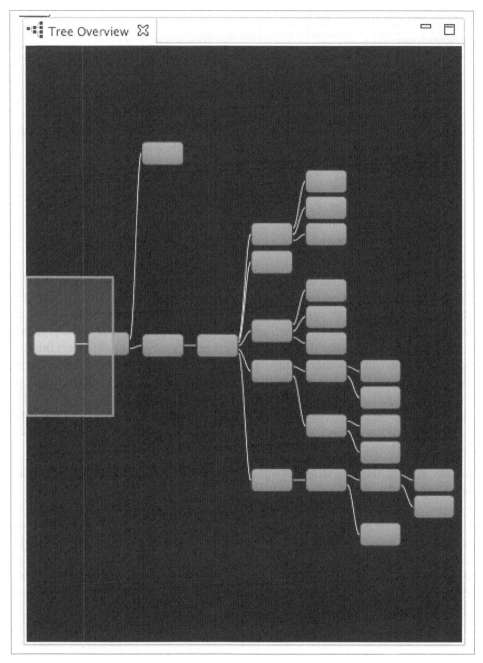

Figure 13-14. Hierarchy View: bad tree

Using the Tree tool to inspect the bad UI

To help identify the exact View components that are causing slow render performance, use the Tree tool (Figure 13-15) to check the different nodes, inspecting their performance indicators. Concentrate on the nodes with red or yellow performance indicators, which can indicate slower performance.

The View Hierarchy window also helps you pinpoint performance issues. By looking at the performance indicators for each node, you can quickly identify the objects that are the slowest to draw. This helps to identify the elements to focus on.

 It is worth noting that red or yellow indicators are not always indicative of a problem. This is particularly true for ViewGroup objects, which have more children and are more complex (and thus take more time to render).

When I look at the bad UI, I see red and yellow dots on many different nodes (in this figure, there are red and yellow dots on a variety of different places in no discernible order). On a high level, this tells me the entire UI is problematic and that the issues aren't isolated to one particular ViewGroup. At this point, I know this layout is probably overly complex and is a candidate for a complete redesign. Next, I will inspect the particular elements with red dots (in this case, there is the TextView that is second from the top, and the EditText that is on the bottom to the very right). In this case, both these elements are simple object types, using an Android base class (TextView). If these were custom Views (i.e., MyCustomTextView), red and yellow dots would point to good places to spend time optimizing. In this case, because these are Android base classes, I know I probably should spend my time elsewhere.

You can also use this tool to identify unused layouts (if you didn't catch them earlier using Lint, described in "Fixing Problems Using Lint" on page 218). Unused layouts in your hierarchy are a common problem with potentially big performance impacts, as each additional ViewGroup makes the measure pass described in "Two-pass layout" on page 201 take more time (and it's already the bulk of the time required to render the screen). It is reasonably easy to identify unused layouts. In this case, there is one Line arLayout (in the middle towards the left) that doesn't show any performance metrics (there is just a blank space where the colored balls and timing information would be). This indicates that it is not being rendered and should be removed.

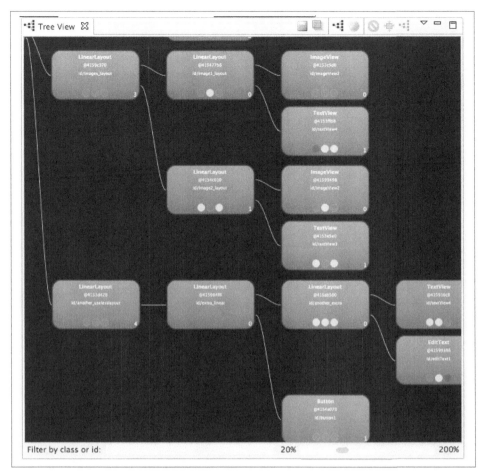

Figure 13-15. Hierarchy View: bad detail

Using the Tree tool to inspect the good UI

The performance indicators in the good UI look much better than the bad one in the Tree View. Most of the indicators in Figure 13-16 are green. The concentration of all the red indicators on my single layout indicates that I don't need to worry about them —the tool has just identified that this path takes the most time to render, which is appropriate because it is the only path.

There are clearly no unused layouts, so that looks great as well. Overall, this layout is much better, which is easy to visualize using this tool.

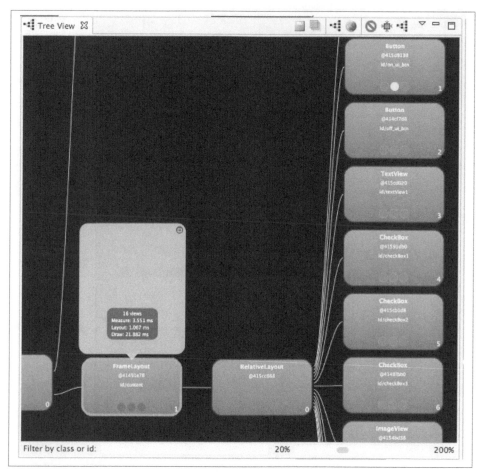

Figure 13-16. Hierarchy View: good detail

Fixing Problems Using Lint

ADT includes a static code analysis tool designed to check source code for potential issues and identify optimization opportunities. It automatically analyzes source code for a variety of criteria. You have likely encountered it before, as it is involved in other aspects of Android development, including writing the business logic (Java classes).

Lint is launched by pressing the little red button on the far right of the Graphical Editor toolbar (▣), which we discussed in the previous chapter (Chapter 12). This number indicates the number of issues Lint has identified. Clicking it will launch the Lint tool (Figure 13-17). You can use this tool to organize and navigate to the various issues it identifies. When you click on an item, the bottom will show additional information about the issue (and offer suggestions about possible fixes).

The right side provides a few buttons that allow you to take action on the item. You can opt to fix it, or if it isn't important to your particular use case, you can tell the tool to ignore it. You can remove instances from the display, specifying whether you would like to remove just one instance ("Suppress Issue"), all instances in this file ("Suppress in Layout"), or all instances in your entire project ("Disable Issue Type").

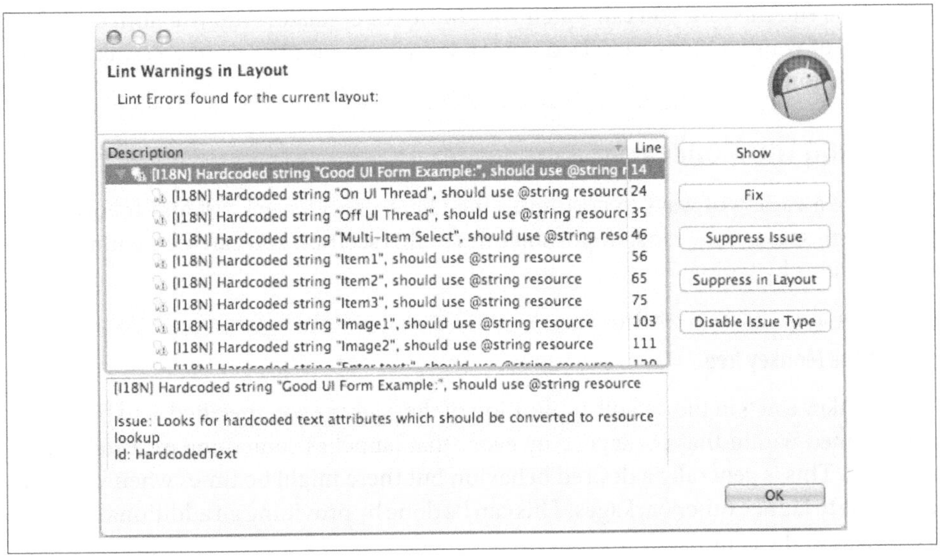

Figure 13-17. Visual Editor using Lint

Application Exerciser Monkey

The Monkey is a tool you run on your device to generate a pseudorandom stream of user interactions and system-level events. It is used to stress-test applications by providing a way to simulate lots of random interactions in a repeatable manner while collecting metrics about crashes or memory issues. This is a great way to test for user interactions that aren't the "normal" ones that you expect (and are already testing for). You can think of it as a tiny virtual primate, whose sole job is to punch and prod your application in an effort to break it.

Monkey runs on your device, which means we will use ADB (see "Android Debug Bridge (ADB)" on page 17) and shell commands to run it remotely. When starting it, you need to provide your package name and the number of events you want to trigger. So if you wanted to run 500 events against the MyPackage app, the command would look like:

```
$ adb shell monkey -p com.foo.MyPackage 500
```

A real example of running this looks like:

```
$ adb shell monkey -p com.tools.demo 500
// activityResuming(com.tools.demo)
// activityResuming(com.tools.demo)
Events injected: 500
## Network stats: elapsed time=36972ms (36972ms mobile, 0ms wifi,
0ms not connected)
$
```

When you run this test, you can watch your device or emulator. You will notice random elements of your UI being exercised as if an imaginary monkey were pressing on your app at random.

Grooming the Monkey

There are a variety of ways to customize the Hierarchy Viewer's test and report. I will go through some of the most important ones in this section. You can see a complete list of all options by typing:

```
$ adb shell monkey --help
```

Letting the Monkey free

The Monkey starts in the default application of the package you specified, and by default is contained within that package. Any event that launches something external will be dropped. This is generally a desired behavior, but there might be times when you want to be able to launch other packages. This can be done by providing an additional package argument to the command:

```
$ adb shell monkey -p com.foo.MyPackage -p com.foo.MyPackage2 500
```

Specifying event types and frequency

It is possible to isolate the types of events that are triggered. You can specify the percentage of a particular event that should be run. This is done with the *event* parameters. So, for instance, if you want to ensure that 50 percent of the events are touch events (a down-up event in a single place on the screen), enter a command like:

```
$ adb shell monkey --pct-touch 50 -p com.foo.MyPackage 500
```

Verbosity level

Depending on your needs, you may want to get back different levels of information from a test run. It is possible to set the verbosity level to indicate how much information you wish to receive. There are three possible levels, based on how many *v*'s you set. Putting a single *v* (the default) provides the least information—basically just information about startup, test completion, and final results. Putting *vv* will also output information during the test run. Lastly, entering *vvv* provides the most information, including details about activities selected or not selected for testing.

If that isn't enough information for you, you can also include the *hprof* argument on the command line. This will dump a large (~5MB) file that can be used by *traceview* (see Chapter 10) for memory profiling.

So to see the most verbose output, enter:

```
$ adb shell monkey -vvv -hprof -p com.foo.MyPackage 500
```

Setting a seed value

A *seed value* allows you to generate the *same* set of random events over and over. This can be useful when you need to duplicate the same set of random events predictably to isolate a particular bug. If you rerun the Monkey with the same seed number, the same exact events will be executed in the same sequence. The seed can be any value, and determines where Monkey starts in its generation of pseudorandom events. So we could choose the seed number 334422 as follows:

```
$ adb shell monkey -seed 334422 -p com.foo.MyPackage 500
```

Monkeyrunner

This tool (which despite the similar name to the tool we just discussed is completely different) is designed to control an Android device from outside of code, simulating how a real user would interact. It provides an API so you can simulate user interactions by issuing commands through a script, or from the command line. This is a powerful tool for simulating and running a consistent set of UI interactions in a repeatable fashion.

The *monkeyrunner* tool is a Java program that can be found with the rest of the tools in the *${android.home}/tools* folder. To run it, create a set of instructions you would like to simulate and feed to the tool. This is a scripted application, so we need to give the tool a list of commands in order for it to run. You can either type the commands one at a time in interactive mode or create a script to run a collection of commands together.

You can do a lot with *monkeyrunner*, which provides a robust automated tooling platform. This tool makes repeating a specific UI easy. This makes it easy to standardize functional tests, which can be run across a variety of devices.

Using Python to Create the Script

Rather than inventing a scripting language for this tool, the creators chose to use an existing language named Python. Python was the logical choice because it is very powerful and popular. It is a dynamic programming language that was designed to focus on creating clear, readable code that is modular and extensible. Python combines functional and object-oriented programming concepts to make it easy to express procedural programs. It is beyond the scope of this book to explain the details of the Python language but we can step through a simple *monkeyrunner* script to show how it can be used. Even if you don't know Python, you should be able to follow along.

Let's step through a simple example that shows how to install an application, launch an activity, take a screenshot of the menu options, and then store the screenshot for later review.

```
#menu_script.py
# Import the monkeyrunner modules we need from com.android.monkeyrunner
import MonkeyRunner, MonkeyDevice

# Connect to a device
device = MonkeyRunner.waitForConnection()

# Install an application to the device
device.installPackage('../ToolsDemo.apk')

# Run a component
device.startActivity(component='com.tools.demo/.MainActivity')

# Press and hold the 'MENU' button
device.press('KEYCODE_MENU', MonkeyDevice.DOWN)

# Take a screenshot
screen1 = device.takeSnapshot()

# Store the screenshot to the filesystem
screen1.writeToFile('screens/menu_buttons.png','png')

# Release the 'MENU' button
device.press('KEYCODE_MENU', MonkeyDevice.UP)
```

You can run this script by starting *monkeyrunner* from the command line with this script as a parameter:

```
$ {android.home}\tools\monkeyrunner menu_script.py
```

When you execute this command, you will be able to watch the actions you scripted on your device as they are happening.

Thanks for Reading!

Well, that's the end of this chapter on UI performance, and the end of the book. With any technology that changes as rapidly as Android does, there will frequently be updates and new information. There's a website with pointers on that at *http://www.mikewolfson.com*. And finally, I'd like to thank you for choosing this book and reading it all the way to the end. In the final analysis, programmers don't write books for fame or financial reward. We write them to share our hard-won knowledge and make the path of other programmers a little bit easier. I hope that this book fulfills that goal for you (and that you recommend it to all your developer friends!).

Index

Symbols

*:s, silencing all other log messages, 98

A

accelerometer, SensorSimulator accelerometer example, 124

actions
Android Actions, in Android Studio default toolbar, 75
common, in Android Studio, 76
Telephony Actions, Emulator Control tab, 118

activities
Activity option in Configuration Chooser, 198
Don't keep activities option, 126
log messages on, 90

Activity Manager, 22

ActivityManager:* tag, 93

ADB (Android Debug Bridge), 17–24
functionality, additional, 22
issuing commands, 19
managing applications on a device, 19
transferring files, 19
querying for device instances, 18
directing command to specific device, 18
finding connected devices, 18
resetting the server, 23

resources for learning more about, 24
shell command, 20–22
interactive mode, 20
one-off mode, 21
retrieving system data, 21
using Activity Manager, 22
starting, 17

ADB driver, downloading, 7

adb logcat command, 97

ADB process, resetting from Devices tool, 50

ADT (Android Developer Tools), ix, 5
ADT Preview Channel, 15
development process, x
File Explorer, 50
Gradle integration, documentation on, 144
leveraging to build great UIs, 171
Lint, 107
requirements for, ix

ADT Template Format Documentation, 65

ADT website, x

Analyzer Tool, 153–155
running, 154
viewing results, 154

Android Attributes, getting information about, 106

android create avd command, 31

Android Debug Bridge (see ADB)

Android Debug Monitor, 152

Android Developer Tools (see ADT)

We'd like to hear your suggestions for improving our indexes. Send email to index@oreilly.com.

About the Author

Mike Wolfson is a passionate mobile designer/developer working out of Phoenix, AZ. He has been in the software field for almost 20 years, and with Android since its introduction. Currently, he develops Android applications for the health care field. He has written a variety of successful apps, and is best known for the "Droid Of The Day" App.

Mike has spent his career helping others learn technology. He currently runs the local Google Developer Group, and has been a lifelong supporter of a variety of other group learning activities. He has spoken about Android and mobile development at a variety of conferences and user groups.

When he is not geeking out about phones, he enjoys the outdoors (snowboarding, hiking, scuba diving), collecting PEZ dispensers, and chasing his young (but quick) daughter.

Colophon

The animal on the cover of *Android Developer Tools Essentials* is a cassowary (genus *Casuarius*), a large, flightless bird that is native to the rainforests of New Guinea and Australia. This genus consists of three species: one is extinct and the rest are living but endangered. It is estimated that only 1,500 cassowaries exist in the entirety of Australia. Like the ostrich and the emu, the cassowary is a ratite, or flightless bird. Although the three species of cassowary differ slightly in size, the Southern cassowary is the largest, with females reaching heights of six and a half feet. Despite their enormous size, cassowaries subsist mainly on fruits that have fallen from trees and will occasionally eat fungus or insects if necessary. They swallow their food whole, sometimes taking in entire bananas or mangos in one gulp.

All species of cassowary are black with bright blue and red necks and hard outgrowths of flesh on the tops of their heads called *casques*. There is much debate about what purpose the casques serve, with theories ranging from protection from falling fruit to an amplifier of the birds' rumbling calls. It is also possible that they allow the bird to forge ahead through dense forest growth, with the casque acting as a battering ram to clear foliage out of the way. The thick feathers that adorn the bird's body are also thought to provide protection from the undergrowth given their unique two-quilled design.

Female cassowaries are much larger than males and are in charge of initiating breeding and courtship. After a female selects a mate, they court for almost a month before breeding. The female will create a nest and lay the eggs, then immediately start off to find another mate. The father then incubates the eggs until they hatch by sitting on them for fifty days. Baby cassowaries are born with tan and white stripes to help them blend in with the detritus on the rainforest floor. The chicks follow their father around for about ten months and learn how to forage fruit and insects. Eventually, the father chases the chicks away so that they can start life on their own and he can breed with another female.

Cassowaries are extremely territorial, so in the wild they are solitary creatures. Generally they are shy around humans, opting to run away rather than be noticed. However, cassowaries can be very dangerous to people and other animals if provoked. Given the rate at which human civilization is encroaching upon cassowary habitats, run-ins with these giant birds are becoming more and more common. In 2003, 150 attacks involving humans were reported, and 75% of these came from instances of people trying to feed the birds. The cassowary's best defense is its dagger-like claws, one on each center toe, which can grow to be four inches long. One kick from a cassowary's powerful legs can slice open all but the toughest hides. Especially in northern Australia, where roads bisect the rainforests, encounters with cassowaries are on the rise. Although large swaths of land are now protected, the future of the cassowary is as unclear as that of the rainforest; both must contend with human development and the environmental effects of global warming.

The cover image is from the Dover Pictorial Archive. The cover font is Adobe ITC Garamond. The text font is Adobe Minion Pro; the heading font is Adobe Myriad Condensed; and the code font is Dalton Maag's Ubuntu Mono.

Get even more
for your money.

Join the O'Reilly Community, and register the O'Reilly books you own. It's free, and you'll get:

- $4.99 ebook upgrade offer
- 40% upgrade offer on O'Reilly print books
- Membership discounts on books and events
- Free lifetime updates to ebooks and videos
- Multiple ebook formats, DRM FREE
- Participation in the O'Reilly community
- Newsletters
- Account management
- 100% Satisfaction Guarantee

Signing up is easy:

1. **Go to: oreilly.com/go/register**
2. **Create an O'Reilly login.**
3. **Provide your address.**
4. **Register your books.**

Note: English-language books only

To order books online:
oreilly.com/store

For questions about products or an order:
orders@oreilly.com

To sign up to get topic-specific email announcements and/or news about upcoming books, conferences, special offers, and new technologies:
elists@oreilly.com

For technical questions about book content:
booktech@oreilly.com

To submit new book proposals to our editors:
proposals@oreilly.com

O'Reilly books are available in multiple DRM-free ebook formats. For more information:
oreilly.com/ebooks

Spreading the knowledge of innovators   oreilly.com

24.99

CPSIA information can be obtained at www.ICGtesting.com
Printed in the USA
LVOW01s0434040913

350802LV00023B/54/P

9 781449 328214